PENGUI

AGAINST

Ian Hamilton wrote biographies of the poets Robert Lowell and Matthew Arnold and the novelist J. D. Salinger. He also published poems and two books of essays, and was the editor of *The Penguin Book of Twentieth-Century Essays*. From 1974 to 1979 he edited the *New Review*. Ian Hamilton died in December 2001.

Against Oblivion

*Some Lives of the
Twentieth-Century Poets*

IAN HAMILTON

PENGUIN BOOKS

PENGUIN BOOKS

Published by the Penguin Group
Penguin Books Ltd, 80 Strand, London WC2R ORL, England
Penguin Putnam Inc., 375 Hudson Street, New York, New York 10014, USA
Penguin Books Australia Ltd, 250 Camberwell Road,
Camberwell, Victoria 3124, Australia
Penguin Books Canada Ltd, 10 Alcorn Avenue, Toronto, Ontario, Canada M4V 3B2
Penguin Books India (P) Ltd, 11 Community Centre,
Panchsheel Park, New Delhi – 110 017, India
Penguin Books (NZ) Ltd, Cnr Rosedale and Airborne Roads,
Albany, Auckland, New Zealand
Penguin Books (South Africa) (Pty) Ltd, 24 Sturdee Avenue,
Rosebank 2196, South Africa

Penguin Books Ltd, Registered Offices: 80 Strand, London WC2R ORL, England

www.penguin.com

First published by Viking 2002
Published in Penguin Books 2003
1

Set in Monotype Bembo
Printed in England by Clays Ltd, St Ives plc

Contents

Author's Note

Some of the 'appraisals' included in this book derive, in ways both large and tiny, from earlier pieces I've composed for newspapers and magazines over a forty-year-plus 'career' of poetry-book reviewing. This being so, I have many editors to thank – more, perhaps, than I can now remember. Some names do stand out, though: Arthur Crook (*TLS*), Karl Miller (*New Statesman*, *Listener*, *LRB*), Alan Ross (*London Magazine*), Mary-Kay Wilmers (*LRB*, post-Miller), Alan Jenkins (*TLS*, post-Crook), Terry Kilmartin (*Observer*), Miriam Gross (also *Observer*, but later *Sunday Telegraph*) and Claire Tomalin (*Sunday Times*). There have been other encouragers and, beyond them, a host of allies and provocateurs; roughly speaking, these people will know who they are, and what they did. Thanks also to Tony Lacey of Penguin Books and to Gillon Aitken, my agent. And special thanks to Patricia Wheatley for her assistance with the final text.

Ian Hamilton
London, 2001

Introduction

Some time ago it was suggested to me that I might try to write an updated, twentieth-century version of Samuel Johnson's *Lives of the Poets*. Like Johnson, I would – it was proposed – compose mini-biographies plus mini-critiques of about fifty modern, or near-modern poets. Like Johnson's, my poets would be dead and, like his, they would have enjoyed substantial reputations when alive. I would not, of course, attempt to rival Johnson's magisterial self-confidence, but on the other hand I would aim to be more conscientious than he was when it came to assembling my information. Johnson, it will be remembered, hated having to find things out – he either knew them already or he didn't. Mostly, of course, he did.

All in all, then, this Johnson update seemed a nice idea, if somewhat gimmicky, and I agreed to have a go. I made a start by checking out Johnson's late-eighteenth-century selection. Indeed, my first discovery was that his selection was not just eighteenth-century, as I had lazily supposed. In addition to his Popes and Swifts there were lives of Milton, Dryden, Cowley and the like. In other words, his fifty or so poets were drawn from two centuries, not one. And the list I had begun compiling, of twentieth-century candidates, had in no time soared towards the fifty mark. Could this be just? Was it really true that the twentieth century had more worthwhile poets than the seventeenth and eighteenth centuries put together?

Continuing my scrutiny of Johnson, I was further nonplussed to find that, out of his selected fifty poets, I was familiar with the work of maybe half a dozen. That is to say, there were about forty poets who had enjoyed fame in two past centuries about whom I knew next to nothing. In a few instances, even their names were quite unknown to me. And here I was, with my fast-growing list of moderns, having a hard time deciding who to leave out: each name on my shortlist appeared to have a decent claim. And so, presumably, it must have seemed to Johnson. But were Johnson's poets really so forgotten, or was it just that I was ignorant? I asked a number of expert, or near-expert acquaintances to tell me everything they knew about Thomas Yalden, Thomas Tickell, Edmund Smith, Elijah Fenton, and so on. Like me, they'd never heard of them. I checked anthologies and reference books, like Margaret Drabble's *Oxford Companion to English Literature*, but with similar results: no Tickell, no Yalden, no Fenton. In some cases, I came across poets who were listed in the *Oxford Companion* simply *because* they had appeared in Johnson's *Lives*. No other claims could be advanced for them, apparently. With the Tickells and the Yaldens, though, not even Johnson's hospitality had been sufficient to protect them from the final darkness. They had pretty well vanished from the map, and it seemed most unlikely that they would ever stage a comeback.

And yet in their lifetimes these same poets had presumably been made to feel, or allowed to feel, that they had talent which might last. At the very worst, they must have been given the idea that they were possessed of some uncommon gift. And they had lived their lives, perhaps, accordingly. Of course, in the eighteenth century, the writing of accomplished verses was often seen as a necessary adjunct to the gentlemanly way of life. At the same time, though, rivalries were intense, as we know from Pope's *Dunciad*, and dreams of immortality were central to the whole business of creative composition.

In the eighteenth century, though, such dreams were not thought to be at odds with society's main drift. Poets were not automatically perceived as oddballs or outsiders. It was not until the nineteenth century that writers of poetry began to see themselves, and to let themselves be seen, as social outcasts. Even as the Romantic poet sanctified his calling, so he was made to feel that what he had to offer was not greatly in demand. And this rejection fed his pride, his sense of splendid separateness. In the twentieth century, how-ever, this separateness was not always felt to be so splendid. One of the essential tenets of so-called poetic 'modernism' was that the serious artist had been banished to the sidelines of a society whose imagination was deadened. From this marginal location, the poet could complain and criticize, if he so chose, or he could cultivate his sense of alienation and write simply for himself, or for his friends, and as obscurely as he wished. What he could not hope for was the kind of central, civilizing social function for which – so he at heart continued to believe – his gifts and insights so crucially equipped him: the kind of function that Matthew Arnold had in mind, or said he had in mind.

In other words, poetry in the twentieth century did not take over from religion, as Arnold none too persuasively predicted that it might. It did not become the source of that 'sweetness and light' which a democratized, industrialized, commercialized society so badly needed in order to counterbalance its own dehumanizing drift. And yet poets continued to write poems, and continued also to insist that what they had to offer was, potentially, of world-altering significance. In practice, as they could all too clearly see, the world did not have much use for them. For some poets, this spurning made it all the more essential that they continue to uphold the faith, in one way or another. Some might retreat into a sort of defiant obscurantism; others might do a deal and seem ready to reduce, or secularize, the pretensions of their craft. On the whole, though, I think it's true to say that poets at the end of the twentieth century were no less convinced of their own value than they had been at the beginning. To which a present-day philistine might well retort: but surely that adds up to one hundred years of wasted effort?

But most poets can't help believing they are poets, and believing, too, that being a poet really matters. And this brings me back to my *Lives of the Poets* project. In spite of my Johnson studies, when I came to plan my update I still found myself with a list of nearly fifty twentieth-century poets, each of whom, it seemed to me, would have to be included in my *Lives*, either on the grounds of reputation, or personal taste, or because their careers had 'literary-historical' significance. Even so, this list of mine was surely far too long. How many of my poets would ultimately go the way of Johnson's? How many had already gone that way? Again, I tested out my list – this time, my moderns list – on a few expert and

near-expert friends. Somewhat to my surprise, about six of the
poets I had listed were utterly unknown. Another dozen had been
heard of but not read. A further dozen had been read but not
remembered: 'Yes, I know the name. I've read him, but what
did he write? Remind me.' Lurking within my list of Lowells,
Berrymans and Plaths, there was a second list, a sub-list, of poets
once admiringly reviewed and perhaps thought of as the next new
thing, but now teetering on the edge of oblivion, an oblivion which
presumably they had spent whole lifetimes seeking to transcend, by
dint of what they took to be their gifts as poets. Did they, within
themselves, suspect or fear that this would be the likely outcome?
And did this in turn affect the way they lived, the way they
wrote?

Some poets, I know, are quite ready to settle for a middle rank,
to trade in their hopes of an illustrious posterity for the sake of a
few plaudits from their current circle. For others, though, such
relegation is an active torment. I recently came across an essay called
'Oblivion' by the American poet Donald Justice – an intelligent
poet who is widely respected in the United States but is in no sense
a 'big-name' figure. He is not, so far as I am aware, much read in
Britain, although Philip Larkin used to drop his name whenever
he, Larkin, was pressed to admit that, yes, from time to time he had
been forced to read the odd transatlantic book of verse.

In his sombre essay, Justice is really concerned to advance, indeed
to rescue the reputations of three American poets he believes have
been wrongly neglected, but before getting down to business he
finds himself brooding on the general predicament of most poets
who, for one reason or another, find themselves consigned to what
he calls the 'underclass' of modern verse. Justice says:

Do not mistake me, I do not have in mind the productions of societies
or amateurs, literary clubs, workshops; I mean the real thing. There may
well be analysable causes behind the oblivion some good writers suffer,
but the causes, whatever they are, remain elusive. There is a randomness
in the operation of the laws of fame that approaches the chaotic.

We can guess, from the tone of his essay, that Justice fears that he himself might fall victim to this chaos, this oblivion.

And yet he has lived most of a lifetime – Justice is now in his seventies – in what he calls a state of 'otherness', a state of believing himself to have been singled out for creativity. He writes about this condition with some eloquence:

Experience teaches one to believe that there is a dimension to the self that all those who are not artists lack; I believe it myself. There is a mysterious and hidden consciousness within the artist of being *other*; there is an awareness of some reality-beyond-the-reality that lures and charges the spirit; it charges and gives power to one's very life.

What do we feel on reading this? Do we feel sorry for Justice, that he should be saddled with such strange convictions? Or do we feel admiring, as he, we suspect, would like us to? Assuming that many poets feel, have felt, as Justice says he does, there is indeed a poignancy in contemplating whole lifetimes given over to a vocation for which the world in general has so little use.

And this poignancy is of course exacerbated, as Justice's essay goes on to make clear, by the knowledge that, every so often, the world in general does take notice of its poets. That is to say, it takes notice of a few of them, and these few it honours with fine prizes and a sort of fame. As a result, the great majority of poets find themselves burdened not just with a vague sense of cultural neglect, but also with a very specific sense of professional exclusion. A sort of career-envy comes into play, and this can have unattractive outcomes. 'Why is poet X so famous when I'm not?' The refrain is horribly familiar.

Many factors are involved in the making of a reputation which will, for a period, outlive its owner. Fashion, I need hardly say, has much to answer for. In itself, fashion is transient, of course, and one of oblivion's most reliable lieutenants. At the same time, though, it *can* assist in the survival of a reputation – or, at any rate, in the survival of a name. For example, who would speak of Hilda Doolittle had she not been part of a once-fashionable movement; who, one might even ask, would speak of C. Day Lewis? To be seen as part of literary history, a poet does not need to have written any worthwhile poems. It can be sufficient that he or she was in the right place at the right time.

This process can, though, work both ways. Just as one can think of certain poets who have profited from a fashionable association, so one can think of others who have suffered damage. When the political poetry of the 1930s went out of vogue, a number of quite worthy figures sank without much trace. Who speaks today of A. S. J. Tessimond, Charles Madge, Drummond Allison, and so on? Such poets were once pigeon-holed as Audenesque, and that was that. When Auden's star declined, theirs disappeared. The same kind of thing happened with the Georgian poets when T. S. Eliot and his cohorts came to power, and to the Apocalyptics of the 1940s once the Movement poets of the 1950s took control.

These ups and downs are to be expected and literary history is full of them. I mean, whatever happened to the nineteenth-century Spasmodics? And maybe we should not shed too many tears for fashion's victims. After all, getting to be fashionable is not usually an accident. Maybe we need these intermittent purges. On the other hand, there are poets who, by keeping to one side of the ins and outs of literary fashion, do find themselves rather more to one side than they'd wish. By holding back, they run the risk of getting lost. Look at almost any twentieth-century anthology of currently 'important' verse, or consult some bygone survey of what's happening to 'poetry now', and you will at once be struck by the rapidity with which oblivion ingests its victims. I have in front of me a copy of Harold Monro's *Some Contemporary Poets* (1920). In his day, Monro was thought to be a fierce critic of new verse and his infrequent recommendations carried weight. The poets he chose for his (briefly) influential 1920s *tour d'horizon* were as follows: A. E. Housman, John Masefield, Walter de la Mare, Ralph Hodgson, W. H. Davies, Charlotte Mew, F. M. Hueffer, Ezra Pound, F. S. Flint, Richard Aldington, Hilda Doolittle (HD), Frederic Manning, Herbert Read, Susan Miles, Max Weber, John Rodker, Lascelles Abercrombie, Gordon Bottomley, W. W. Gibson, Ronald Ross, Aldous Huxley, Siegfried Sassoon, Osbert Sitwell,

Sacheverell Sitwell, Edith Sitwell, G. K. Chesterton, Hilaire Belloc, J. C. Squire, W. J. Turner, Edward Shanks, John Freeman, Robert Nichols, Robert Graves, Gerald Gould, Fredegond Shove, Rose Macaulay, John Drinkwater, Alfred Noyes, James Stephens, Padraic Colum, Joseph Campbell, Shane Leslie, D. H. Lawrence, Anna Wickham, Helen Parry Eden, Frances Cornford. That's about fifty poets for whom Monro was ready to make admiring claims. (In an Appendix, he lists another ninety whom he would have included had he had the space!) Fifteen years later came Michael Roberts's *Faber Book of Modern Verse*, which offered sixty poets as essential to an understanding of the modern 'period' (i.e., 1936–45), but of Roberts's sixty, only Lawrence, the Sitwells and Ezra Pound had appeared on Monro's list.

Admittedly, Roberts's book was meant to promote the new modernistic poets, but even so, lip service to the past could have been a touch more courtly. All of a sudden, something like fifty moderns had gone missing, and would remain missing until a few of them were included in Philip Larkin's 1973 *Oxford Book of Twentieth Century Verse* – a pious, almost patriotic, rescue act which has since showed few signs of permanence.

What, then, of the poets on my list, the poets 'covered' (though not always admiringly) in this end-of-century appraisal. It does seem a fair bet that in, say, one hundred years from now, about half of the poets I have chosen to consider in *Against Oblivion* will have become lost to the general view. They will be marked down as 'forgotten' or as irrevocably 'minor' – a designation which no living poet ever likes to live with. I have my own ideas about who will be forgotten and who won't, and my prejudices can be inferred, without much trouble, from my text. I could, of course, be wrong. It could even be said that I am likely to be wrong. We'll see – or, rather, we won't see. And then, of course, one has to mention the poets I might have/ should have included on my list. For instance, randomly picking names from old anthologies, one comes across the following: George Barker, Laurence Binyon, Basil Bunting, Roy Campbell, Donald Davie, W. H. Davies, Walter de la Mare, James Dickey, Ralph Hodgson, Patrick Kavanagh, Laurie Lee, John Masefield, Edgar Lee

Masters, Edwin Muir, Norman Nicholson, George Oppen, Robert Penn Warren, Laura Riding, Edwin Arlington Robinson, Delmore Schwartz. And one could think of twenty more.

It will be noticed that four rather more celebrated names are also not included on my list: Hardy, Yeats, Eliot and Auden. For these four, it appears to me, oblivion presents no threat. There can be no disputing either their mastery or their supremacy, as the twentieth century's most gifted poetic presences, and those most likely to endure. Dozens of critical encomia have already been heaped on them, and there are numerous biographies. In this book, the presence of Hardy, Yeats, Eliot and Auden can be felt throughout. They overshadow modern poetry in all its several strands and they impose a twofold influence: as encouraging exemplars or as giant-sized inhibitors. As my account proceeds, these four names crop up repeatedly, so that one soon comes to accept, for instance, that every Anglo-American poet who postdated Eliot was haunted by *The Waste Land*, and thus felt it a duty to construct large-scale diagnoses of the century's cultural predicament. You can take the work of almost any poet in this book and point to ways in which it has been shaped by the need to 'settle with' the shades of one or another of the exemplary four. Thus, poets of 'inspiration', of melody and magic and the dark unconscious, will look repeatedly to Yeats; poets who saw it as their duty to be 'public' or 'political' have to imitate Auden and then struggle to be free of him; poets who wish to resist the encroachment of mid-Atlantic modernism, and to connect their own endeavours to some 'native' English line, will feel the need to call on Hardy. In other words, it is hard to think of a twentieth-century poet who would not have written differently had these great overshadowers not lived. And since all four of them wrote their best work during the first three decades of the century, a map of that century turns into a complicated intermeshing of repudiation and submission. Some of this I attempt to disentangle in *Against Oblivion*.

Ian Hamilton
London, spring 2001

Rudyard Kipling

1865–1936

'I am not a poet and never shall be,' wrote Rudyard Kipling, and since his death in 1936 even his most admiring readers have tended to agree, or half-agree. What Kipling wrote in stanzas was not 'poetry' but 'verse': this, on the whole, has been the verdict and it can probably be traced back to Eliot's 1941 attempt to resurrect a reputation which had fallen into disrepair. (During the 1930s, to admire Kipling was, for left-wing critics, akin to having a soft spot for Hitler.)

'He is a master of a mixed form,' said Eliot, gamely trying to make out a case for Kipling's thumping, jaunty rhythms, his balladeering swagger, his formal and yet not quite 'poetic' skilfulness, and so on. Eliot seems to have meant that Kipling's verse should not, could not be held in isolation from the prose, and that if we were seeking the subtleties and obliquities which Eliot's own writings had led us to revere, we should seek them in this writer's stories and not in his verse. At the same time, though, the verse – for all the tum-te-tum complacency of its technique – was often powered by energies carried over from the fiction: not least an attention-holding narrative prowess more nineteenth-century than modernistic. Some of Eliot's own earliest work aspired to, or glanced wistfully towards, the neatnesses of narrative or drama, and sometimes in his famous 1941 preface to *A Choice of Kipling's Verse* he seems somewhat to envy his subject's freedom from literary-historical constraints or obligations – his way of taking and enjoying liberties which Eliot, the archmodernist, was forced to think of as belonging to the realm of 'verse'.

How strange it must have seemed to Kipling's older readers to witness his decline from public favour and his post-1940s semireconstruction. At one time, Kipling's stock could scarcely have stood higher. His winning of the Nobel Prize in 1907 (he was the first English writer to have carried off this honour) marked the climax to a remarkable and swift ascent to youthful eminence. From the moment almost of Kipling's first appearance on the London literary scene in the early 1890s, he had been acknowledged as a 'natural'. Stevenson called him 'too clever to live', and Tennyson saw him as 'the only one with the divine fire'. Even Henry James admitted that Kipling was 'the star of the hour'.

Born in Bombay in 1865, Kipling came from a cultivated colonialist background – his father was an author and his mother a relative, by marriage, of Burne-Jones – and he had first exercised his literary gifts as a sketch-writing (and verse-writing) journalist in India, where, at the age of seventeen, he had been reunited with his parents (who, well-meaningly, had had him raised in England since the age of six). Kipling's childhood years were a nightmare of cruel foster-parents and cranky public schools, and for him returning to India was like a return to some lost paradise: his eyes were wide and he missed nothing. In India, Kipling wrote the sketches he included in *Plain Tales from the Hills* and some of the verses that appeared in his immensely popular *Barrack Room Ballads*, verses in which imperialist pride is allied with a feeling for the sturdy merits of the English working classes – i.e., the put-upon, forbearing Empire 'Tommy'. Kipling's dialect-poems, once adored for their colloquial verve, can now seem tediously mannered (as in 'When 'Omer smote 'is bloomin' lyre'), and one is never quite persuaded that the barracks are where he belongs, or thinks that he belongs. The soldiers Kipling really felt in tune with were of officer material, young subalterns who exemplified those qualities of courage, decisiveness and leader-like resourcefulness on which, so he believed, the British Empire had been built.

Kipling's imperialistic loyalties had deepened into permanence during his early years in India, but most of his adult life was spent in England, on his estate in Sussex. He married Carrie Wollcott, an American, in 1892 and lived for a short while in Vermont, but had a miserable time in that lost corner of the Empire. In Sussex, many thought, his life was no less joyless, even though the literary honours continued to pile up throughout his middle age. His wife was a dominant, organizing type and Kipling – especially after the death of his only son in World War One – was ready enough to let her run his life for him: administering his literary affairs, vetting his social contacts. Kipling came to view himself rather as Carrie viewed him: as a national treasure, or icon. Gradually, the pair of them drifted off into a kind of marmoreal reclusiveness, with Carrie fierce in her protectiveness and Rudyard 'wrung dry by domesticity' (as somebody observed) and brought low, from time to time, with stomach cramps. Many great honours were rebuffed (the Order of Merit, the Poet Laureateship), and so too were many would-be worshippers, but Kipling was allowed to travel quite extensively throughout his later years, and he was always ready to perform pious services for the War Graves Commission – and also, of course, to pen patriotic poems for *The Times*. He devoted much care and energy to the writing of a history of his dead son's army regiment. By the late 1920s, when this work appeared, his political sympathies had become increasingly right-wing, and his literary reputation plummeted accordingly. As another war approached, Kipling deplored the weakness of those politicians who hoped somehow to avoid it. For him, the country's real leaders, the strong men, had been killed in World War One.

Even as Kipling's critical standing declined, his popular reader-ship continued to be vast, and during the war years his patriotic verses were much praised. Kipling, it should be remembered, first made his appearance in the 1890s, and he was welcomed by many readers then as a heartening alternative to post-Romantic decadence. This Kipling was no drooping lily, nor was he out to drub the bourgeoisie. He was a man of action rather than of ideas; he was machine-mad, ocean-going, boyishly excited by heroic values – a man's man, not at all a disaffiliated cissy. Kipling, of course, played up this persona, but at the same time it was genuine; he loved to stir and entertain a massive audience and his uncannily absorbent feel for the rhythms of music-hall ballads and Methodist hymn-tunes gave his verse a thoroughly seductive air of off-the-cuff immediacy. Kipling's verse rarely seemed to have been pondered, even when it tended to the ponderous – as now and then it did, when he was feeling unusually sagacious.

And it was this ability to reach for the verse-tap (or so it seemed) that made Kipling such a stunningly effective public poet, or verse-writer. Today, it is the public Kipling whom we are likely to find most difficult to set aside. Poems like 'If' may not stand up to a great deal of sceptical examination, but it's power to stir is more than just nostalgic: it tunes into some self-perfecting impulse which, perhaps, we all wish we had never lost. Something similar could be claimed for more strictly 'occasional' pieces like 'Recessional' (written for Queen Victoria's second Jubilee in 1897), and even for pro-Empire works like 'The Native-Born', 'The White Man's Burden' and 'For all We Have and Are'. Lines about 'lesser breeds without the law' may be hard to stomach these days, but it is still worth our while trying to work out what Kipling meant when he said this or that now-awful thing. For instance, the much-derided 'Recessional' was seen by him as a fervent plea for national humility. Shortly after writing it, he also wrote:

This is no ideal world but a nest of burglars, and we must protect ourselves against being burgled. All the same, we have no need to shout and yell and ramp about our strength because that is a waste of power, and because other nations can do the advertising better than we can. The big smash is coming one of these days, sure enough, but I think we shall pull through not without credit. It will be common people – the third-class carriages – that'll save us.

And this – lest we forget – was written a few days before the birth of Kipling's doomed son, John.

The Long Trail

There's a whisper down the field where the year has
    shot her yield,
    And the ricks stand grey to the sun,
Singing: 'Over then, come over, for the bee has quit
    the clover,
    And your English summer's done.'

      You have heard the beat of the off-shore wind,
      And the thresh of the deep-sea rain;
      You have heard the song – how long? how long?
      Pull out on the trail again!
Ha' done with the Tents of Shem, dear lass,
We've seen the seasons through,
And it's time to turn on the old trail, our own trail,
    the out trail,
Pull out, pull out, on the Long Trail – the trail that
    is always new!

It's North you may run to the rime-ringed sun
    Or South to the blind Horn's hate;
Or East all the way into Mississippi Bay,
    Or West to the Golden Gate –
      Where the blindest bluffs hold good, dear lass,
      And the wildest tales are true,
      And the men bulk big on the old trail, our own
        trail, the out trail,
      And life runs large on the Long Trail – the trail
        that is always new.

The days are sick and cold, and the skies are grey and
    old,
  And the twice-breathed airs blow damp;
And I'd sell my tired soul for the bucking beam-sea
    roll
  Of a black Bilbao tramp,
    With her load-line over her hatch, dear lass,
    And a drunken Dago crew,
    And her nose held down on the old trail, our
      own trail, the out trail
    From Cadiz south on the Long Trail – the trail
      that is always new.

There be triple ways to take, of the eagle or the snake,
  Or the way of a man with a maid;
But the sweetest way to me is a ship's upon the sea
  In the heel of the North-East Trade.
    Can you hear the crash on her bows, dear lass,
    And the drum of the racing screw,
    As she ships it green on the old trail, our own trail,
      the out trail,
    As she lifts and 'scends on the Long Trail – the
      trail that is always new?

See the shaking funnels roar, with the Peter at the fore,
  And the fenders grind and heave,
And the derricks clack and grate, as the tackle hooks the
    crate,
  And the fall-rope whines through the sheave;
    It's 'Gang-plank up and in,' dear lass,
    It's 'Hawsers warp her through!'
    And it's 'All clear aft' on the old trail, our own
      trail, the out trail,
    We're backing down on the Long Trail – the trail
      that is always new.

O the mutter overside, when the port-fog holds us tied,
   And the sirens hoot their dread,
When foot by foot we creep o'er the hueless, viewless
    deep
  To the sob of the questing lead!
    It's down by the Lower Hope, dear lass,
    With the Gunfleet Sands in view,
    Till the Mouse swings green on the old trail, our
      own trail, the out trail,
    And the Gull Light lifts on the Long Trail – the
      trail that is always new.

O the blazing tropic night, when the wake's a welt of
    light
  That holds the hot sky tame,
And the steady fore-foot snores through the planet-
    powdered floors
  Where the scared whale flukes in flame!
    Her plates are flaked by the sun, dear lass,
    And her ropes are taut with the dew,
    For we're booming down on the old trail, our
      own trail, the out trail,
    We're sagging south on the Long Trail – the trail
      that is always new.

Then home, get her home, where the drunken rollers comb,
   And the shouting seas drive by,
And the engines stamp and ring, and the wet bows reel
    and swing,
  And the Southern Cross rides high!
    Yes, the old lost stars wheel back, dear lass,
    That blaze in the velvet blue.
    They're all old friends on the old trail, our own
      trail, the out trail,
    They're God's own guides on the Long Trail –
      the trail that is always new.

Fly forward, O my heart, from the Foreland to the
    Start –
  We're steaming all too slow,
And it's twenty thousand mile to our little lazy isle
  Where the trumpet-orchids blow!
    You have heard the call of the off-shore wind
    And the voice of the deep-sea rain;
    You have heard the song – how long? – how
      long?
    Pull out on the trail again!

The Lord knows what we may find, dear lass,
And The Deuce knows what we may do –
But we're back once more on the old trail, our own
    trail, the out trail,
We're down, hull-down, on the Long Trail – the trail
    that is always new!

If

If you can keep your head when all about you
  Are losing theirs and blaming it on you,
If you can trust yourself when all men doubt you,
  But make allowance for their doubting too;
If you can wait and not be tired by waiting,
  Or being lied about, don't deal in lies,
Or being hated, don't give way to hating,
  And yet don't look too good, nor talk too wise:

If you can dream – and not make dreams your master;
  If you can think – and not make thoughts your aim;
If you can meet with Triumph and Disaster
  And treat those two impostors just the same;

If you can bear to hear the truth you've spoken
    Twisted by knaves to make a trap for fools,
Or watch the things you gave your life to, broken,
    And stoop and build 'em up with worn-out tools:

If you can make one heap of all your winnings
    And risk it on one turn of pitch-and-toss,
And lose, and start again at your beginnings
    And never breathe a word about your loss;
If you can force your heart and nerve and sinew
    To serve your turn long after they are gone,
And so hold on when there is nothing in you
    Except the Will which says to them: 'Hold on!'

If you can talk with crowds and keep your virtue,
    Or walk with Kings – nor lose the common touch,
If neither foes nor loving friends can hurt you,
    If all men count with you, but none too much;
If you can fill the unforgiving minute
    With sixty seconds' worth of distance run,
Yours is the Earth and everything that's in it,
    And – which is more – you'll be a Man, my son!

Charlotte Mew

1869–1928

Almost everything about Charlotte Mew seems to have been rather wincingly small-scale, including Mew herself who, according to one contemporary description, 'was very small, only about four feet ten inches, very slight, with square shoulders and tiny hands and feet'. This description is by Alida Monro, the wife of Harold Monro, who in 1921 was to publish Mew's first book of poems, *The Farmer's Bride*, under the then-prestigious Poetry Bookshop imprint. Alida Monro also describes her first meeting with the future author: 'When she came into the shop she was asked, "Are you Charlotte Mew?", and her reply, delivered characteristically with a slight smile of amusement, was "I am sorry to say I am."' With some people, this response might have been taken as sheer affectation. With Charlotte Mew, though, the regret seemed genuine: this woman really didn't enjoy being who she was.

Even in the world of poetry politics, Mew kept always to the margins. When everyone else was worrying about Georgianism versus Modernism, she seemed to take no notice. And yet her work, as if by accident, was not old-fashioned. There is an obliqueness of intent and an exactness of language in her writing which could

easily have earned her admission to Pound's school of Imagistes –
and almost did. Had she been fully taken up by Pound, he would
have wanted her to modernize her diction and to be less feelingful
about the countryside, but happily this never happened. For Mew,
the writing of poetry had nothing much to do with schools and
counter-schools. By the time she got going as a poet – around 1913
– she was already in her forties, and although by then she had
printed a few things in magazines (short stories, mostly), she had
no real presence on the London literary scene. And this seemed not
to bother her at all.

Mew certainly saw herself as an outsider, but her outsiderism –
her sense of being 'other' – did not wholly derive from her belief
in an artistic destiny. Her feelings of estrangement from the social
norm were partly to do with her undeclared lesbianism, but they
also related to her fear that she was fated to go mad. Insanity ran in
her family and at any moment, so she feared, her number might
come up:

> Here, in the darkness, where this plaster saint
>   Stands nearer than God stands to our distress,
> And one small candle shines, but not so faint
>   As the far lights of everlastingness
> I'd rather kneel than over there, in open day
>   Where Christ is hanging, rather pray
>   To something more like my own clay,
>   Not too divine . . .

Charlotte Mew was born in London in 1869, the daughter of an
architect. There were seven children of the Mew marriage, and
Charlotte was the third. Of the other six, three died in childhood
and two fell victim to schizophrenia: her elder brother, Henry, and
her younger sister, Freda, were taken off to mental hospitals. Henry
died in 1901 but Freda lived on until 1958 and was often visited in
hospital by Charlotte. There was also a mad uncle in the background. Persistently Mew asked herself: is insanity inherited? A
sense of shame, and of imminent disintegration, is omnipresent in

her work. In the poem quoted above, for instance, she speaks of madness as 'the incarnate wages of man's sin'. She was religious but in a private, anguished way. Even as she prayed, she hoped to exempt herself from the divine jurisdiction that might ultimately banish her into the realm of lunacy. Some of her most ardent and unshapely prayer-poems (of which she wrote a few) are actually prayers for what she guessed might be the equilibrium of godlessness, the sanity of non-belief. 'I do not envy Him his victories', she claims – speaking of God – because 'His arms are full of broken things':

> When I first came upon him there
> Suddenly, on the half-lit stair,
> I think I hardly found a trace
> Of likeness to a human face
> In his. And I said then
> If in His image God made men,
> Some other must have made poor Ken –
> But for his eyes which looked at you
> As two red, wounded stars might do.

Mew's inner life was turbulent indeed. Externally, however, her day-to-day biography was pretty uneventful – no doubt deliberately so (why risk adventuring beyond the boundaries of custom and routine?). There was a mild scandal when Charlotte developed a mostly suppressed passion for the novelist May Sinclair, but no great public repercussions. After her parents died, and with money hard to come by, Charlotte lived with her sister Anne in Bloomsbury and then in Camden, with Anne working as a picture restorer and Charlotte making the odd timid foray into literary London. From time to time, they took in lodgers. And then, in 1927, Anne died of cancer, and with this blow Charlotte finally fell victim to the insanity she had always dreaded. Early in 1928, she was admitted to hospital and a month later she died, having swallowed a bottle of disinfectant. When doctors tried to save her, she said to them: 'Don't keep me. Let me go.'

After her death, and with Auden and Co. just around the corner, Charlotte Mew's reputation as a poet sank, and over the next thirty years or so it all but disappeared – and this in spite of Thomas Hardy having called her 'the best living woman poet'. It was not until the 1960s, when, post-Lowell and post-Plath, there was a renewed responsiveness to the glamour of poetic instability, that Mew came to be acknowledged as an original of lasting value. Even so, her reputation still hangs by a thread. Her output was slender, she was attached to no fashionable schools and movements, she is missing from certain widely taught anthologies, she offers little to biographers. In other words, she is a perfect candidate for posterity's disdain. Perhaps, with her, posterity will not run true to form. Let's hope it doesn't. She is worth preserving, even though her admirers can more easily point to compelling lines and stanzas in her work than to whole finished poems. In this sense, perhaps her work did suffer from her shyness, from lack of exposure to the scrutiny of sympathetic critics. On the other hand her shyness, her obliquity, quite often seems to guarantee her authenticity. All in all, in her case, I think we ought to make the most of what we have.

Pécheresse

Down the long quay the slow boats glide,
  While here and there a house looms white
Against the gloom of the waterside,
  And some high window throws a light
  As they sail out into the night.

At dawn they will bring in again
  To women knitting on the quay
Who wait for him, their man of men;
  I stand with them, and watch the sea
  Which may have taken mine from me.

Just so the long days come and go.
  The nights, ma Doué! the nights are cold!
Our Lady's heart is as frozen snow,
  Since this one sin I have not told;
  And I shall die or perhaps grow old

Before he comes. The foreign ships
  Bring many a one of face and name
As strange as his, to buy your lips,
  A gold piece for a scarlet shame
  Like mine. But mine was not the same.

One night was ours, one short grey day
  Of sudden sin, unshrived, untold.
He found me, and I lost the way
  To Paradise for him. I sold
  My soul for love and not for gold.

He bought my soul, but even so,
    My face is all that he has seen,
His is the only face I know,
    And in the dark church, like a screen,
    It shuts God out; it comes between;

While in some narrow foreign street
    Or loitering on the crowded quay,
Who knows what others he may meet
    To turn his eyes away from me?
    Many are fair to such as he!

There is but one for such as I
    To love, to hate, to hunger for;
I shall, perhaps, grow old and die,
    ·With one short day to spend and store,
    One night, in all my life, no more.

Just so the long days come and go,
    Yet this one sin I will not tell
Though Mary's heart is as frozen snow
    And all nights are cold for one warmed too well.
    But, oh! ma Doué! *the nights of Hell!*

The Farmer's Bride

Three Summers since I chose a maid,
Too young maybe – but more's to do
At harvest-time than bide and woo.
    When us was wed she turned afraid
Of love and me and all things human;
Like the shut of a winter's day,
Her smile went out, and 'twasn't a woman –
    More like a little frightened fay.
        One night, in the Fall, she runned away.

'Out 'mong the sheep, her be,' they said,
'Should properly have been abed';
But sure enough she wasn't there
Lying awake with her wide brown stare.
So over seven–acre field and up–along across the down
We chased her, flying like a hare
Before our lanterns. To Church–Town
    All in a shiver and a scare
We caught her, fetched her home at last
    And turned the key upon her, fast.

She does the work about the house
As well as most, but like a mouse:
    Happy enough to chat and play
    With birds and rabbits and such as they,
    So long as men–folk keep away.
'Not near, not near!' her eyes beseech
When one of us comes within reach.
    The women say that beasts in stall
    Look round like children at her call.
    I've hardly heard her speak at all.

Shy as a leveret, swift as he,
Straight and slight as a young larch tree,
Sweet as the first wild violets, she,
To her wild self. But what to me?

The short days shorten and the oaks are brown,
    The blue smoke rises to the low grey sky,
One leaf in the still air falls slowly down,
    A magpie's spotted feathers lie
On the black earth spread white with rime,
The berries redden up to Christmas-time.
    What's Christmas-time without there be
    Some other in the house than we!

She sleeps up in the attic there
Alone, poor maid. 'Tis but a stair
Betwixt us. Oh! my God! the down
The soft young down of her, the brown,
The brown of her – her eyes, her hair, her hair!

Robert Frost

1874–1963

Robert Frost was wary of biography but by no means disdainful of its power to damage even the most sturdily based literary reputation. When, in the 1930s, the life writers began knocking on his door, he greeted them with hospitable evasions and false leads. He enjoyed the attention but was determined to control it. 'I want you to understand me wrong,' he used to say. The important thing, in his view, was to 'keep the over-curious out of the secret places of my mind'.

Frost, after all, at that time had an image to protect. In the eyes of his large readership, he was the loveable New England farmer-bard, tough-minded, independent, genial – and quintessentially American. This self-presentation had been nurtured at countless public readings and book signings, and Frost was not going to let biography disrupt it. In 1939, he appointed his own official Boswell, one Lawrance Thompson – a youthful and admiring critic who could, Frost thought, be kept on a tight leash.

For the next twenty-five years Thompson served as Frost's factotum, accompanying the poet on his travels and assisting, when required, in the continuing ascent of his prestige and celebrity. At the start of Frost's poetic career, which had not begun until he was past forty, academic modernists had tended to see him as a hayseed neo-Georgian. He had spent time in England and had hung out there, not with Pound and Eliot, but with discredited figures like Lascelles Abercrombie and Wilfred Gibson. And before that, in America, he had dithered from job to job – farmer, schoolteacher, newspaper editor, and so on – and had seemed to have learned little from his truncated Harvard education.

During the 1930s, the leftist literary establishment shunned Frost as crankily right-wing. By sheer force of determination, though, he stuck to his own line, his own hauntingly distinctive 'speaking voice', a voice both metrical and colloquial, a voice that owed nothing to modernism and yet never seemed antique or self-consciously poetical. Now and then Frost jawed on tiresomely and was always too fond of the cracker-barrel aphorism, but every so often he achieved an intimate, intense and yet forbearingly intelligent dramatic forcefulness of just the kind which, we imagine, modernists like Ezra Pound were dreaming of when they compiled their lists of Dos and Don'ts. Poems like 'Birches', 'Stopping by Woods on a Snowy Evening', and even longer works like 'Home Burial' could scarcely be dismissed as neo-Georgian:

> My long two-pointed ladder's sticking through a tree
> Toward heaven still,
> And there's a barrel that I didn't fill
> Beside it, and there may be two or three
> Apples I didn't pick upon some bough.
> But I am done with apple-picking now.
> Essence of winter sleep is on the night,
> The scent of apples: I am drowsing off.
> I cannot rub the strangeness from my sight
> I got from looking through a pane of glass
> I skimmed this morning from the drinking trough
> And held against the world of hoary grass.
> It melted, and I let it fall and break.
> But I was well

Upon my way to sleep before it fell,
And I could tell
What form my dreaming was about to take . . .

By the end of his long life, Frost had effectively bridged the gap between his popular readership and the highbrow élite. When Lionel Trilling, in 1960, called Frost a 'terrifying' poet, there were many protests from adoring fans, but everybody must have known what Trilling meant:

> The people along the sand
> All turn and look one way.
> They turn their back on the land.
> They look at the sea all day.
>
> The land may vary more;
> But wherever the truth may be –
> The water comes ashore,
> And the people look at the sea.
>
> They cannot look out far.
> They cannot look in deep.
> But when was that ever a bar
> To any watch they keep?

It is difficult to imagine anything more terminally desolate, and yet the strain, the edginess, the shrewdness of the poem in the end derive from a resistance to the terminal – and from a grim conviction that it's better to know where you stand than attempt to turn away. Many of Frost's finest poems are about barriers and separations, and the best of them express a futile yearning for conditions to be otherwise. And it was something of this sort, presumably, that Trilling had in mind.

At Frost's death in 1963, aged eighty-eight, he was without question America's most valued poet: a popular bestseller who was regularly praised by Randall Jarrell. He read his work at Kennedy's inauguration and in the last year of his life was sent to Russia as an ambassador for no-nonsense Yankee values.

All this Grand Old Man activity was, of course, observed and noted down by Lawrance Thompson. When Frost died, it was generally assumed that his disciple's biography, when it appeared, would be a hymn of praise. It turned out to be quite the reverse. During his long years of trusted flunkeydom, Thompson had come to despise Frost – and to despise his own role in Frost's life. (He was also having an affair with Kay Morrison, Frost's long-serving mistress.) The first two volumes of his 2,000-page *Life* portrayed Frost as a mean-minded self-advancer, corrupt in his literary-political manoeuvres, close to madness in his vengefulness and spite. Far from being a disinterested rustic, forever communing with the soil and with dumb animals, Frost had spent many of his hours plotting his next Pulitzer, sucking up to powerful critics, heading off any competition that seemed likely to get in his way.

And in his private life, he had been just as unpleasantly self-centred. His personal tragedies – the early deaths of four of his six children, one of them by suicide; the slow surrender to insanity of his only sister; the embittered remoteness of the wife he had more or less bullied into marriage – all these were presented by Thompson as the to-be-expected offshoots of Frost's monomaniacal pursuit of literary fame.

The biography held nothing back, or so it seemed (although Thompson made no mention of his dealings with Kay Morrison), and was almost gloatingly well-documented. Even the index headings bristled with hostility, with entries under headings like 'Hate', 'Jealousy', 'Fear', 'Charlatan', 'Retaliations, Poetic', and so on. By the end of it, the poet's nice-guy reputation lay in ruins. Reviewers of Thompson's book denounced Frost as monstrous, near-demonic. One even claimed that 'a more hateful human being cannot have lived'.

In some quarters, though, the standing of Frost's poetry was actually enhanced by Thompson's revelations. For one thing, the work's essential bleakness could be more openly discussed. And knowing the poet to have been devious in life, critics could all at once perceive a sly obliqueness in the verse. All this did wonders for Frost's highbrow reputation, and in the past few years there have been at least three biographies which, in one way or another, have set themselves to tone down Thompson's harsh portrayal. In the most recent, by Jay Parini, Frost comes across as conscientious and dignified in the face of his life's several tragedies. As for the careerism: yes, Frost enjoyed his fame, but so what? Why shouldn't a chap try to get ahead?

Such rehabilitative labours will not restore Frost to his earlier status as America's fireside bard. Frost-mottos like 'Good fences make good neighbours' were once read as inspiring affirmations of Yankee self-reliance. Post-Thompson, Frost's adoring public had to face the fact that self-reliance is often indistinguishable from self-centredness, from simple un–American misanthropy. After all, Frost also told his readers to 'Keep off each other, and keep each other off'.

After Apple-Picking

My long two-pointed ladder's sticking through a tree
Toward heaven still,
And there's a barrel that I didn't fill
Beside it, and there may be two or three
Apples I didn't pick upon some bough.
But I am done with apple-picking now.
Essence of winter sleep is on the night,
The scent of apples: I am drowsing off.
I cannot rub the strangeness from my sight
I got from looking through a pane of glass
I skimmed this morning from the drinking trough
And held against the world of hoary grass.
It melted, and I let it fall and break.
But I was well
Upon my way to sleep before it fell,
And I could tell
What form my dreaming was about to take.
Magnified apples appear and disappear,
Stem end and blossom end,
And every fleck of russet showing clear.
My instep arch not only keeps the ache,
It keeps the pressure of a ladder-round.
I feel the ladder sway as the boughs bend.
And I keep hearing from the cellar bin
The rumbling sound
Of load on load of apples coming in.
For I have had too much
Of apple-picking: I am overtired
Of the great harvest I myself desired.
There were ten thousand thousand fruit to touch,
Cherish in hand, lift down, and not let fall.
For all

That struck the earth,
No matter if not bruised or spiked with stubble,
Went sure to the cider-apple heap
As of no worth.
One can see what will trouble
This sleep of mine, whatever sleep it is.
Were he not gone,
The woodchuck could say whether it's like his
Long sleep, as I describe its coming on,
Or just some human sleep.

Stopping by Woods on a Snowy Evening

Whose woods these are I think I know.
His house is in the village though;
He will not see me stopping here
To watch his woods fill up with snow.

My little horse must think it queer
To stop without a farmhouse near
Between the woods and frozen lake
The darkest evening of the year.

He gives his harness bells a shake
To ask if there is some mistake.
The only other sound's the sweep
Of easy wind and downy flake.

The woods are lovely, dark and deep,
But I have promises to keep,
And miles to go before I sleep.
And miles to go before I sleep.

Edward Thomas

1878–1917

Two events are said to have transformed Edward Thomas from
Hack Writer to Important Poet: the outbreak of World War One
and Thomas's friendship with Robert Frost. Thomas was thirty-six
in 1914 and had indeed spent the past fourteen years earning his
living as a professional wordsmith: thirty prose books (rural
sketches, travel guides, biographies) as well as several hundred essays
and reviews had issued from his pen, and for long stretches of this
prose career he had been perilously poor. In 1915, his enlistment
freed him from his treadmill and, with Frost's encouragement, he
wrote – in two and a half years – the ninety or so poems on which
his reputation is now based.

It is an extraordinary tale and on the whole it stands up to
inspection: Frost and the war did have a massive influence on
Thomas's late flowering as a poet. The problem, however, is that
this version of the Thomas life tends to skip past the fourteen
years as if they had been largely wasted – and this must beg at
least two questions: how 'hack' was Thomas's hack writing, and
could the poems have happened as they did if his first adult years
had been lived differently? By all accounts (including the account

given by his widow), Thomas spent most of those years in a state
of abject misery. He had married very young – his wife-to-be,
Helen, became pregnant when he was still an undergraduate at
Oxford – and he discovered early on that he had little, if any,
taste for domesticity and fatherhood. As an offshoot of this
discontent he turned against his wife, with whom at first he had
shared the most fervent of romantic aspirations. Their dream of
a love-cottage in the country gave way to a daily round of
penny-pinching drudgery. Instead of the envisaged life of leisured
creativity, Thomas found himself condemned to a regime of
frantic Grub Street hustling. Helen Thomas has recorded scenes
from the marriage which portray her writer-husband as explosively
depressed, prone to black rages and deep silences, constantly dis-
appearing on lengthy research missions or on work-seeking trips to
London.

Thomas's background was middle class (he was born in Lambeth
of Welsh parents – his father was a civil servant – and he attended
St Paul's School before going on to Lincoln College, Oxford),
and the indignities of poverty were hard for him to bear. More
profoundly, though, he disliked his own dislike of married life. On
Helen's side, in spite of poverty and children and numerous house
moves, romantic passion had not dimmed; nor had her belief in
Edward's 'genius'. For him, though, something had been lost:

> My eyes scarce dare meet you
> Lest they should prove
> I but respond to you
> And do not love.

The sense of loss that suffuses his relationship with Helen is central
to the poems he eventually wrote. In these, the loss is not just
personal; it has to do with an imperilled rural England. But
Thomas's unhappiness began at home. The mediocrity of married
life, together with – as he saw it – the mediocrity of his career,
turned him into a self-lacerating moaner. Many poets have had to
cope with dreary marriages, shortage of money and a too-heavy

load of third-rate literary labour; with Thomas, though, self-pity has become the stuff of legend.

It's true enough, though, that his work load was spectacular: in two months of one year he wrote forty-one book reviews, even as he toiled to meet the deadline on his latest book commission. Thomas was efficient – he usually delivered on time – but he was also fairly slapdash: most readers of his *Oxford* or *Beautiful Wales* or *The Heart of England* have found it easy to identify the corner-cuttings and space-fillings that Thomas now and then resorted to. And here it is important to remember that it was he who chose this arduous career. 'Couldn't he have worked in a bank?' asked Philip Larkin. 'Apparently not. One cannot help thinking that Thomas was that unfortunate character, a "man of letters", to whom no hardship or humiliation outweighs the romance of scraping a living from the printed word.' And, of course, 'romance' is the key word. Just as Thomas saw the romance draining from his once splendid love of Helen, so he witnessed the erosion of his youthful fantasies about the 'literary life'.

He remained faithful to Helen, though. For him, it was infidelity enough that he should be so miserable. From time to time, he would try to recapture what had gone, and Helen never doubted his commitment (if his eye roved, as once or twice it did, she was complaisant: her aim always was to cheer him up). So too, in a way, with what he wrote. He complained constantly about this or that low-grade commission, but he never seems to have considered a change of career, and with at least some of his prose books there were flickers of a genuine engagement with the task in hand:

From that bleak and yet pleasant scene I turned with admiration to a farmhouse on the other side of the road. It stood well above the road, and the stone wall enclosing its far-yard followed the irregular crown of the steep slopes. This plain stone house, darkened, I think, by a sycamore, and gloomy, above Nettlebridge, seemed to me a house of houses. If I could draw, I would draw this and call it 'A House'. For it had all the spirit of a house, farm and fortress in one, grim without bellicosity, tranquil, but not pampered.

Thomas's literary heroes were writers like Richard Jefferies and George Borrow, and a large part of his hack-frustration came from his conviction that, given a bit more time and money, his own writings about rural Britain might some day have achieved true excellence. As with his marriage, one might say, Thomas was utterly committed to the idea of a writing life, but only now and then did the reality live up to expectations: a sense of thwartedness became for him the desolating norm.

In his college days, Thomas had written poetry, but once he had become a full-time writer he gave up: although his poetry reviews were in demand, nobody was hiring him to turn out poems. It was the intervention of Frost in 1914 that caused him to look again at some of his prose writings and to see in them, from time to time, the outlines of good poems. And the example of Frost's own work, so grounded in narrative and observation, was also heartening. And then came the outbreak of war, and Thomas's enlistment: even as he was freed from the worst of his hack-obligations, so he was made to focus, with intensity, on the idea of loss: the loss of his own life and therefore too the loss of everything this life of his had lacked – indeed, the loss, perhaps, of that deep, settled rural England which he had not, or so he thought, been given time to honour and explore. Many of the poems Thomas wrote in his last years – he was killed in France in 1917 – can easily be read as efforts to repair or circumvent this English loss, by force of fond-remembered detail (see 'Adlestrop', 'Old Man', and many others). Some losses, though, were not to be repaired.

No One So Much As You

No one so much as you
Loves this my clay,
Or would lament as you
Its dying day.

You know me through and through
Though I have not told,
And though with what you know
You are not bold.

None ever was so fair
As I thought you:
Not a word can I bear
Spoken against you.

All that I ever did
For you seemed coarse
Compared with what I hid
Nor put in force.

My eyes scarce dare meet you
Lest they should prove
I but respond to you
And do not love.

We look and understand,
We cannot speak
Except in trifles and
Words the most weak.

For I at most accept
Your love, regretting
That is all: I have kept
Only a fretting

That I could not return
All that you gave
And could not ever burn
With the love you have,

Till sometimes it did seem
Better it were
Never to see you more
Than linger here

With only gratitude
Instead of love –
A pine in solitude
Cradling a dove.

Adlestrop

Yes, I remember Adlestrop –
The name, because one afternoon
Of heat the express-train drew up there
Unwontedly. It was late June.

The steam hissed. Someone cleared his throat.
No one left and no one came
On the bare platform. What I saw
Was Adlestrop – only the name

And willows, willow-herb, and grass,
And meadowsweet, and haycocks dry,
No whit less still and lonely fair
Than the high cloudlets in the sky.

And for that minute a blackbird sang
Close by, and round him, mistier,
Farther and farther, all the birds
Of Oxfordshire and Gloucestershire.

Wallace Stevens

1879–1955

Although it is commonplace nowadays for Wallace Stevens to be ranked as one of the major modern poets, it is rare to hear him or his works spoken of with great affection. He is admired, and often imitated, but not even his most ardent fans seem able to get close to the personality behind the poems. And this was how Stevens wanted it to be. In his lifetime, he made sure that other people were kept at arm's length, and although he gave the impression of caring little for posterity, it would have pleased him to know that his invisibility was durable. He had no wish for readers who would find him likeable. Of Robert Frost, he once said: 'His work is full (or said to be full) of humanity.' Using the Stevens lexicon, there could have been no more withering disparagement.

From the beginning, Stevens's remoteness was a source of irritation to his critics, and in some quarters it remains so to this day. He did not publish his first book, *Harmonium*, until he was in his forties, although he had been writing and publishing in magazines for over twenty years. 'A book of poems', he used to say, 'is a damned serious affair.' There was in this an implied disdain for the hustling of his contemporaries, and one or two of them took it amiss. After all, they would say, it was easy for Stevens to take his time: he came from a well-off Pennsylvania background, had studied at Harvard, qualified as a lawyer and risen to become Vice-President of an insurance company. He lived in a big house in Connecticut and wrote his poems on his way to work. He had no exposure to the rigours of the freelance literary life, no divorces, no breakdowns, no upheavals. In short, so the indictment ran, he took no risks. Nobody then knew that Wallace Stevens had been told by his doctor that he would probably die in his forties. The problem was high blood pressure.

Harmonium was a somewhat dandified affair, cryptic, unyielding and yet 'gaudy'. It was full of show-off dictionary words like 'fubbed' and 'princox', 'girandoles' and 'carked', and it exhibited a modish Francophilia – this last was widely mocked, because Stevens had never been to Europe and took all his holidays in Florida. There was also a vein of conceited playfulness on show, in titles like 'The Paltry Nude Starts on a Spring Voyage', 'The Emperor of Ice Cream', 'Thirteen Ways of Looking at a Blackbird', and a weird jungle-exoticism, 'a dreaming of tigers/in red weather', that seemed to derive more from the travel brochure than from any intense personal imaginings. The manner throughout was urbane, and the tone ranged from the chuckling-oblique to the mellifluous-sublime. There are lines in Stevens that are silly and boring, but almost none that are incompetent. 'No one else,' one early critic wrote, 'monocled and gloved, can cut so faultless a figure standing in his box at the circus of life.'

Harmonium was a commercial failure, even by the standards of poetry publishing: it sold fewer than a hundred copies. For five or six years afterwards, Stevens gave up writing poetry and concentrated on consolidating his career in business. When he did start publishing again, he was careful to do so in limited editions from small presses. It was not until 1936 that he reappeared in the market-place, when Knopf brought out his second volume, *Ideas of Order*, the book that is usually taken to signal his move away from dandy-aestheticism into the 'philosophical' mode for which he is now probably best known. Stevens was approaching sixty when this second book appeared, and would live for another twenty years – years in which he published four more books and became a revered and prize-laden American poet. He never retired from his insurance company: 'It gives a man character', he said, 'to have this daily contact with a job.'

Remarkably, Stevens's *Collected Poems* runs to over 500 pages. Remarkable, yes, but looked at more closely, Stevens's late productivity is not really all that puzzling. It can seem to have been an irresistible function of those theories he settled on in the mid-1930s and scarcely changed thereafter, theories which held the writing of poetry to be inseparable from the continuance of life – his own life, but also any human life that would seek to call itself 'worth living'. It was this vast claim for poetry that became the subject of his poems. 'After one has abandoned a belief in God,' he wrote, 'poetry is that essence which takes its place in life's redemption.' It was not that we should all be writing poetry – what mattered was that all humans should develop to the full their 'ways of seeing': 'The sea is loveliest by far in the abstract when the imagination can feed upon the idea of it. The thing itself is dirty, wobbly and wet.'

The imagination was godless, but had the power to be godlike: not godlike in the sense of issuing commandments or telling us how to behave, but in its processes, in the activity of its own compositions ('the poem of the act of the mind') and in its enrichment of the perceptible, existing world, its enrichment of 'the thing itself'. It was this process of enrichment that Stevens came to describe as the Supreme Fiction, although he was always careful to describe his poems as 'notes towards' that fiction.

In the thirties and the war years, there were those who saw this whole notion as a supreme self-indulgence and were angered by Stevens's rapt aloofness from the common struggles of the day. Asked in a questionnaire, 'As a poet what distinguishes you, do you think, from an ordinary man?', Stevens replied, 'Inability to see much point to the life of an ordinary man.' His critics were not appeased by the poet's willingness to add, 'The chances are an ordinary man himself sees very little point to it.'

Postwar, it was easier for readers to digest Stevens's talk about the supremacy of the imagination and, having digested it, some critics were able to look back to the poems of *Harmonium* and detect in them, behind the gaudiness, a sense of near-intolerable loss, or lack. Stevens was a natural believer but he had the spiritual aristocrat's contempt for beliefs that were lazily or sentimentally espoused. *Harmonium* pulls faces at middle-class America and its inherited religion, but behind the mockery there was a blank. No longer believing, what do I believe? Reread thus, a poem like 'Sunday Morning' can seem less than fully committed to its own majestic cadences, and we are drawn also to shift bare, desolate pieces like 'The Snow Man' closer to the centre of the stage. Here the poet is merely 'the listener, who listens to the snow/ And, nothing himself, beholds/ Nothing that is not there,/ and the nothing that is'.

Like other sorts of worshipper, Stevens was not afraid of monotony, or repetition, or an obscurity which even the most finely tuned eavesdropper will not find easy to decipher. His critics have continued to complain, with some justice, that he had little or no interest in the dramatic, the social, the autobiographical. And it is surely because we know all this that we are likely to respond so readily to the unexpectedly heartfelt final act in Stevens's 'non-drama': the poems he wrote at the very end of his life, poems in which he was obliged to face the fact which had all along both mocked and energized his fictions:

> It makes so little difference, at so much more
> Than seventy, where one looks, one has been there before.
>
> Woodsmoke rises through the trees, is caught in an upper flow
> Of air and whirled away. But it has often been so.

From another poet, this might sound merely defeated. From Stevens, who had 'been there before' so often and with such an excited vitality of mind, it comes across as touchingly courageous.

And this final surge of poignancy must surely make us all the more
alert to what was heroic in Stevens's monotonies and repetitions:

> The man-hero is not the exceptional monster,
> But he that of repetition is most master.

Disillusionment of Ten o'Clock

The houses are haunted
By white night-gowns.
None are green,
Or purple with green rings,
Or green with yellow rings,
Or yellow with blue rings.
None of them are strange,
With socks of lace
And beaded ceintures.
People are not going
To dream of baboons and periwinkles.
Only, here and there, an old sailor,
Drunk and asleep in his boots,
Catches tigers
In red weather.

Large Red Man Reading

There were ghosts that returned to earth to hear his phrases,
As he sat there reading, aloud, the great blue tabulae.
They were those from the wilderness of stars that had
    expected more.

There were those that returned to hear him read from the
    poem of life,
Of the pans above the stove, the pots on the table, the tulips
    among them.
They were those that would have wept to step barefoot into
    reality,

That would have wept and been happy, have shivered in the
    frost
And cried out to feel it again, have run fingers over leaves
And against the most coiled thorn, have seized on what was
    ugly

And laughed, as he sat there reading, from out of the purple
    tabulae,
The outlines of being and its expressings, the syllables of its
    law:
Poesis, *poesis*, the literal characters, the vatic lines,

Which in those ears and in those thin, those spended hearts,
Took on colour, took on shape and the size of things as they
    are
And spoke the feeling for them, which was what they had
    lacked.

William Carlos Williams

1883–1963

William Carlos Williams is these days more often discussed as a
founding figure in the history of modernist technique than as the
author of distinguished individual poems, and it is easy enough to
see why this is so: not only was Williams a key dissenting figure in
the early days of Imagism, but his dissent has had a lasting influence
on the entire course of twentieth-century American poetry. At the
same time, though, there is still a case for wondering how gifted
Williams would have seemed if he had written in iambic penta-
meter, or if he had served his apprenticeship in London. Even as
academics ponder Williams's historical significance, they can't help
sounding just a little condescending: Williams, in spite of his great
influence as a technician, is still widely represented as the American
roughneck to Pound's metropolitan sophisticate.

And this, to be sure, was Williams's own chosen stance during
the early years of his career. 'Before meeting Ezra Pound is like
BC and AD,' he once testified, and it was from his unconvinced
encounters with Pound's Eurocentric modernism that he evolved
his attachment to what he called 'the American grain'. Before
Pound, Williams was writing 'Keatsian sonnets' and dabbling

reluctantly in Whitmanesque. What Pound provided was the elementary principle that Williams would go on to promote throughout his life: that notion of direct, unadorned particularity sloganized in his now celebrated 'Say it! No ideas but in things.'

For a time, Williams was a willing recruit to Pound's Imagist enterprise. Pound and Williams (and HD) had met as co-students at the University of Pennsylvania, and Williams was at first attracted by Pound's iconoclastic verve. He was more practical than Pound, though, and more humbly down to earth. He was not at the university to study poetry. His field was medicine, and the 'things' that demanded his direct scrutiny were immediate and close to home. He soon enough lost patience with Pound's medievalist nostalgia. Why go to ancient European texts for guidance? The real task was to make American poetry distinctively American.

In his Prologue to *Kora in Hell* (1920), Williams formally announced his repudiation of Pound's line, and in response Pound wrote him off as a provincial: 'an old village cut-up'. (Less endearingly, Pound also called Williams a 'dago immigrant', and thus not authentically 'American': Williams's mother was Puerto Rican.) It was, said Pound, 'doubly lamentable that the two halves of what might have made a fairly decent poet should be sequestered and divided by the buttocks of the arse-wide Atlantic ocean'. Williams did not have Pound's taste for rollicking invective, but he did have an immovable persistence. More and more, he came to regard the modern movement as enslaved by those foreign influences which had from the start disfiguringly limited America's cultural ambitions. When Eliot published *The Waste Land* in 1922, Williams saw the work as a betrayal: 'I had to watch him carry my world with him, the fool, to the enemy.'

In pleading for 'no ideas but in things', Williams was also pleading, it turned out, for an elimination of 'lyrical interference' – by which he seemed to mean that the eye should meet the subject with an innocent directness, as if for the first time, with no cultural preconceptions, no ironies, no footnotes. By way of this somewhat puritanical approach, the American poet could escape his Puritan inheritance and for the first time see his native land for what it was

– a new world of promise and discovery, but also a 'hard, truculent mass' into which poetry had so far made few inroads.

As R. P. Blackmur once observed, Williams the documentarist (or innocent explorer) too often 'calls attention to what we are already in possession of', and in much of his work there is a decent, unilluminating factuality – too many things, too few ideas, one could almost say. Much of his subject matter was drawn directly from his stable but eventful daily life as a medical practitioner in Rutherford, New Jersey, where he settled in 1920 and remained until his death in 1963. A conscientious doctor and a steadfast husband to Florence (whom he married in 1912 and who features in several of his poems), Williams is probably the least scandalous of modern poets. Every so often, his decency flares up into distress, and the best of his short poems are about other people, people for whom he was the local doctor (see 'To Waken an Old Lady' or 'The Widow's Lament in Springtime'):

> Thirtyfive years
> I lived with my husband.
> The plumtree is white today
> with masses of flowers.
> Masses of flowers
> load the cherry branches
> and color some bushes
> yellow and some red
> but the grief in my heart
> is stronger than they
> for though they were my joy
> formerly, today I notice them
> and turn away forgetting.

But Williams also had *Cantos*-sized ambitions. His long poem, *Paterson*, began appearing in 1946 and was still in progress at the poet's death, almost twenty years later. The general effort of this interminable work was to unfold an individual sensibility in terms of its American environment, local, historical and cultural. Williams 'searched for a city', he said, a city not too big and not too small, but possessing a 'colonial history'. As well as verse, the work includes numerous passages of prose – local historical records, personal letters, and so on. The method is passively cumulative – i.e., no 'lyrical interference' – and Williams compared its languid progress to that of the local river, the Passaic: 'I took the river as it followed its course down to the sea; all I had to do was follow it and I had a poem.'

Even more than his Americanist content, Williams's technical peculiarity has been promiscuously imitated. In the 1930s, he helped to found the Objectivist Press, which was a late retort to Imagism (Pound's movement enjoyed a small rebirth at the beginning of that decade). Williams and his co-objectivists announced that 'there is no such thing as free verse'. All verse, they said, had to obey 'a measure of some sort'. Their own *vers*, which appeared to be entirely *libre*, was actually responding to rules that ran much deeper than mere 'counted syllables'. The Williams measure was, he claimed, dictated by the action of his breath when he was in the act of writing. On the page, the effect is as one might expect: staccato, broken, short of wind. In one poem, the late 'Asphodel, that Greeny Flower', this limp-along effect makes for a halting spontaneity in which the sheer effort of expression is 'measured' by the poem's layout:

> I thought the world
> stood still.
> At the altar
> so intent was I
> before my vows,
> so moved by your presence
> a girl so pale
> and ready to faint
> that I pitied
> and wanted to protect you

As I think of it now,
            after a lifetime,
                        it is as if
a sweet-scented flower
            were poised
                        and for me did open.
Asphodel
            has no odor
                        save to the imagination
but it too
            celebrates the light.

This is a rare success, though. Habitually, the reader's impulse is to rearrange a Williams down-the-page trickle into prose, as with:

There is
the
microscopic
anatomy
of
the whale

or, in another poem, although here we'd need some commas:

whom I myself
ignorant
as I was taught

to read the poems

The triple space signifies a stanza break: the deepest of deep breaths.

The Widow's Lament
in Springtime

Sorrow is my own yard
where the new grass
flames as it has flamed
often before but not
with the cold fire
that closes round me this year.
Thirtyfive years
I lived with my husband.
The plumtree is white today
with masses of flowers.
Masses of flowers
load the cherry·branches
and color some bushes
yellow and some red
but the grief in my heart
is stronger than they
for though they were my joy
formerly, today I notice them
and turn away forgetting.
Today my son told me
that in the meadows,
at the edge of the heavy woods
in the distance, he saw
trees of white flowers.
I feel that I would like
to go there
and fall into those flowers
and sink into the marsh near them.

From *Asphodel, That Greeny Flower*

Book 1

Of asphodel, that greeny flower,
        like a buttercup
                upon its branching stem –
save that it's green and wooden –
        I come, my sweet,
                to sing to you.
We lived long together
        a life filled,
                if you will,
with flowers. So that
        I was cheered
                when I came first to know
that there were flowers also
        in hell.
                Today
I'm filled with the fading memory of those flowers
        that we both loved,
                even to this poor
colorless thing –
        I saw it
                when I was a child –
little prized among the living
        but the dead see,
                asking among themselves:
What do I remember
        that was shaped
                as this thing is shaped?
while our eyes fill
        with tears.
                Of love, abiding love

it will be telling
    though too weak a wash of crimson
        colors it
to make it wholly credible.
    There is something
        something urgent
I have to say to you
    and you alone
        but it must wait
while I drink in
    the joy of your approach,
        perhaps for the last time.

D. H. Lawrence

1885–1930

The outline of Lawrence's life is thoroughly familiar – indeed, its general shape is echoed in the *curricula vitae* of quite a few modern poets: the escape from a provincial background, the philistine father, the culture-vulture mother, the eventual flight into a guilty, rootless eloquence. D. H. Lawrence was born in Eastwood, Nottinghamshire, in 1885. His father was a coal-miner, his mother a middle-class schoolteacher. D. H., the clever son, won scholarships at the local high school and went on to university in Nottingham, and from there became a schoolmaster and apprentice writer. He published his first novel at the age of twenty-six, and two years before that began publishing poetry in London periodicals. In 1912 he eloped with the German wife of a university professor, and married her in 1914. Persecuted as suspected spies during the 1914–18 war, the Lawrences fled England for several years of fidgety world travel: Sicily, Australia, New Mexico. During these years, Lawrence became well known as the author of novels such as *Sons and Lovers* and *Women in Love*. In 1925, the couple returned to England, in time for the banning of *Lady Chatterley's Lover*. Lawrence died, aged forty-five, in 1930.

Lawrence's poetry has often been sidelined as 'careless', 'hurried' or 'slapdash', or as belonging to a lower rank of creativity than his fiction. His standing as a novelist has always surpassed his standing as a poet, and when the author himself talked about his verses he tended to emphasize their hasty composition. For Lawrence, though, haste was no sin. He was proud of his spontaneity, and boasted of his attachment to the 'instantaneous'. In part this emphasis was literary-political, a way of reproaching his supposedly 'revolutionary' verse-contemporaries – and in particular those Imagists who wanted to recruit him to their ranks. In Lawrence's view, the free verse of the Imagists was merely pretending to be free. Although they had broken with tight metrics, these so-called pioneers had not really broken with poetry's time-honoured commitment to ideals of 'finish' or 'perfection'. The marmoreal tradition lingered.

Lawrence's own poetry had no yearnings of this kind: it was, he claimed, an expression of 'the instant'; it was 'quick'; it had 'no satisfying stability'; it was 'like plasm'; it 'let the demon say its say'.

. . . Give me nothing fixed, set, static. Don't give me the infinite or the eternal: nothing of infinity, nothing of eternity. Give me the still, white seething, the incandescence and coldness of the incarnate moment: the moment, the quick of all change and haste and opposition: the moment, the immediate present, the Now. The immediate moment is not a drop of water running downstream. It is the source and issue, the bubbling up of the stream. Here, in this very instant moment, up bubbles the stream of time, out of the wells of futurity, flowing on to the oceans of the past. The source, the issue, the creative quick.

His early, and persisting, hero was the abundant and untethered Whitman ('that great, fierce poetic machine'). It was from Whitman that he learned to travel down the long, colloquial line as though it were some thrilling, if prosodic, open road. And Lawrence also thrilled to Walt's gigantic egotism, his dramatic vigour, his refusal to be yoked by cultural sophistications. 'Whitman, the one pioneer,' Lawrence called him. 'Ahead of all poets, pioneering into the wilderness of unopened life . . . Beyond him, none.'

At best, the Whitman influence permitted Lawrence a stirringly impassioned directness of address that has no real precedent in English: a talking voice that sounds like talk. At worst, the influence encouraged noisy, narcissistic sprawl. But even in Lawrence's most rambling and bombastic slabs of pulpitry, we hardly ever get a sense of something false, or of an over-effort to impress. The dullness – when it comes – is genuine. Was Lawrence writing to be heard, or overheard? When we think we know the answer to that question, it is usually because the poet knows it too. With Lawrence, the reader is never quite an eavesdropper, never quite an addressee, but something in between. Lawrence's long lines, like Whitman's, are not easily achieved: although they seem unstoppable, they do get stopped, and Lawrence is not often felt to be at the mercy of his own loquacity:

> And I thought of the albatross,
> And I wished he would come back, my snake.
>
> For he seemed to me again like a king,
> Like a king in exile, uncrowned in the underworld,
> Now due to be crowned again.
>
> And so, I missed my chance with one of the lords
> Of life,
> And I have something to expiate;
> A pettiness.

But Lawrence's universe can soon get claustrophobic, with its relentless atmosphere of confrontation, its perpetual oppositions: between 'phallic consciousness' and 'cerebral sex consciousness', between spontaneous feeling and dithering intellectualism, between heart and head, the sun and the rain, the this and the that. Lawrence leaves no space for indecision and has little patience with the tentative – at any rate where humans are concerned. He needed to be in a state of rage: not just for the sake of the subject matter but also because rage offered him structures for survival. His oppositional polemics masked a deep misanthropy. For all his talk of human feelings, Lawrence hated being human, hated humans. Hence the splenetic and not often very funny verse 'satires', or messages of hate, like 'How Beastly the Bourgeois Is' or 'The Oxford Voice'; hence the deep reverence for animals and plants. The tenderness and humility one finds in Lawrence's bat poems, or his tortoise poems, or his much-anthologized 'The Snake' are not easy to locate in his transactions with the human world, except when that human world is of the past, and lost.

Lawrence often talked of a 'new life', by which he meant a next life. Death is depicted as a 'merging' even more exalted and intense than that of man and woman ('for the great mergers, woman at last becomes inadequate'), and nowhere is this death-love more powerfully expressed than in Lawrence's magnificent last poems, and in particular his 'Ship of Death', written a few months before his own tubercular demise. Misanthropy brought out the best in Lawrence: both as a rage-filled polemicist and as a rapt observer of non-human beauty – or of beauty which humans had neglected or repressed. Few poets can have anticipated their own liberation from ill temper with the benign impatience to be gone that went into the building of this strange, unhappy writer's ship of death:

> Build then the ship of death, for you must take
> the longest journey, to oblivion.
>
> And die the death, the long and painful death
> that lies between the old self and the new.

Snake

A snake came to my water-trough
On a hot, hot day, and I in pyjamas for the heat,
To drink there.

In the deep, strange-scented shade of the great dark
        carob-tree
I came down the steps with my pitcher
And must wait, must stand and wait, for there he was at
        the trough before me.

He reached down from a fissure in the earth-wall in the
        gloom
And trailed his yellow-brown slackness soft-bellied
        down, over the edge of the stone trough
And rested his throat upon the stone bottom,
And where the water had dripped from the tap, in a
        small clearness,
He sipped with his straight mouth,
Softly drank through his straight gums, into his slack
        long body,
Silently.

Someone was before me at my water-trough,
And I, like a second comer, waiting.
He lifted his head from his drinking, as cattle do,
And looked at me vaguely, as drinking cattle do,
And flickered his two-forked tongue from his lips, and
        mused a moment,
And stooped and drank a little more,
Being earth-brown, earth-golden from the burning
        bowels of the earth
On the day of Sicilian July, with Etna smoking.

The voice of my education said to me
He must be killed,
For in Sicily the black, black snakes are innocent, the
    gold are venomous.

And voices in me said, If you were a man
You would take a stick and break him now, and finish
    him off.

But must I confess how I liked him,
How glad I was he had come like a guest in quiet, to
    drink at my water-trough
And depart peaceful, pacified, and thankless,
Into the burning bowels of this earth?

Was it cowardice, that I dared not kill him?
Was it perversity, that I longed to talk to him?
Was it humility, to feel so honoured?
I felt so honoured.

And yet those voices:
If you were not afraid, you would kill him!

And truly I was afraid, I was most afraid,
But even so, honoured still more
That he should seek my hospitality
From out the dark door of the secret earth.

He drank enough
And lifted his head, dreamily, as one who has drunken,
And flickered his tongue like a forked night on the air,
    so black,
Seeming to lick his lips,
And looked around like a god, unseeing, into the air,
And slowly turned his head,
And slowly, very slowly, as if thrice adream,

Proceeded to draw his slow length curving round
And climb again the broken bank of my wall-face.

And as he put his head into that dreadful hole,
And as he slowly drew up, snake-easing his shoulders,
    and entered farther,
A sort of horror, a sort of protest against his
    withdrawing into that horrid black hole,
Deliberately going into the blackness, and slowly
    drawing himself after,
Overcame me now his back was turned.

I looked round, I put down my pitcher,
I picked up a clumsy log
And threw it at the water-trough with a clatter.

I think it did not hit him,
But suddenly that part of him that was left behind
    convulsed in undignified haste,
Writhed like lightning, and was gone
Into the black hole, the earth-lipped fissure in the
    wall-front.
At which, in the intense still noon, I stared with
    fascination.

And immediately I regretted it.
I thought how paltry, how vulgar, what a mean act!
I despised myself and the voices of my accursed human
    education.

And I thought of the albatross,
And I wished he would come back, my snake.

For he seemed to me again like a king,
Like a king in exile, uncrowned in the underworld,
Now due to be crowned again.

And so, I missed my chance with one of the lords
Of life.
And I have something to expiate;
A pettiness.

Piano

Softly, in the dusk, a woman is singing to me;
Taking me back down the vista of years, till I see
A child sitting under the piano, in the boom of the
     tingling strings
And pressing the small, poised feet of a mother who
     smiles as she sings.

In spite of myself, the insidious mastery of song
Betrays me back, till the heart of me weeps to belong
To the old Sunday evenings at home, with winter
     outside
And hymns in the cosy parlour, the tinkling piano our
     guide.

So now it is vain for the singer to burst into clamour
With the great black piano appassionato. The glamour
Of childish days is upon me, my manhood is cast
Down in the flood of remembrance, I weep like a child
     for the past.

Ezra Pound

1885–1972

Everyone who thinks at all about modern poetry sooner or later has to take a view of Ezra Pound. As Auden – no admirer – once confessed, there are 'very few living poets who could say their work would have been exactly the same if Mr Pound had not lived'. Most of those 'living poets' are now dead, but Auden's point is not to be disputed.

Pound was born in Hailey, Idaho in 1885, but spent most of his childhood in Pennsylvania. He attended the University of Pennsylvania and seemed all set for a career in academia when, in 1908, he moved to London. He lived in London for twelve years – twelve crucial years in the inauguration of so-called 'modernism', an inauguration masterminded by Pound. It was Pound who invented Imagism and who promoted the early work of T. S. Eliot and campaigned against the censors on behalf of Joyce. His own verse during this period changed from vapid archaism to the melodious-colloquial, but much of it was offered as translation – from the Provençal, from Old English, Italian, Chinese, Latin. Some people derided him for the sloppiness of his 'translations'; others praised him for his 'renewal' of old texts. And this was always the way of things with Pound: on the one hand there were those who saw him as a charlatan, on the other those who hailed him as modern poetry's Messiah.

For Pound's disciples, of whom there are still several, Auden's talk about Pound's influence would seem to be the faintest of faint praise. For hard-line Poundians, Ezra represents the one true source, his unending *Cantos* the wondrously scornful exemplum for all who would pretend to 'make it new'. For Pound's detractors, though, Auden would appear to have quite shirked the central point. For hard-line anti-Poundians, the poet's rabid anti-Semitism, his open support of Fascism during the war, the incoherent megalomania that marks so much of what he wrote, are what we ought to focus on. Here surely, such might say, is one instance where a poet's politics must be allowed to cancel out his poems.

In between these two dubious positions, there is another, smaller Pound on offer: Pound the literary impresario, the one whose energy and self-assurance brought literary Georgianism to its knees and established new ground rules for the modern poet:

1. Direct treatment of the 'thing', whether subjective or objective.
2. To use absolutely no word that does not contribute to the presentation.
3. As regards rhythm: to compose in sequence of the musical phrase, not in sequence of the metronome.

Some of Pound's battle cries – 'Make it new!'; 'Poetry must be at least as well-written as prose' – seem fairly simplistic nowadays, but at the time they engendered a useful bustle of self-scrutiny among the older guard. And Pound did have new poems to hand that seemed to reinforce the slogans – poems by T. S. Eliot in particular. Without Eliot, much of Pound's propaganda might easily have fallen flat.

In this approach to Pound, the poet-publicist is cast in a heroic role, practical and down-to-earth where others are timid and bumbling, sacrificing his own genuine but modest gifts in order to promote the larger gifts of others – a super-agent for the difficult-

to-sell. Pound's phoney scholarship, his often nonsensical mani-
festos, his fake-bohemian self-presentation: all can be forgiven
because so often, in those early days, he got it right. He backed
some duds, but he also backed some formidable winners – Eliot
and Joyce, most notably, but also Lawrence and Wyndham Lewis,
and his influence was felt by Yeats and Frost.

Those who admire Pound chiefly because of what he did for
others tend to see the rest of his life – from, say, his reworking of
Eliot's *The Waste Land* until his death in 1972 – as a sorry postscript
to those splendid London years. First came the mad economics,
then the support of Mussolini and the broadcasts from war-time
Italy, and then the most pitiable image of all: Pound caged in an
internment camp near Pisa in 1945, under indictment by the US
Government for treason and still muttering belligerently about
Jewish world conspiracies. Then followed the twelve years in a
Washington mental hospital (which Pound seems to have enjoyed
much of the time, with visits from admirers and controversies about
his winning of prizes and inclusion in anthologies), and after that
his return to Italy and a period of slow disintegration. Pound's years
of freedom in Italy had little of the kingly aspect that had marked
his sojourn in Washington. There were still visits from admirers,
but Pound at this stage had lost, or given up, the will to preach –
indeed, for long stretches during these rather pitiful last years, he
refused to say anything to anyone. He'd said enough.

When Pound the youthful impresario is praised, Pound the poet
tends to get less than he deserves. The *Cantos* are seen as a gigantic
folly – which, for most of their vast, incoherent length they surely
are: the kind of folly that might be expected from a great promoter
who ends up with nothing to promote except himself. Energies that
had once cowed editors like Margaret Anderson and Harriet Monroe
into accepting poems they did not understand were pumped into
the construction of a 'major work', which the whole world found
incomprehensible but somehow got bullied into taking seriously.

And yes, the idea of Pound the bully does fit with Pound the
Fascist and with Pound the mogul of the avant-garde. It does not
fit, however – except by some narrative of respite – with the

delicate, hesitant, exalted moments in Pound's verse. Such moments are few and far between, but they are both dignified and humble when they happen – and touching also in their non-modernist attachment to diction which, thanks to the proselytizing Pound, was out of date, or made to seem so:

> See, they return; ah, see the tentative
>> Movements, and the slow feet,
>> The trouble in the pace and the uncertain
>> Wavering!
>
> See, they return, one, and by one
> With fear, as half-awakened;
> As if the snow should hesitate
> And murmur in the wind,
>> And half turn back;
> These were the 'Wing'd-with-Awe,'
>> Inviolable.

Most often, moments of this kind can be encountered in his early verse, but they occur throughout his work – even, sometimes, in the *Cantos*; see in particular, his *Canto 81*:

> 'Master thyself, then others shall thee beare'
>> Pull down thy vanity
> Thou art a beaten dog beneath the hail,
> A swollen magpie in a fitful sun,
> Half black half white
> Nor knowst'ou wing from tail
> Pull down thy vanity
>> How mean thy hates
> Fostered in falsity,
>> Pull down thy vanity,
> Rathe to destroy, niggard in charity,
> Pull down thy vanity,
>> I say pull down.

Even at his early propagandist peak, Pound's poetry nearly always lagged behind his theories – often it seemed to offer good examples of the kind of stuff he said he didn't want. But then Pound was always at his best when he stopped thinking, when he let himself follow his own ear. William Carlos Williams, Pound's earliest literary friend but by no means his constant fan, could never understand how such a noisy crackpot could be 'possessed of the most acute ear for metrical sequences, to the point of genius, that we have ever known'.

Francesca

You came in out of the night
And there were flowers in your hands,
Now you will come out of a confusion of people,
Out of a turmoil of speech about you.

I who have seen you amid the primal things
Was angry when they spoke your name
In ordinary places.
I would that the cool waves might flow over my mind,
And that the world should dry as a dead leaf,
Or as a dandelion seed-pod and be swept away,
So that I might find you again,
Alone.

Further Instructions

Come, my songs, let us express our baser passions,
Let us express our envy of the man with a steady job
        and no worry about the future.
You are very idle, my songs.
I fear you will come to a bad end.
You stand about in the streets,
You loiter at the corners and bus-stops,
You do next to nothing at all.

You do not even express our inner nobilities,
You will come to a very bad end.

And I?
I have gone half cracked,
I have talked to you so much that
                              I almost see you about me,
Insolent little beasts, shameless, devoid of clothing!

But you, newest song of the lot,
You are not old enough to have done much mischief,
I will get you a green coat out of China
With dragons worked upon it,
I will get you the scarlet silk trousers
From the statue of the infant Christ in Santa Maria
      Novella,
Lest they say we are lacking in taste,
Or that there is no caste in this family.

Hilda Doolittle ('HD')

1886–1961

It was Ezra Pound who persuaded Hilda Doolittle to call herself 'HD', and it was Pound who, in 1910, urged the twenty-four-year-old beauty (his one-time flame) to quit her devout Moravian homestead in Bethlehem, Pennsylvania (where she was born in 1886) and join him in his Euro-modernist adventuring in London. It is hard to deny that, without Ezra's assistance, this thinly gifted poet would probably not now be the subject of two full-length biographies. Nor would her trivia, translations and hitherto-unpublished jottings be distending a 600-page *Collected Poems*. But then, if anything at all instructive emerges from HD's life, it is that literary success does not always depend on literature. At certain periods in history it has been quite enough to have been in the right place at the right time – and to have looked the part.

Certainly, Hilda Doolittle seems to have had the kind of appearance that might help to launch a literary fashion. 'Ethereal', 'faun-like', 'luminous': such is the slack-jawed vocabulary that gets trundled out in almost every account of her. She was tall, almost six foot, and she dressed herself with much poetical taste and daring. Her demeanour was abstracted, strangely unreachable, with a hint of the bisexual. Over the years she managed to inspire some truly dreadful prose. Here is one of her admirers trying to explain what really went on between HD and Ezra Pound:

There was another Hilda who would flit in and out of the woods, her face changing in a mist, her moods altering with each dryad challenge, just as his troubadour self might appear fickle as it searched the world; they were alike.

Well, so much for the image. As for the time and place, there can be little doubt that in 1912 any young poet who happened not to be in London was missing an important rendezvous with the next one hundred years or so of English studies. Not to be swept up by Ezra was to risk getting pigeon-holed as Georgian or reactionary. Pound in 1912 had already created a small stir in London literary circles and he was anxious to make his impact felt back home in the United States. As if on cue, the American Doolittle began to show him verses which, although strenuously 'Hellenic' in subject matter, were none the less uncluttered, static and hard-edged: they were (or almost were) the kind of thing that Pound had just begun campaigning for:

> Dryads
> haunting the groves,
> Nereids
> who dwell in wet caves,
> for all the white leaves of olive-branch,
> and early roses,
> and ivy wreaths, woven gold berries,
> which she once brought to your altars,
> bear now ripe fruits from Arcadia,
> and Assyrian wine
> to shatter her fever.

Pound seized her manuscripts, signed them 'HD, Imagiste' and mailed them off to *Poetry* (Chicago). All at once, he had his movement (he also seized the works of Richard Aldington, HD's then husband), and HD had her place in literary history. From this point on, whatever else this poet did or did not do, she could not be omitted from any reliable account of the origins of modern verse. She was an Imagist.

But what else *did* she do? Not much, seems to be the uninfatuated answer — not much, that is, so far as her writing is concerned. Her verse remained uncluttered but its moment swiftly passed. Lack of clutter soon came to seem like lack of substance, and when in due course HD abandoned her Greek draperies, there was nothing to disguise a tiresome self-absorption:

> I wanted to say I was sorry,
> but why should I? but anyway
> I did want to say I was sorry
> but how could I? who was I?

HD's autobiographical fiction, a godsend to chroniclers of her various psychic upheavals, offers an unappealing mix of cosmic breathiness and fiddling narcissism.

After Imagism, HD continued writing for another forty years (she died in 1961), but even the most ardent biographer would have to agree that hers was not an admirable literary life. Her tangled relationship with the lesbian philanthropist Winifred Bryher, her sessions of analysis with Sigmund Freud, her love affairs with worshipful disciple figures, her tireless manipulation of those whom she believed she had ensnared, her dabblings in cinema and spiritualism: all these goings-on have interest of a kind, but not enough to justify the reverence of post-feminist biographers. 'The life of HD', says one of these, 'cannot be scrutinized without taking into consideration her various brews of Egyptology, Hellenic studies, tarot, astrology, numerology, and psycho-analysis.' This verdict seems to rule out several likely scrutineers — and, tellingly, it makes no mention of her verse.

Sea Rose

Rose, harsh rose,
marred and with stint of petals,
meagre flower, thin,
sparse of leaf,

more precious
than a wet rose,
single on a stem –
you are caught in the drift.

Stunted, with small leaf,
you are flung on the sand,
you are lifted
in the crisp sand
that drives in the wind.

Can the spice-rose
drip such acrid fragrance
hardened in a leaf?

Evening

The light passes
from ridge to ridge,
from flower to flower –
the hepaticas, wide-spread
under the light
grow faint –
the petals reach inward,
the blue tips bend

toward the bluer heart
and the flowers are lost.

The cornel–buds are still white,
but shadows dart
from the cornel–roots –
black creeps from root to root
each leaf
cuts another leaf on the grass,
shadow seeks shadow,
then both leaf
and leaf-shadow are lost.

Marianne Moore

1887–1972

In the mid-1950s, Marianne Moore – by then in her mid-sixties – was surprised by an approach from the Ford Motor Company of Detroit. Ford was planning to launch a new style of motor car, but could not settle on a name for it: would Ms Moore be willing to deploy her well-known powers of curious inventiveness to come up with a car name that would convey 'some visceral feeling of elegance, fleetness, advanced features and design'?

Moore was thoroughly delighted to be asked. Her poems, with their neat syllabic packaging, were nothing if not elegant and for three decades had been thought of in poetic circles as both worldly and 'advanced': for some, much too advanced. As a young poet in the 1920s, she had been a prominent figure in the modernist movement: promoted by Ezra Pound, encouraged by T. S. Eliot, befriended by HD, a denizen of Greenwich Village. Born in 1887, Moore was the daughter of an unsuccessful engineer who took little interest in his daughter's upbringing – Moore's childhood was spent in the house of her maternal grandfather, a Presbyterian minister. Moore's mother, a lastingly key figure in her life, housekept for her father and saw to it that her two children had a decent education.

Marianne's brother became a chaplain in the Navy and Marianne herself studied biology at Bryn Mawr. After Bryn Mawr, she tried her hand at several jobs: tutor, secretary, librarian.

A literary career was not envisaged and had it not been for the sometimes oppressive urgings of HD, Moore's poetry might have remained unnoticed. She herself made no great claims for it. Her jagged typographical layouts, her byzantine sentence-structures, even her syllabic patternings: all of these seemed to betoken a superior offhandedness. Was this poetry or prose? Moore seemed neither to know nor to care, so long as what she wrote was 'genuine':

> There is a great amount of poetry in unconscious
>   fastidiousness. Certain Ming
>   products, imperial floor coverings of coach-
>   wheel yellow, are well enough in their way but I have
>   seen something
>   that I like better – a
>   mere childish attempt to make an imperfectly
>   ballasted animal stand up,
>   similar determination to make a pup
>   eat his meat from the plate.

As it turned out, Moore won prizes and plaudits throughout the 'experimental' 1920s, and in 1926 she became editor of an influential New York literary magazine, *The Dial*. By 1940, she was generally recognized as America's leading 'woman poet'. And by the time of Ford's bizarre request, she was heavily garlanded with prizes, honorary degrees, academic sinecures, and so on.

It was not just her celebrity, however, that had attracted Ford. Moore was known to take pride in her down-to-earthness. She knew about science and machines and she took a benign interest in popular culture. She liked baseball and boxing, circuses and zoos. Although semi-reclusive and stunningly well-read, she also had a powerful streak of silliness, or whimsicality. The Ford assignment tickled her no end.

As things turned out, Ford invented its own name for the car –

'Edsel' was the final choice – and anyway the whole project was a failure: the new model bombed. But Moore's correspondence with the company was printed in the *New Yorker* and was much enjoyed by literary types. Indeed, it still occupies a small niche in the history of poetry's transactions with the world of commerce. It also happened to highlight some of the key features of Moore's hard-to-define giftedness: her sly obliquity, her mischievously arch abstractedness, her appetite for transient Americana.

But then, for Marianne Moore the writing of letters was never just a chore. For most of her long life – she died in 1972, aged eighty-five – she put as much energy into her letters as she did into her verse. She sometimes wrote as many as fifty letters in a single session, and rarely were her letters brief. In her later years, it could be said, letter-writing became a significant aspect of her creativity – quite often, she turned letters into poems, and her epistolary style became similar to her poetic style, and vice versa. The upshot was not always to be welcomed. Although some of her set-piece descriptions – of animals, objects, peculiar events – do benefit from having been tried out in letters, there also seems to be a way in which some of the proudly circuitous locutions which often make the poems tedious and irritating were greatly encouraged by her letter-writing prose. Neither in the poems nor in the letters do we get much sense of an addressee:

> flowers are curious. Some wilt
>   in daytime and some close at night. Some
> have perfume; some have not. The scarlet much-quilled
>   fruiting pomegranate, the African violet,
>   fuchsia and camellia, none; yet
>   the house-high glistening green magnolia's velvet-
> textured flower is filled
>   with anesthetic as inconsiderate as
>   the gardenia's.

It is often as though Moore is keeping herself company, or attempting to divert herself from an encroaching sense of tedium or pointlessness.

As editor of *The Dial*, Moore encouraged the 1920s avant-garde, but she also did her best to curb its self-aggrandizements. She sometimes removed weak lines from poems she had accepted and replaced them with neat strips of dots, and in general she backed away from literary pretentiousness. To her, George Saintsbury was as much of a hero as James Joyce and Ezra Pound, and she was not afraid to say so.

For most of her adult life, post-*Dial*, Moore lived quietly in Brooklyn with her mother. A trip to the zoo or to the Dodgers was a big event. Although we can deduce that she was probably of lesbian disposition (in her writings, she often casts herself as 'he'), there is no evidence that she had love affairs. She scrutinized her friends' entanglements rather as she scrutinized their poems: wryly, from a distance, and with an occasional flicker of reproach. But then, if she did have love affairs, she would almost certainly not have put them in her poems – nor, even, in her letters.

Critics and Connoisseurs

There is a great amount of poetry in unconscious
    fastidiousness. Certain Ming
        products, imperial floor coverings of coach-
    wheel yellow, are well enough in their way but I have
        seen something
            that I like better — a
                mere childish attempt to make an imperfectly
                    ballasted animal stand up,
                similar determination to make a pup
                    eat his meat from the plate.

I remember a swan under the willows in Oxford,
    with flamingo-colored, maple-
        leaflike feet. It reconnoitered like a battle-
    ship. Disbelief and conscious fastidiousness were
        ingredients in its
            disinclination to move. Finally its hardihood was
                not proof against its
            proclivity to more fully appraise such bits
                of food as the stream

bore counter to it; it made away with what I gave it
    to eat. I have seen this swan and
        I have seen you; I have seen ambition without
    understanding in a variety of forms. Happening to stand
        by an ant-hill, I have
            seen a fastidious ant carrying a stick north, south,
                east, west, till it turned on
            itself, struck out from the flower bed into the lawn,
                and returned to the point

from which it had started. Then abandoning the stick as
   useless and overtaxing its
      jaws with a particle of whitewash – pill-like but
   heavy – it again went through the same course of procedure.
                  What is
         there in being able
            to say that one has dominated the stream in an
                  attitude of self-defense;
            in proving that one has had the experience
               of carrying a stick?

The Monkeys

winked too much and were afraid of snakes. The zebras, supreme in
their abnormality; the elephants with their fog-colored skin
   and strictly practical appendages
      were there, the small cats; and the parakeet –
         trivial and humdrum on examination, destroying
      bark and portions of the food it could not eat.

I recall their magnificence, now not more magnificent
than it is dim. It is difficult to recall the ornament,
   speech, and precise manner of what one might
      call the minor acquaintances twenty
         years back; but I shall not forget him – that Gilgamesh among
      the hairy carnivora – that cat with the

wedge-shaped, slate-gray marks on its forelegs and the resolute tail,
astringently remarking, 'They have imposed on us with their pale
   half-fledged protestations, trembling about
         in inarticulate frenzy, saying
      it is not for us to understand art; finding it
   all so difficult, examining the thing

as if it were inconceivably arcanic, as symmetrically
     frigid as if it had been carved out of chrysoprase
  or marble – strict with tension, malignant
     in its power over us and deeper
          than the sea when it proffers flattery in exchange for hemp,
     rye, flax, horses, platinum, timber, and fur.'

Robinson Jeffers

1887–1963

Robinson Jeffers was known to be contemptuous of literary fashions, but even so he would probably not have been amused to learn that his own poetry is nowadays most often talked about in terms of audience response, and of how that response fluctuated throughout the course of his disdainfully single-track career.

In the 1920s, Jeffers was widely hailed as America's great new poet, a heartening, home-grown alternative to mid-Atlantic modernists like Pound and Eliot. Jeffers, it was contended, had restored to modern verse some of its cherished but now vandalized glories and responsibilities: he was both high-prophetic and low-readable. He was a primitive who was familiar with the classics; he had no taste for ironic brevities. His response to urban-industrial unpleasantness was to avoid it altogether. He even chose to live in California. Instead of trying to construct alliances with Europe, Jeffers took his lead from Whitman: vitality and amplitude were hymned at the expense of precision and sophistication.

But Jeffers's background, it so happened, was peculiarly cosmopolitan. Born in Pittsburgh in 1887, he was the son of a theology professor who taught him Greek and Latin at an early age and then sent him to a string of European boarding schools, where he learned Italian, French and German. In 1903, his family moved to California; Jeffers enrolled at the University of Southern California, and there met and fell in love with Una Custer, a married woman. Thwarted in his courtship, Jeffers travelled in Europe for a time, but eventually returned to the West Coast, married Una – who was by now divorced – and, with the help of a legacy, moved with her to the coastal town of Carmel, where he lived in semi-isolation for the ensuing five decades of his lengthy life. He died in 1963.

Jeffers's career as a poet started slowly. At the peak of his prestige he was already in his thirties and had been publishing for several years, to modestly favourable reviews. It was not until the publication of *Tamar* and *Roan Stallion*, two lengthy narratives, that he began to be regarded as a significant American original. And the acclaim, when it arrived, was wildly fulsome. He was bracketed with Sophocles and Shakespeare, and for a period was routinely viewed as 'one of the very few poets of the early Twentieth Century that the Twenty-First will read'. His picture appeared on the cover of *Time* magazine, where he was lauded as 'one to rank with the greatest poets of all generations'.

Although Jeffers was vaunted by traditionalist critics, it is worth noting that, but for an accident of history, he could easily have been recruited by the London modernists. In 1912, he planned to quit America for Europe, as so many US artists did around that time, but the threat of war discouraged him. Instead (rejected for active service in that war) he made for Carmel and there built – with his own hands – the tower-house that became his permanent, and to outsiders thoroughly unwelcoming, address. Perched on a cliffside, this austere dwelling offered splendid views of what would soon become the standard properties of Jeffers's verse: rocks, sea-birds, beaches, tides. When the Jeffers cult was riding high, admirers found in the remote discomfort of his lodgings a guarantee of his poetic authenticity, his fierce rejection of the present tense. Many of his best-known poems sanctified the non-human self-sufficiency of rocks and hawks, and it has to be conceded that his tireless eye for oceanic detail and expanse is one of his most lasting strengths.

Poems like 'November Surf ', 'Evening Ebb' and 'The Purse-Seine'
show Jeffers at his most steadily and most impressively observant:

> The ocean has not been so quiet for a long while; five night-herons
> Fly shorelong voiceless in the hush of the air
> Over the calm of an ebb that almost mirrors their wings.

The risk in all this steady looking was, of course, monotony, but
Jeffers always seemed indifferent to the possibility that what he
wrote might actually be boring: he was, after all, an oracle and
oracles tend to repeat themselves. The non-human views scanned
so obsessively by Jeffers were not just views; in each of them, and
in their cumulative sameness, we are meant to find instruction, we
are meant to understand that, by comparison, the human world is
botched and blind. This oracular, doctrine-giving self-assurance
was what some readers in the postwar 1920s were most thrilled by:
humans, they were happy to be told, had brutally laid waste to
their most lofty possibilities. Some of this had come to Jeffers via
Whitman, some via Lawrence, some via Nietzsche. Jeffers, from
his cliffside, was calling for a renewal of man's ancient and now
broken kinship with the world of nature. He called his philosophy
'inhumanism'.

As with Lawrence, it is not easy to distinguish meliorative fervour
from bilious misanthropy. And when Jeffers turned his gaze from
falcons to females this difficulty deepened. In the 1920s there was a
general readiness to be beguiled by close-up sexual candour, and
Jeffers's getting-back-to-nature vehemence somewhat too readily
attached itself to themes of incest and bestiality. Looking back on
Tamar and *Roan Stallion*, and on their spectacular contemporary
success, the suspicion is that spicy-sounding subject matter had
more bearing on Jeffers's audience-appeal than his grim, vitalist
'philosophy'.

And maybe Jeffers himself half-feared that this was so. The drift
of his post-1920s work was towards more abstract sermonizing. But
'inhumanism', as a blueprint for living, found few takers in the
1930s. Nor was there much appetite for flinty individualism. The

new cry was for togetherness. On this score, Jeffers was deemed to be irrelevant, if not a little dangerous. And this judgement coincided with the emergence of New Critics like Ransom and Yvor Winters, for whom Jeffers's simple-minded message-mongering seemed, well, the reverse of complex. Jeffers – to his credit, some might say – seemed not to notice the steep falling-off in his prestige. Maybe he noticed, and just didn't care. During the 1940s he ranted unpatri- otically against America's involvement in the war and by 1948, with the appearance of *The Double Axe*, he was so out of touch with currently modish dispositions that his publishers had to issue a disclaimer: 'Random House feels compelled to go on record with its disagreement over some of the political views pronounced by the poet in this volume.' There followed a critical neglect of Jeffers that lasted for some twenty years. It was not until the Vietnam era that readers were prepared to acknowledge that Jeffers's 'anti- Americanism' was chiefly anti-war (Jeffers feared that America's imperialistic ambitions would end in ruin – not least because Americans were not, by nature, colonists). In the 1960s, such thinking was not reckoned to be hateful.

Jeffers did not live to see this mild revival of his fortunes and it seems unlikely that his reputation will ever regain its 1920s peak. His slack technique, his vatic yet overbearing tone, together with the monotony of his content – all these are likely to keep his work in a glass case for years to come. But even so, there does seem to be a new, and altogether welcome willingness at least to acknow- ledge the integrity of Jeffers's descriptive pieces, and also to look for signs of what he might have done had he not felt himself to be burdened with elevated bardic duties (see the moving lines on his dead wife – Una died in 1950 – that preface the long narrative called 'Hungerfield').

When Una died, Jeffers contemplated suicide, but decided instead to stick to what he called 'my own thirty-year-old decision: who drinks the wine/ Should take the dregs; even in the bitter lees and sediment/ New discovery may lie'. Jeffers made no new discoveries but he never lost his willingness to 'take the dregs'. For this alone, perhaps, he is owed a second reading.

Evening Ebb

The ocean has not been so quiet for a long while; five
    night-herons
Fly shorelong voiceless in the hush of the air
Over the calm of an ebb that almost mirrors their wings.
The sun has gone down, and the water has gone down
From the weed-clad rock, but the distant cloud-wall rises.
   The ebb whispers.
Great cloud-shadows float in the opal water.
Through rifts in the screen of the world pale gold gleams,
    and the evening
Star suddenly glides like a flying torch.
As if we had not been meant to see her; rehearsing behind
The screen of the world for another audience.

Gray Weather

It is true that, older than man and ages to outlast him,
    the Pacific surf
Still cheerfully pounds the worn granite drum;
But there's no storm; and the birds are still, no song;
    no kind of excess;
Nothing that shines, nothing is dark;
There is neither joy nor grief nor a person, the sun's
    tooth sheathed in cloud,
And life has no more desires than a stone.
The stormy conditions of time and change are all
    abrogated, the essential
Violences of survival, pleasure,
Love, wrath and pain, and the curious desire of
    knowing, all perfectly suspended.
In the cloudy light, in the timeless quietness,

One explores deeper than the nerves or heart of nature,
    the womb or soul,
To the bone, the careless white bone, the excellence.

Rupert Brooke

1887–1915

Sneering at the Georgian poets has long been a classroom reflex, the obligatory first step towards extolling Eliot and the complex urbanism of genuinely 'modern' verse. 'Weekend pastoralism', 'false rusticity', 'glib technique', 'the worship of trees and birds': this has been the customary charge-sheet, and it does of course bear quite a bit of truth. 'Glib technique' was probably the major problem but, as to subject matter, the Georgians saw themselves as no less anxious than the modernists to break free of late-Victorian restraints: they saw themselves as pioneering a new realism.

Historically, the Georgian Poetry anthologies were simultaneous with Imagism, Futurism, Vorticism and the like. And certainly the first collections were assembled by Edward Marsh in a spirit of revolutionary fervour. As Marsh saw things, Georgianism and Imagism were just two different ways of expressing a pervasive discontent with what had gone before. He could with justice have argued that early Pound was more tuned into the 1890s than many of his own contributors. He could also have pointed out that T. E. Hulme, the first theorist of Imagism, sat alongside Henry Newbolt on the committee that voted Rupert Brooke's 'Grantchester' as the best poem published in *Poetry Review* in 1912. There were many such overlaps, and Harold Monro's Poetry Bookshop was where all the younger poets of the day, Georgians and Imagists, rubbed shoulders.

It is also true, of course, that Marsh loathed free verse and that Harold Monro refused to publish 'The Love Song of J. Alfred Prufrock'. But this was just one group of poets fighting with another for supremacy, and Georgianism was in truth much more despised by the old guard than by the Pound/Hulme faction. And Marsh certainly did not believe himself to be old-fashioned. On the contrary, he stood for a new earthiness and candour, so he thought. John Masefield and Arthur Bottomley set the standard, and so too did Rupert Brooke, with his seasick 'A Channel Passage':

> Do I forget you? Retchings twist and tie me,
>   Old meat, good meals, brown gobbets, up I throw.
> Do I remember? Acrid return and slimy,
>   The sobs and shudders of a last year's woe.
> And still the sick ship rolls. 'Tis hard, I tell ye
> To choose 'twixt love and nausea, heart and belly.

Old buffers were more shocked by the Georgians' nasty subject matter than they were by Eliot's efforts in *vers libre*, of which they tended to know next to nothing.

It was the First World War, as much as Ezra Pound, that put paid to the Georgians – or confirmed them in the now accepted stereotype. The war offered actual squalor and brutality; from now on, to be shocked meant to be shell-shocked. Seen from the rat-infested trenches, the Georgians' vaunted 'realism' seemed ludicrously tame and self-indulgent. Escapes into the English countryside seemed no less other-worldly than, say, Swinburne.

The later Georgian anthologies (the series ran until 1922) could have included Owen, Sassoon, Rosenberg and other front-line poets, but they didn't. Marsh, after all, was Winston Churchill's private secretary. Squire, Shanks and Freeman were the favoured names and it was probably these later books (together with Squire's

anti-experimental fulminations in the *Mercury*) that won the movement its lasting reputation for complacency. The 'realists', it seemed
evident, had no means of coping with the real thing, and no wish
to try.

The career of Rupert Brooke nicely encapsulates this narrative.
At first viewed as a morbid brutalist, Brooke was eventually installed
as the golden boy of volunteer war fervour, this last on the strength
of his War Sonnets and the infatuated PR work of Edward Marsh,
who would become Brooke's executor after the poet's death in
1915 (he died of a mosquito bite and saw no active service). Born
in 1887, the son of a Rugby housemaster, Brooke from the start
seemed destined for a golden future of some kind. Gifted and
good-looking, he knew how to make the most of his assets; even
at school he was a tireless poseur, one of his favourite roles being
that of the doomed prodigy, the flawed beauty of exquisite and
perhaps unhealthy promise. Both at school and later on in Cambridge, he nurtured an image of faintly decadent malaise, of death-
inclined aestheticism: 'Do not be surprised', he wrote, 'to hear that
I am found dead some day on the Close, a self-thrust dagger in my
heart, a volume of Swinburne pallidly open before me.'

This adolescent death-wish, real or false, became a constant
feature of the Brooke self-presentation. Heading for the recruitment
office, he declared: 'I really think large numbers of male people
don't want to die, which is odd.' And to John Drinkwater: 'Come
and die. It'll be great fun.' Brooke was more afraid of growing old
than of dying. In all his love relationships, he sought refuge from
the adult world and could turn babyishly nasty when rejected. In
1912, after yet another sexual setback (although much desired by
men, Brooke fell in love with women), he succumbed to a somewhat theatrical nervous breakdown and fled to America, and then to
the South Seas, from where he bombarded his timorous love-object
with suicide threats and coarse recriminations. His trip to the South
Seas, he said, was like 'getting back to childhood', and so too,
afterwards, was his recruitment: 'The eye grown clearer and the
heart.'

Hence the war-welcoming sonnets that would make his name,

sonnets in which military combat was envisaged as a purifying rite of passage, an escape from 'a world grown old and cold and weary'. One of Brooke's recurring fears was that he would become a 'greying literary hack, mumbling along in some London suburb'. This never happened, but even if it had we would still be reading Brooke's 'The Soldier' – a poem which, for all its studied charm, did fix for ever that moment in British history when adolescent moodiness made contact with the nation's practical requirements, and engendered a bloodbath.

> If I should die, think only this of me:
> > That there's some corner of a foreign field
> That is for ever England.

Winston Churchill wrote Brooke's obituary in *The Times*:

The thoughts to which Rupert Brooke gave expression in the very incomparable war sonnets which he has left behind will be shared by many thousands of young men moving resolutely and blithely forward into this, the hardest, cruellest, and the least-rewarded of all the wars that men fought. They are a whole history and revelation of Rupert Brooke himself. Joyous, fearless, deeply instructed, with classic symmetry of mind and body, he was all that one would wish England's noblest sons to be in days when no sacrifice but the most precious is acceptable, and the most precious is that which is most freely proferred.

Quite so, but all the same, one can't help wondering how the poet of 'A Channel Passage' would have coped with those disgusting trenches. If Brooke had turned into Wilfred Owen, Edward Marsh would certainly have printed the results in *Georgian Poetry*.

A Memory

Somewhile before the dawn I rose, and stept
  Softly along the dim way to your room,
  And found you sleeping in the quiet gloom,
And holiness about you as you slept.
I knelt there; till your waking fingers crept
  About my head, and held it. I had rest
  Unhoped this side of Heaven, beneath your breast.
I knelt a long time, still; nor even wept.

It was great wrong you did me; and for gain
Of that poor moment's kindliness, and ease,
And sleepy mother-comfort!
                                   Child, you know
How easily love leaps out to dreams like these,
Who has seen them true. And love that's wakened so
Takes all too long to lay asleep again.

The Soldier

If I should die, think only this of me:
  That there's some corner of a foreign field
That is for ever England. There shall be
  In that rich earth a richer dust concealed;
A dust whom England bore, shaped, made aware,
  Gave, once, her flowers to love, her ways to roam,
A body of England's, breathing English air,
  Washed by the rivers, blest by suns of home.

And think, this heart, all evil shed away,
  A pulse in the eternal mind, no less

Gives somewhere back the thoughts by England
   given;
Her sights and sounds; dreams happy as her day;
   And laughter, learnt of friends; and gentleness,
      In hearts at peace, under an English heaven.

Conrad Aiken

1889–1973

Conrad Aiken is probably best studied nowadays as an arch-victim of the convulsion of self-doubt that afflicted most poets who began writing in the first two decades of the century. Aiken, as a young man of thoroughly traditional literary inclinations, found himself – by accident – embroiled in the first throes of modernism's fear that poetry had maybe (thanks to technology and mass-communication) had its day; that, at the very least, this ancient art would soon be forced to yield much of its time-honoured prestige and authority. Aiken, it could certainly be said, came to believe that modern poets were faced with a stark choice: between extinction and self-renovation. And, as a result, he found himself condemned to a lifetime of generic indecision. Aiken wanted modern poetry to be different from what had gone before, to branch out in compelling new directions, but he could never quite decide how such a branching-out could best be served.

Poets, Aiken believed, should learn from Freud and set themselves to give voice to the quotidian unconscious: if this made for trivia and tedium, so be it. They should learn from the Symbolists to construct worlds 'shimmering with ambivalence and ambiguities': if this made for obscurity, too bad. They should learn too from

Santayana to go in search of 'philosophies of the universe' and from modern music that ideas need not be explicit – they can resonate: why not a poem-symphony, or, come to that, a *Four Quartets*?

It was perhaps Aiken's early contact with T. S. Eliot that first set him on these questing paths. Born in Georgia in 1889, Aiken endured a troubled, not to say horrific childhood. At the age of eleven, he saw his father shoot his mother dead and then commit suicide. Parentless, he went to live with a great-aunt in New England, attended a good school there and did well. In 1907, he enrolled at Harvard, which is where he met Eliot, a co-student. The two of them shared an interest in off-colour limericks and the works of Théophile Gautier ('There was a lot of interchange', claimed Aiken later on. 'The juice flowed both ways'), and it was Aiken who famously told Ezra Pound that 'there was a guy at Harvard doing funny stuff' whom Pound might usefully watch out for.

When Eliot left for London, Aiken stayed put and in 1914 produced a first book of verse which was, in his own later summing-up, a 'dead steal' from John Masefield. It was not until 1916 (by which date Eliot's London fame was in its infancy) that Aiken became a modernist convert – or at any rate a convert to the cause of Novelty. He had read Freud by now and discovered what he called 'a veritable gold-mine of consciousness'. 'I swallowed Freud early', he would testify, 'and then pursued him in every direction.'

Aiken also began to devote himself to literature full time (a teaching spell at Harvard in the 1920s ended with his dismissal on the grounds of 'moral turpitude': he was, by all accounts, a zealous womanizer), and began publishing impenetrable dream-poems, some of these organized – so he would claim – as 'musical struc-tures'. A kind of murmuring monotony became the best-known feature of his efforts to claim for poetry a new mode of eloquence, a mode that would 'transcend' the limitations of mere language rather as the unconscious might transcend the limitations of in-telligence and common sense. Some readers heard the voice of Swinburne in these lush outpourings rather more clearly than they heard the voice of Freud, but it was Aiken's habit – post-conversion – to attach an up-to-date 'experimental' gloss to whatever happened from his pen. In spite of a generally baffled audience-response, he was given a Pulitzer Prize in 1930 (the first of many such awards to come his way), and by the mid-1930s he was firmly established as a senior, still-questing literary figure.

During the 1920s and 1930s, Aiken lived in Britain for long stretches, on and off – for a time in Henry James's Rye – but the British tended to see him as a rather tiresome Joyce-derivative. He also served for a period as a companion-mentor-watchdog to the apprentice alcoholic Malcolm Lowry: Lowry's rich, despairing father hired Aiken for this task, but there are some who believe that the Consul in Lowry's *Under the Volcano* has Aiken-like ingredients. Gradually – and by sheer force of visibility, it seems – Aiken turned himself into what he himself described as 'an almost unique phenomenon, a poet who has acquired a Reputation, or a Position, or what have you, without ever being caught in the act' – the act being, presumably, the composition of a worthwhile poem. With Aiken, marks were awarded for conscientiousness and 'experimentation' and, in the end, for a remarkable profusion. The never-unimpressive quantity of Aiken's output was assisted by the mellifluous vagueness of his content: nobody could quite make sense of what he wrote, but most were ready to settle for the belief that Aiken himself knew what he was about – and with poetry's destiny in doubt there was, especially in the 1920s, an eagerness to be reassured by noble-sounding plans of action. Conrad Aiken might be hard to take but he was always seeking to be new, and novelty seemed to afford, for poetry, some prospect of survival.

Aiken was also a loquacious autobiographer, in both fiction and non-fiction (see *Blue Voyage* and *Ushant*), and his persistent self-absorption seemed to open up new zones of exploration for the unnerved and bewildered modern poet. And it helped too that Aiken was a busy operator in the literary-political arena; throughout the middle period of his career he was a ubiquitous reviewer in the magazines and was usually available for the issuing of dicta and the staffing of prize panels. Aiken's commitment to the imperilled cause of poetry was never in doubt, and Randall Jarrell was perhaps the most generous and accurate of contemporary critics when he described him as 'a kind of Midas: everything he touches turns to verse'.

During the 1930s, Aiken's Freudianism counterbalanced his distaste for the prosy ins and outs of political in-fighting, and he would later attack the followers of Auden for their 'little dexterities, negative safety and indoor marxmanship'. When the 1940s came along, he began to bang the drum for a 'new romanticism', and to call for a resurgence of 'gusto': 'For God's sake, let's let in the whole romantic shebang again; it's about time.' By the 'romantic shebang' he seems to have meant Dylan Thomas – another sonorous obscurantist with links to Freudian interiors. For Aiken, the example of Thomas permitted scope for poeticizing self-inflation. But Thomas's rhetoric, however difficult to fathom, was rarely sleep-inducing, and Aiken was never able to emulate the Welshman's histrionics. The impression persisted that Aiken, for all his industry, was not so much a trail-blazer as an adjustable disciple-type – an attendant lord, as Prufrock would have said – but estimable, none the less, and probably quite useful.

In old age, though, Aiken began to seem less useful, and – understandably, perhaps – less well-adjusted to his secondary role. Always large and talkative, he was now spoken of as garrulous and fat, a kind of wordy Buddha-figure, as one critic put it. And he developed a late reputation for asperity, for laying into currently inflated reputations. American poetry, he pronounced not long before his eightieth birthday, had come to a 'temporary pause', and he, Aiken, had no time for then-fashionable types like Robert Lowell and Allen Ginsberg, although each of these poets should, it might be thought, have fitted with one or another of his own lifelong tendencies: either the self-exploratory or the declamatory. Harsh judgements were also issued at the expense of novelists Saul Bellow and Vladimir Nabokov: 'no style or taste' was found in either one of them. Aiken's critical ardour was now directed towards comic strips, he said, and the short fictions of John O'Hara. A few years before his death in 1973, Aiken composed his own obituary-in–verse, as if to demonstrate that, in spite of everything, there had been no diminution of his appetite for philosophical enquiry:

> Separate we come,
> separate we go.
> And this be it known is all
> that we know.

From *Preludes for Memnon—2*

Two coffees in the Español, the last
Bright drops of golden Barsac in a goblet,
Fig paste and candied nuts . . . Hardy is dead,
And James and Conrad dead, and Shakspere dead,
And old Moore ripens for an obscene grave,
And Yeats for an arid one; and I, and you —
What winding sheet for us, what boards and bricks,
What mummeries, candles, prayers, and pious frauds?
You shall be lapped in Syrian scarlet, woman,
And wear your pearls, and your bright bracelets, too,
Your agate ring, and round your neck shall hang
Your dark blue lapis with its specks of gold.
And I, beside you — ah! but will that be?
For there are dark streams in this dark world, lady,
Gulf Streams and Arctic currents of the soul;
And I may be, before our consummation
Beds us together, cheek by jowl, in earth,
Swept to another shore, where my white bones
Will lie unhonored, or defiled by gulls.

What dignity can death bestow on us,
Who kiss beneath a streetlamp, or hold hands
Half hidden in a taxi, or replete
With coffee, figs and Barsac make our way
To a dark bedroom in a wormworn house?
The aspidistra guards the door; we enter,
Per aspidistra — then — *ad astra* — is it? —
And lock ourselves securely in our gloom
And loose ourselves from terror . . .

Edna St Vincent Millay

1892–1950

During the 1920s, Edna Millay was lauded as the *femme fatale* of Greenwich Village, fabled for her beauty, her promiscuity, her lyrical bravado. She was also famous for her loyalty to antique literary forms – in particular, the sonnet. For Greenwich Villagers of Millay's epoch, the sonnet was ready to be pensioned off. Millay, though, showed little interest in technical experimentation. Outrageously and scornfully progressive in the conduct of her daily life, she was staunchly conservative in her approach to matters of poetic form. Her diction, too, was scarcely up-to-date colloquial. And yet somehow she appeared no less innovative than many of the so-called 'moderns'. But then Millay was a woman, a 'new freewoman', and this, it seems, was novelty enough.

Born in Maine in 1892, of parents who soon afterwards became divorced, she studied at Barnard ('this hell hole', as she typically described it), and then Vassar. By the time she took her degree, she already had a reputation as a poet (she had been writing verses since the age of five), and Greenwich Village beckoned. In no time at all, Millay was lauded as a female Scott Fitzgerald, and her books became bestsellers. As well as poems, she wrote verse plays (in which she liked to act) and novels (under a pseudonym). In 1923, she won a Pulitzer Prize and astonished her sub-bohemian admirers by marrying a Dutch businessman and resolving to clean up her act. She and her new husband retired to a farmhouse in New York State, where they attempted to construct a quiet life.

Perhaps this marriage to Eugene Boissevain was, rather like Millay's attachment to the sonnet form, a way of fixing limits to her volatility. In the early 1920s, with youth, beauty, fame and drink to urge her on, she was, by all accounts, a dazzling but unstable presence on the literary scene. In the ensuing two decades, though, her reputation went into steep decline. Her war poems of the 1940s showed a sorry falling off from the spontaneity and craftsmanship of her heyday. She was by this stage an alcoholic and susceptible to nervous breakdowns. She died in 1950 at the age of fifty-eight.

The sonnet form, Millay once said, made Wordsworth 'pull up his socks, told him to shut up, etc', and it may have had a similar usefulness for her. It constrained her innate unruliness and yet at the same time, within limits, it allowed her to roam free. For us, the upshot still seems thoroughly remarkable: an old form was injected with new vigour – and this at a time when old forms were in modish disrepute. Millay's audience was on a scale undreamed of by modernists like Pound and Eliot, and for this alone she came in for a good deal of resentment from self-consciously 'radical' reviewers (Malcolm Cowley, for example, railed against her 'baby talk'). But her popularity is not difficult to fathom; readers were reassured by her familiar structures even as they were excited by the impassioned eloquence that these structures just about managed to contain.

Millay's life seems to have functioned within a similar polarity between chaos and constraint. Her best poems were love poems; it was for love adventures that she first became notorious. And she did indeed have many lovers, of both sexes (a total of eighteen by 1920, one biographer has reckoned), and some of them – like Edmund Wilson and John Reed – were famous figures of the day. And yet none of them seems to have altogether conquered her. According to the memoirs of her victims, she was almost

Byronically unfaithful: 'What lips my lips have kissed, and where
and why/ I have forgotten.'

These victims, though, seem rather to have gloried in her wild
inconstancy, and to have decided in the end, with Edmund Wilson
(whom she pulverized), that Millay was 'a creature too noble, too
courageous and too brilliant for the ordinary mind'. And Millay
herself enjoyed such humble verdicts. There is a vein of jaunty
sexual triumphalism running through much of her early work. She
revelled in the power of her 'Large mouth/ Lascivious' and her
'long throat, which will someday be strangled'. And, of course, the
most famous of all Millay's lines cannot have reassured her legion
of admirers:

> My candle burns at both ends;
>   It will not last the night;
> But ah, my foes, and oh, my friends –
>   It gives a lovely light!

This hedonistic boastfulness can sometimes seem pre-packaged.
More typically, and more authentically, Millay tended to portray
herself in poems as distraught and victimized: see pieces like 'Hearing your words', 'Now by this moon' and 'Sweet love, sweet thorn'.
Even at its most heartfelt, though, there is something impersonal in
her distress: we don't really believe, and nor does she, that Lover
A or Lover B can help her much. The real torturer is Death, or the
idea of Death. Death is unfailingly constant; Death means what it
says. Sexual passion is, at best, a way of keeping the real enemy at bay:

> Love is not all: it is not meat nor drink
> Nor slumber nor a roof against the rain;
> Nor yet a floating spar to men that sink
> And rise and sink and rise and sink again.
> Love can not fill the thickened lung with breath,
> Not clean the blood, nor set the fractured bone . . .

An indignant, almost regal death-defiance is often at the centre of Millay's sexual bravado, and it can make for a heart-piercing pathos. 'I am not resigned', she writes in 'Dirge Without Music': not resigned, that is, 'to the shutting away of loving hearts in the hard ground'. She will deal with death, she boasts, as she would deal with an insistent and unwanted suitor:

> With all my might
>   My door shall be barred
> I shall put up a fight
>   I shall take it hard

Edna Millay wrote too much and was absurdly overrated in her day (the sonnets in *Fatal Interview* were ranked alongside those of Donne and Sidney). There was an inevitable backlash in the 1940s, when she was largely written off as cheaply histrionic. Her artificial diction, with its grating 'ah's and 'nay's, together with a breast-beating shrillness which too often faltered into bathos: such criticisms were legitimate and by and large can still be held against her. At the same time, though, we can now identify about a dozen poems in which, by some strange alchemy, her weaknesses can be perceived as strengths – or, at any rate, as evidence of an impressive courage. Millay was not like anybody else, and this perhaps will be her final ranking: a weird original; and at her best transfixingly old-fashioned and 'advanced'.

Hearing Your Words,
and Not a Word Among Them

Hearing your words, and not a word among them
Tuned to my liking, on a salty day
When inland woods were pushed by winds that flung them
Hissing to leeward like a ton of spray,
I thought how off Matinicus the tide
Came pounding in, came running through the Gut,
While from the Rock the warning whistle cried,
And children whimpered, and the doors blew shut;
There in the autumn when the men go forth,
With slapping skirts the island women stand
In gardens stripped and scattered, peering north,
With dahlia tubers dripping from the hand:
The wind of their endurance, driving south,
Flattened your words against your speaking mouth.

Dirge Without Music

I am not resigned to the shutting away of loving hearts in the hard
    ground.
So it is, and so it will be, for so it has been, time out of mind:
Into the darkness they go, the wise and the lovely. Crowned
With lilies and with laurel they go; but I am not resigned.

Lovers and thinkers, into the earth with you.
Be one with the dull, the indiscriminate dust.
A fragment of what you felt, of what you knew,
A formula, a phrase remains, – but the best is lost.

The answers quick and keen, the honest look, the laughter, the
     love, –
They are gone. They are gone to feed the roses. Elegant and curled
Is the blossom. Fragrant is the blossom. I know. But I do not approve.
More precious was the light in your eyes than all the roses in the
     world.

Down, down, down into the darkness of the grave
Gently they go, the beautiful, the tender, the kind;
Quietly they go, the intelligent, the witty, the brave.
I know. But I do not approve. And I am not resigned.

Hugh MacDiarmid

1892–1978

Hugh MacDiarmid was the pseudonym of Christopher Murray Grieve, born 1892, the son of a Dumfriesshire postman. Trained as a teacher, MacDiarmid served in the 1914–18 War and later became a journalist. Or, rather, C. M. Grieve did. For a time during the 1920s, Grieve/MacDiarmid led a double literary life: C. M. Grieve wrote articles in magazines calling for a revitalized Scots diction and Hugh MacDiarmid put Grieve's notions into practice, or attempted to. Later on, as MacDiarmid's verse became more prosy, the prosaic Grieve fell largely silent.

One of Hugh MacDiarmid's better-known poems is called 'The Kind of Poetry I Want', and there is a sense in which the entire Grieve/MacDiarmid output could be gathered under a single heading of this kind. MacDiarmid was always more concerned with programmes than with actual poems – indeed, his programmes rarely gave poetry much of a chance. He rejected what he called 'the irresponsible lyricism in which sense impressions/Are employed to substitute ecstasy for information' and declared himself in favour of 'a poetry which fully understands that the era of technology is an established fact'. He urged the Scots to return to the 'old Gaelic days'. And these glum dicta were offered up as poetry.

Easy enough to fly flags, of course, and this was the late – or middle-period – MacDiarmid speaking, the MacDiarmid who in the 1930s abandoned the synthetic Scots in which he had composed such engaging early oddities as *A Drunk Man Looks at the Thistle* (1926), and declared himself to be a Marxist. His 'First Hymn to Lenin' appeared in 1931. But with MacDiarmid the programmatic, trouble-making bent was always paramount. He saw himself as 'the catfish that vitalizes the other torpid denizens of the aquarium'. Even his stitched-together Scots was politically angled: Mac-Diarmid was a founder-member of the Scots Nationalist Party (which expelled him when he joined the Communists). In *Who's Who*, he listed his 'recreation' as 'Anglophobia', and he was never happier than when he was belabouring 'Anglicized mediocrities who are continually debauching the public taste'.

When MacDiarmid began to write in English, he was praised for attempting to turn poetry into a vehicle for 'ideas', and for his welcoming of 'scientific knowledge'. His opponents, and those who regretted his abandonment of Lallans, complained that the post-1930 MacDiarmid had merely granted himself a licence to lay down the law. The success of the kind of poetry MacDiarmid said he wanted depended finally on the quality of the intelligence it sought to exhibit. In this department, he was distinctly unimpressive. We could perhaps tolerate the flatness of his delivery, the general poverty of imagery and verbal subtlety, if we could locate at the centre of it all a mind of real distinction, or even a body of half-surprising insights. But MacDiarmid was always better at telling his readers what they needed than he was at actually supplying it:

> Clear thought is the quintessence of human life,
> In the end its acid power will disintegrate
> All the force and flummery of current passions and pretences,
> Eat the life out of every false loyalty and craven creed,
> And bite its way through to a world of light and truth.

It was this kind of banality that time and again brought MacDiarmid's theorizing down to earth, and it was no surprise when in his old age he became better known for his turbulent contentiousness (and his occasional plagiarisms) than for his actual poems. 'I'll hae nae hauf-way hoose but aye be whaur/Extremes meet' was the proud boast of his youth and, like most of his work, it sounds better in Scots, or in his patchwork of forgotten Lowlands dialects. Lallans was a good vehicle, he believed, for bellicose argumentation: 'Dunbar not Burns' was one of his battle cries, and he clearly yearned for the olden days, the very olden days, when writers could be flyters and get praised for the magnificent woundingness of their invective.

Scotland may well be grateful to MacDiarmid for his early efforts to achieve a Scots Renaissance, but to the unkilted reader there still seems something quaint, and rather bogus, in the dredged-up archaisms of literary Lallans. Encountering, in one of his Scots works, a reference to 'mither-fochin scones', we turn to the Glossary that comes with his *Collected Poems* and discover there that, in MacDiarmid's Scotland, 'to foch' means 'to turn (used of scones on a griddle)'. Tell *that* to the Gorbals. If poetry cannot be wrung from the language Scotsmen speak, no amount of nostalgic pedantry is likely to bring about the cultural reflowering for which MacDiarmid said he yearned. Even so, better – perhaps – the fake-Scots of this bad-tempered poet's youth than the prosy dreariness of his maturity.

Old Wife in High Spirits

In an Edinburgh Pub

An auld wumman cam' in, a mere rickle o' banes, in a faded black
    dress
And a bonnet wi' beads o' jet rattlin' on it;
A puir-lookin' cratur, you'd think she could haurdly ha'e had less
Life left in her and still lived, but dagonit!

He gied her a stiff whisky – she was nervous as a troot
And could haurdly haud the tumbler, puir cratur;
Syne he gied her anither, joked wi' her, and anither, and syne
Wild as the whisky up cam' her nature.

The rod that struck water frae the rock in the desert
Was naething to the life that sprang oot o' her;
The dowie auld soul was twinklin' and fizzin' wi' fire;
You never saw ocht sae souple and kir.

Like a sackful o' monkeys she was, and her lauchin'
Loupit up whiles to incredible heights;
Wi' ane owre the eight her temper changed and her tongue
Flew juist as the forkt lichtnin' skites.

The heich skeich auld cat was fair in her element;
Wanton as a whirlwind, and shairly better that way
Than a' crippen thegither wi' laneliness and cauld
Like a foretaste o' the graveyaird clay.

Some folk nae doot'll condemn gie'in' a guid spree
To the puir dune body and raither she endit her days
Like some auld tashed copy o' the Bible yin sees
On a street book-barrow's tipenny trays.

A' I ken is weel-fed and weel-put-on though they be
Ninety per cent o' respectable folk never hae
As muckle life in their creeshy carcases frae beginnin' to end
As kythed in that wild auld carline that day!

Wilfred Owen

1893–1918

The story of Wilfred Owen is well known. Before the 1914–18 War he was a lush, sub-Keatsian romantic; his juvenilia gives little hint of an unusual giftedness. In terms of then-current poetry fashions, the young Owen was contentedly behind the times – unaware, it seems, of Pound and Eliot and other metropolitan excitements. It was the war experience, the unanticipated horror of trench-combat, that turned him into the poet we now value so highly and respond to with such gratitude – gratitude because, more than any other poet of a century darkened by two mighty wars, he was able to tell us what war felt like and would feel like.

Owen experienced the war first-hand and his war poems swarm with ugly detail. He also experienced the editorial guidance of Siegfried Sassoon and, in terms of his eventual achievement, this too was all-important. When Owen was sent to Craiglockhart Hospital in 1917, Sassoon was already there – the hospital's most celebrated inmate. Sassoon had already had his own poetic habits altered by the experience of warfare. Like Owen, he had started out as a romantic bard. After a few hair-raising months on the front line, he had become a bitter and effective satirist. As a result of his well-publicized protests against the conduct of the war, he had been consigned to Craiglockhart for psychiatric observation.

So too, by 1917, had Wilfred Owen. Owen was Sassoon's junior by some six years. Born in 1893, the son of a railwayman, his childhood had been dominated by the fervent attentions of his mother, a strict Calvinist. The thought was that Wilfred might take holy orders, but he was forced to withdraw from university because of lack of funds, and in any case his faith had begun to falter by the time he enlisted in the Army in 1915. Owen was trained as an officer and joined action on the Western Front early in 1917. By June of the same year, he was back in Britain, a victim of shell shock, and it was at this point that he met Sassoon. The war poems for which Owen is now famous were composed between August 1917 and September 1918. He was killed in November 1918, having rejoined his regiment a few months earlier. His death came a week before the Armistice.

In 1920, Sassoon oversaw the publication of a book of Owen's poems – by this date, ironically, Sassoon's own satiric blasts against warmongering were felt to have outlived their usefulness. Owen's war poems were more durable than those of his adviser, and not just because they were more skilfully composed – Owen's use of pararhyme was innovative and, thanks largely to Sassoon, he had contrived to purge his work of nineteenth-century poeticisms. The chief difference between the two was one of sensibility, or – in the words of Owen's well-known manifesto – a sense of 'pity'. Sassoon's anger was political: he was angry about *this* war. Owen's was more broadly elegiac: he was angry about the human blindness and stupidity that caused men, time and time again, to go to war, to mutilate each other in the name of some uncomprehended principle. Owen really did feel for the 'doomed youth' of his celebrated 'Anthem':

> What passing-bells for these who die as cattle?
>   Only the monstrous anger of the guns.
>   Only the stuttering rifles' rapid rattle
> Can patter out their hasty orisons.

> No mockeries now for them; no prayers nor bells,
>   Nor any voice of mourning save the choirs, –
> The shrill, demented choirs of wailing shells;
>   And bugles calling for them from sad shires.

Writing about Wilfred Owen, Philip Larkin once fell to musing on the way we usually respond to the 'war poet' phenomenon. However hard we try, he says, and however admirable the actual works under consideration, there is still something in us that withholds from them the highest praise: 'a poet's choice of subject', we're inclined to say, 'should seem an action not a reaction'. Poets, in other words, should choose their subjects and not be chosen by them. 'The Wreck of the Deutschland', says Larkin, 'would have been markedly inferior, we feel, if Hopkins had been a survivor from the passenger list.'

To some extent, this might be true of our response to Wilfred Owen, just as it might be true of our response to Sylvia Plath. At the same time, though, we like to think of our best poets as having been possessed by some deep impulse to articulate. We like to think of Larkin in this way. Perhaps the best way of valuing what Owen did is to compare his poems with those of other poets who were compelled to eloquence by having to live through a war. Again, we are led back to Owen's sensibility, to the essential selflessness of his response, and to his staunch commitment to the actual shaping of good poems. And to speak of selflessness is to remark also on the homosexual element that energized his sense of 'pity'. For Owen, these dead youths represented a defiling of male beauty, even when – as in 'Strange Meeting' – that beauty issued from the other side, the so-called enemy:

> 'Strange friend,' I said, 'here is no cause to mourn.'
> 'None,' said that other, 'save the undone years.
> The hopelessness. Whatever hope is yours,
> Was my life also; I went hunting wild
> After the wildest beauty in the world,
> Which lies not calm in eyes, or braided hair,

> But mocks the steady running of the hour,
> And if it grieves, grieves richlier than here.
> For by my glee might many men have laughed,
> And of my weeping something had been left,
> Which must die now. I mean the truth untold,
> The pity of war, the pity war distilled.

It is perhaps this feeling for the bodies of the dead that makes Owen's war poetry more moving than Sassoon's. Sassoon, a homosexual, felt the same way, no doubt, but more statistically than Owen, and with less generosity of spirit.

Critics have lately argued that it was Owen's willingness to acknowledge his own homosexuality that enabled him to write with new assurance. If so, he was in this respect also indebted to Sassoon. Sassoon was rich, posh and well-connected and he was at pains to introduce the boy Owen to his London circle of smart gays (a circle that included Robert Ross, the loyal friend of Oscar Wilde). The months between Owen's leaving of Craiglockhart and his return to the front-line action were spent in − shall we say? − sophisticated company, and perhaps enabled him to look at what he'd been through earlier, in France, with a new candour, a new willingness to get at what it was that had thrown him off balance. If this is true, those few months can now be viewed as crucial to the poet's spectacular 'convulsion into greatness' (see Dominic Hibberd: *Wilfred Owen, The Last Year*).

As poetic life stories go, few single years can have been more fruitful than Wilfred Owen's 1917−18. What might he have gone on to achieve, if he had lived? This question rather brings us back to Larkin's musings. If Owen had been free to choose his subject, what would that subject have turned out to be? It could scarcely, at the time, and with his mother in attendance, have been to do with personal relationships. Perhaps, like Sassoon, he would have written his prose memoirs of the war and saved his verse for Nature and Religion. Perhaps his heartsore precision would have softened into mild-mannered 'observation'. Or would he have fallen in with

Auden, and paraded his fascination with technique? Perhaps our uncertainty about his prospects does lend support to Larkin's tentative conjecture.

Dulce et Decorum Est

Bent double, like old beggars under sacks,
Knock-kneed, coughing like hags, we cursed through
        sludge,
Till on the haunting flares we turned our backs
And towards our distant rest began to trudge.
Men marched asleep. Many had lost their boots
But limped on, blood-shod. All went lame; all blind;
Drunk with fatigue; deaf even to the hoots
Of tired, outstripped Five-Nines that dropped behind.

Gas! GAS! Quick, boys! – An ecstasy of fumbling,
Fitting the clumsy helmets just in time;
But someone still was yelling out and stumbling,
And flound'ring like a man in fire or lime . . .
Dim, through the misty panes and thick green light,
As under a green sea, I saw him drowning.

In all my dreams, before my helpless sight,
He plunges at me, guttering, choking, drowning.

If in some smothering dreams you too could pace
Behind the wagon that we flung him in,
And watch the white eyes writhing in his face,
His hanging face, like a devil's sick of sin;
If you could hear, at every jolt, the blood
Come gargling from the froth-corrupted lungs,
Obscene as cancer, bitter as the cud
Of vile, incurable sores on innocent tongues, –
My friend, you would not tell with such high zest
To children ardent for some desperate glory,
The old Lie: Dulce et decorum est
Pro patria mori.

Futility

Move him into the sun –
Gently its touch awoke him once,
At home, whispering of fields half-sown.
Always it woke him, even in France,
Until this morning and this snow.
If anything might rouse him now
The kind old sun will know.

Think how it wakes the seeds –
Woke once the clays of a cold star.
Are limbs, so dear achieved, are sides
Full-nerved, still warm, too hard to stir?
Was it for this the clay grew tall?
– O what made fatuous sunbeams toil
To break earth's sleep at all?

E. E. Cummings

1894–1962

E. E. Cummings – or 'e.e. cummings', as he insisted he be called –
was the first poet to perceive that the typewriter could be used as a
creative tool, and he is now chiefly famous for the typographical
layout of his work, his prankish way with brackets, commas,
ampersands, and so on. The idea of such visual gimmickry was to
project an infantile, wide-eyed 'philosophy' of innocence. Cummings, unflaggingly throughout a long career, promoted a head-on
collision between, on the one hand, simple-hearted spontaneity
and, on the other, duplicitous sophistication: scarcely a novel confrontation, but then Cummings's 'novelty' was really a matter of
display. Over the years, he published several hundred poems in
which springtime, flowers and children were set against an evil,
grown-up world of money, politics and war, and if his layouts had
been more conventional, he would probably have been ignored.
There were lyrical poems in which Cummings postured as a child;
there were satirical squibs in which he railed against the iniquities
of 'manunkind'. In neither vein did he sound thoroughly convincing. A friendly smile of half-assent was the required response to
lines like:

O sweet spontaneous
earth how often have
the
doting

   fingers of
prurient philosophers pinched
and
poked

thee
, has the naughty thumb
of science prodded
thy

   beauty

Here, Cummings's typographical playfulness is relatively diffident. In many other of his works, the fooling tends to the berserk:

ump-A-tum
; tee-die
UM-tuM
tidl
   -id
umptyumpty (oo-
   ting
Bam-
   ;do)
, chippity

(This is from a poem that begins 'theys sO alive (who is / ?niggers)'. Commentators nowadays solemnly fast-forward to the typographical 'experiments' of poets like Charles Olson and other figures connected to the 1960s Black Mountain school of poets, and hail Cummings as the progenitor of current avant-garde breathologies.

Cummings would have been delighted by such recognition; for him, as he once said, it was a 'supreme pleasure to have done something FIRST'.

When Cummings's zany typogames first appeared in the 1920s, they were greeted with much general bafflement, but they were prized by the self-conscious modernists of Greenwich Village and *The Dial*. In these circles, the young Cummings was regarded as a hero-figure. Pen portraits of the time pay tribute to his 'gay icono-clasm, his elegant courtesy, his quick generosities, his gleeful mis-chief'. According to John Dos Passos, Cummings was 'the hub' of Greenwich Village literary circles, many of whose members had been his admiring Harvard classmates just a few years earlier. At Harvard, Cummings had made himself notorious for a 1915 com-mencement address in which he had defended the 'New Art' of Matisse, Stravinsky, Gertrude Stein and other much-frowned-upon performers of that epoch.

Even at college, Cummings had been impressively self-assured. His father was a Harvard lecturer (also a Unitarian minister) and Edward Estlin had been born in Cambridge, Mass., in 1894. From the start, he bore the superior air of a New England brahmin – a brahmin who delighted in subversion but was noted also for his academic brilliance. In 1917, Cummings (who, at this stage, saw himself primarily as a painter) joined the Ambulance Corps and was despatched to France. In the same year, though, he was arrested by the French on suspicion of disloyalty (something to do with one of his friends having written some anti-war letters to the anarchist Emma Goldman). For four months, Cummings was interned in what he later called 'a concentration camp'. The experience would be described in his semi-fictional prose book, *The Enormous Room* (1922). In 1918, though, news of it added lustre to his reputation as a Village wit; his war, it was agreed, had been distinctly avant-garde.

In 1923, Cummings published his first book of verse, *Tulips and Chimneys*, and then set off for Paris, where he planned to study painting (a book of Cummings's pictures would appear in 1931 and later on, back in America, he held several one-man shows). In Paris, though, his reputation among the resident American 'Lost

Generation' was as an unorthodox new poet. He became friendly with Malcolm Cowley and Hart Crane – and, of course, Dos Passos – and was known for his engaging prankishness. In *Exiles' Return*, Malcolm Cowley remembers a Dada-ish moment when he, Cowley, decided to make a bonfire of various 'bad books':

We talked about bad books while the smoke grew blacker: then Cummings proved he was a better Dada-ist . . . by walking over and urinating on the fire.

In 1931, Cummings – who was already divorcing his second wife and was about to meet his third – made a tourist's trip to Russia, and described the experience in an anti-collectivist prose work called *Eimi*. This publication, needless to say, earned him few friends in the leftist 1930s. Indeed, there was, in this decade, a good deal of resistance to the Cummings presence: both to his seeming levity and to the sentimental individualism of his politics, as expressed in his several verse attacks on the phenomenon of what he called 'mostpeople': i.e., democratized, dehumanized mankind. Left-wing critics were not appeased by Cummings's fondness for down-and-outs and rugged disaffiliates, and with the emergence of the New Criticism's appetite for brainpower and complexity there was impatience too with his tub-thumping simple-heartedness. As Clive James would later say: 'Cummings had few doubts, few fears, spilled few beans and didn't seem to suffer much. What century did he think he was living in?'

Cummings's reputation in the academies never entirely recovered from the critical assaults it suffered at the hands of Allen Tate and R. P. Blackmur (who noted that in two books Cummings used the word 'flower' seventy times, and each time with, it seemed, a different meaning. 'The question is', said the persuasive Blackmur, 'whether or not the reader can possibly have shared the experience Mr Cummings has had of this word.') Even so, Cummings is still read and still valued for his typographical high-jinks. Long before his death in 1962, there were signs of a new readership for whom his winning simplicities had a direct appeal, and even hostile critics of the 1950s were ready to acknowledge the seductiveness of some of his more juvenile (yet sonorous) grammatical disruptions: 'my father moved through dooms of love/ through sames of am through haves of give'; 'nobody, not even the rain, has such small hands'.

'Who pays any attention to the syntax of things will never wholly kiss,' wrote Cummings (in a different layout), and this primitivist slogan was much heeded in the 1960s, when Beat poets like Lawrence Ferlinghetti and Gregory Corso responded to his naïve charms. But emulating Cummings has proved difficult for most of his would-be successors, both technical and spiritual. By the sixties, cultural prankishness was getting to be humdrum, and many a leaden theory had by then attached itself to poetry's on-the-printed-page theatricalities. Cummings was indeed, just as he'd hoped, the very First, but there are grounds now for wishing that he'd been the First and Last.

my sweet old etcetera
aunt lucy during the recent

war could and what
is more did tell you just
what everybody was fighting

for,
my sister

isabel created hundreds
(and
hundreds) of socks not to
mention shirts fleaproof earwarmers

etcetera wristers etcetera, my

mother hoped that

i would die etcetera
bravely of course my father used
to become hoarse talking about how it was
a privilege and if only he
could meanwhile my

self etcetera lay quietly
in the deep mud et

cetera
(dreaming,
et
   cetera, of
Your smile
eyes knees and of your Etcetera)

My Father Moved Through Dooms of Love

my father moved through dooms of love
through sames of am through haves of give,
singing each morning out of each night
my father moved through depths of height

this motionless forgetful where
turned at his glance to shining here;
that if (so timid air is firm)
under his eyes would stir and squirm

newly as from unburied which
floats the first who, his april touch
drove sleeping selves to swarm their fates
woke dreamers to their ghostly roots

And should some why completely weep
my father's fingers brought her sleep:
vainly no smallest voice might cry
for he could feel the mountains grow.

Lifting the valleys of the sea
my father moved through griefs of joy;
praising a forehead called the moon
singing desire into begin

joy was his song and joy so pure
a heart of star by him could steer
and pure so now and now so yes
the wrists of twilight would rejoice

keen as midsummer's keen beyond
conceiving mind of sun will stand,
so strictly (over utmost him
so hugely) stood my father's dream

his flesh was flesh his blood was blood:
no hungry man but wished him food;
no cripple wouldn't creep one mile
uphill to only see him smile.

Scorning the pomp of must and shall
my father moved through dooms of feel;
his anger was as right as rain
his pity was as green as grain

septembering arms of year extend
less humbly wealth to foe and friend
than he to foolish and to wise
offered immeasurable is

proudly and (by octobering flame
beckoned) as earth will downward climb,
so naked for immortal work
his shoulder marched against the dark

his sorrow was as true as bread:
no liar looked him in the head;
if every friend became his foe
he'd laugh and build a world with snow.

My father moved through theys of we,
singing each new leaf out of each tree
(and every child was sure that spring
danced when she heard her father sing)

Then let men kill which cannot share,
let blood and flesh be mud and mire,
scheming imagine, passion willed,
freedom a drug that's bought and sold

giving to steal and cruel kind,
a heart to fear, to doubt a mind,
to differ a disease of same,
conform the pinnacle of am

though dull were all we taste as bright,
bitter all utterly things sweet,
maggoty minus and dumb death
all we inherit, all bequeath

and nothing quite so least as truth
– i say though hate were why men breathe
because my father lived his soul
love is the whole and more than all

Robert Graves

1895–1985

Robert Graves's reputation reached its peak in the late 1950s / early 1960s, when attempts were made to see him as the product of a 'native line' in modern verse, a line connecting the traditional virtues of Georgianism (virtues of clarity and formal neatness which had been abruptly swept aside by mid-Atlantic modernists like Pound and Eliot) with the metrical good sense that had prevailed throughout the 1950s. The effort seemed distinctly strained, but it was not difficult to understand the impulse to recruit Graves to some school or line. He seemed a lonely eminence, not modern and not vilifiably old-fashioned, and by 1960 he'd been writing verse for almost fifty years. Where did he fit?

In truth, Graves liked to stand aloof from literary groupings. He had appeared in Edward Marsh's anthologies of Georgian poetry, but in the 1920s he had promoted experimentalists like E. E. Cummings. There were traces of Thomas Hardy in his work, but Eliot and Auden seemed to have passed him by. When Graves did give voice to his opinions about modern poetry, he was invariably scathing about his contemporaries and juniors (see his notorious Clark Lectures in the 1950s). The poets he liked were usually poets who seemed to wish to write like him. For much of his life, he did not live in Britain, and his preferred stance was one of lofty, hard-to-reach sagacity.

Graves was born in 1895, of Irish–German background. His father was the noted folk-poet A. P. Graves. Schooled at Charterhouse, Graves served in the Army before Oxford, and was wounded fairly badly on the Western Front. For years afterwards, he would complain of postwar neurasthenia. During the war, he married Nancy Nicholson, sister of the painter Ben and a ferocious feminist, and it was during this first marriage that Graves underwent an early training in submissiveness, a training that intensified in 1925 when he encountered Laura Riding, an American poet even more steely and dictatorial than Nancy. Graves's marriage ended soon after he met Riding, and for the next fifteen years or so, he danced to Riding's tune. At first, the pair of them engaged in joint literary projects, bombarding the establishment with diatribes and squibs. Riding was the guiding force behind these critical assaults, and Graves was more than ready to be guided. To him, Riding was the ultimate Muse figure, the Strong Woman he was bound to serve, and serve her he did – even to the extent, in later years, of helping her to be unfaithful. From his experience of being bossed about by Riding, he evolved that matriarchal reading of world history that would later be enshrined in his White Goddess theories.

In 1929, Riding attempted suicide after one of her Graves-arranged love affairs collapsed, and she and Graves decided to quit Britain for Majorca, where they had plans to set up a community of disciples whose task would be to study the whole matter of male–female relationships. Applicants were warned in advance that 'the female mind is the judge and the male mind the subject of judgement'. To Robert Graves this grim arrangement seemed entirely fair. Quite a few visiting disciples were less sanguine. One of them depicted Graves as being 'like a small boy dancing attendance on a rich aunt of uncertain temper'; he was treated 'like a dog'.

The Majorcan experiment ended in 1936, and Graves was soon

afterwards released from daily servitude to Riding (although the memory of her dominance would never cease to haunt him). He married for a second time and, with his new and altogether docile wife, went back to Majorca, where he became a prolific author of popular prose works like *I, Claudius* and *Wife to Mr Milton*. By the 1950s, these prose works subsidized his poetry-writing life and a lot of his energy was spent haggling with publishers and agents about money. Graves's prose books had, from the start, aimed to be unorthodox in their treatment of historic themes, and Graves clearly took some pleasure in needling the scholars, but it was not long before they began edging towards crankiness, especially when they touched on anthropology and myth. Graves's Riding-derived theories about woman-worship became the subject of prose discourse. Graves had discovered 'the most ancient theme in the world', he said. As a poet it was his task to devote his gifts to worshipping a Muse, or female Love-Goddess: a refusal of the goddess's commands would be a rejection of poetry itself, and would be sinful. In his prose book *The White Goddess*, Graves tried to equip these notions with scholarly support, an effort that was met with general bafflement.

For Graves, the main trouble with living out his goddess theories on a daily basis was that his wife, Beryl, was not really goddess material. For one thing, she was too nice to him. As a result, Graves began looking for post-Riding Muses. Between 1950 and 1975, he declared himself to be in love four times – each time with a young girl who failed to understand what was required of her. There was, it seems, no sexual component in any of these strange infatuations: it was the Muse's task to dominate the poet and it was the poet's duty to obey. With each girl, Graves was plunged into a very public state of torment. The girls, of course, quite failed to measure up and after a while each backed away from her Muse-obligations. Letters poured out from Majorca, urgent meetings were arranged, crisis discussions were demanded, and throughout all this upheaval Graves took it for granted that his wife, his friends, even the girl's boyfriends, would be ready with their sympathy for his obsession

– or high duty, as he'd call it. According to Randall Jarrell, Graves had turned into his own Laura Riding. With nobody on hand to give him a hard time, he had to do it by himself.

Graves has been praised as a love poet, even though we rarely feel that his poems are addressed to any particular loved person. They are, of course, addressed to the demanding Muse and this quite often means that they end up sounding both regimental and / or abject, depending on the current whim of his Strong Woman. As with all poems written to a theory, Graves's love lyrics nearly always have an air of managerial efficiency, even when the speaker of the poem is supposed to be forlorn. Although Graves's chosen role as lover/poet was that of a sufferer, it is hard to detect in his work a vulnerable human voice. When it comes to matters of love, Graves speaks, offputtingly, as an 'expert':

> Lovers in the act dispense
> With such meum-teum sense
> As might warningly reveal
> What they must not pick or steal,
> And their nostrum is to say:
> 'I and you are both away'.

> After when they disentwine
> You from me and yours from mine,
> Neither can be certain who
> Was that mine whose I was you.
> To the act again they go
> More completely not to know.

With Graves, it must be said, a knowledge of the life does tend to undermine one's admiration of the work. Or, to put it differently: with Graves, a reading of the work yields little about how he lived. Who, for example, would guess from reading his biography that some of his best verses (written, no doubt, when the Goddess slumbered) were attractively relaxed and comical:

So many feats they did to admiration:
With their enormous throats they sang louder
Than ten cathedral choirs, with their grand yards
Stormed the most rare and obstinate maidenheads,
With their strong-gutted and capacious bellies
Digested stones and glass like ostriches.
They dug great pits and heaped huge mounds,
Deflected rivers, wrestled with the bear
And hammered judgements for posterity –
For the sweet-cupid-lipped and tassel-yarded
Delicate-stomached dwellers
In Pygmy Alley, where with brooding on them
A foot is shrunk to seven inches
And twelve-pence will not buy a spare rib.
And who would judge between Ogres and Pygmies –
The thundering text, the snivelling commentary –
Reading between the covers he will marvel
How his own members bloat and shrink again.

The Foreboding

Looking by chance in at the open window
   I saw my own self seated in his chair
With gaze abstracted, furrowed forehead,
   Unkempt hair.

I thought that I had suddenly come to die,
   That to a cold corpse this was my farewell,
Until the pen moved slowly upon paper
   And tears fell.

He had written a name, yours, in printed letters:
   One word on which bemusedly to pore –
No protest, no desire, your naked name,
   Nothing more.

Would it be tomorrow, would it be next year?
   But the vision was not false, this much I knew;
And I turned angrily from the open window
   Aghast at you.

Why never a warning, either by speech or look,
   That the love you cruelly gave me could not last?
Already it was too late: the bait swallowed,
   The hook fast.

With Her Lips Only

This honest wife, challenged at dusk
At the garden gate, under a moon perhaps,
In scent of honeysuckle, dared to deny
Love to an urgent lover: with her lips only,

Not with her heart. It was no assignation;
Taken aback, what could she say else?
For the children's sake, the lie was venial;
'For the children's sake', she argued with her
     conscience.

Yet a mortal lie must follow before dawn:
Challenged as usual in her own bed,
She protests love to an urgent husband,
Not with her heart but with her lips only;
'For the children's sake', she argues with her
     conscience,
'For the children' – turning suddenly cold
     towards them.

Hart Crane
1899–1932

Hart Crane was born in Ohio in 1899, and came from a respectable, non-literary background. His father was a manufacturer of chocolate, and little Hart might easily have carved out a career in candy. At the age of sixteen, though, he had one of his verses accepted by a New York magazine and seems to have decided there and then that poetry was his destiny. And for him, this was the highest of high callings, involving a rejection of all modes of life that did not directly serve, or wait upon, his genius.

Crane's businessman father was sympathetic but not too sympathetic. He was keen that Hart should get some kind of college education. Crane's parents, though, were at each other's throats, and he tended, early on, to side with his mother, who was more 'poetic' – i.e., more excitable – than his father, who was always thinking about money. Right from the start, then, there was for Crane a hard-to-handle conflict between Art and Mammon. At seventeen, he left home for New York and there plunged at once into the arty-bohemian world of Greenwich Village, then at its infant worst, a world in which genius was taken for granted as a kind of ticket of admission – and a world too of week-long drinking sprees and self-consciously abandoned sexual frolics. Crane was homosexual, he discovered, and was anxious to prove that he had stripped himself of all mid-Western inhibitions.

Indeed, the whole drift of Crane's new life seemed to have less to do with personal fulfilment than with the thrill of shocking his staid relatives back home, and in particular his dad. Outrageous social conduct became, for him, a measure, or an aspect, of his genius. Over the ensuing years, he plunged ever more deeply into promiscuity and booze. Money was, of course, a constant problem. Crane's background, thanks to his father, had been middle-class well-off, and he was accustomed to living fairly well. And now, a wild-man poet in New York, he needed cash to pay for books, alcohol and breakages – and, now and then, for overnight accommodation. For a time, he took odd jobs in advertising or, with an ill grace, accepted work in his father's candy factory. During one happy stretch, he was in receipt of hand-outs from an indulgent New York millionaire. In Crane's mind, hand-outs were no insult to his pride. As he saw it, the world really did owe him a living. Indeed, the world – by not whole-heartedly warming to his writings – was racking up a debt, and should be made to pay. Unfortunately, Crane felt rather the same way about several of his literary friends and admirers. Possessed of lesser gifts than his, they too, he felt, were there to serve and support. Epic quarrels and precarious reconciliations became for Crane the stuff of daily life – and most of it was fuelled by his steadily deepening dependence on the bottle.

Although Crane felt himself to be living on a timeless, other-worldly plane, he was also hungry for immediate, this-worldly plaudits, and in particular for the kind of blinding literary triumph that even Ohio might greet with something like respect. When drunk – which, during his adult life, was nearly all the time – he would (according to a friend), 'weep and shout, shaking his fist: "I am Baudelaire; I am Whitman; I am Christopher Marlowe; I am Christ!"' When his first book, *White Buildings*, appeared in 1926, he was greeted on all sides as a gifted lyric poet: densely obscure but winningly euphonious. For Crane, though, it was not enough to be thought of merely as a gifted lyric poet. This was the age of

The Waste Land, and every would-be poet with pretensions to 'significance' had to be sagely and inclusively responsive to the new machine age: poets had a duty to confront the Zeitgeist. Crane's ambition was to write a Zeitgeist epic which, as he believed, would counterbalance Eliot's pessimism. His aim was to 'take as much of [Eliot's] erudition and technique as I can absorb and assemble towards a more positive and ecstatic goal'. He planned a poem of eight sections called *The Bridge*, with which he hoped to articulate what he called 'a myth of America' by, as he put it, 'building a bridge between so-called classical experience and many divergent realities of our seething confused cosmos of today'.

Although Crane wished to answer *The Waste Land* with an eruption of Whitmanesque, New World ebullience, the debt to Eliot's work was cripplingly evident in places, and altogether *The Bridge*'s effortful 'ambition' ran counter to Crane's actual gifts. If anything, it encouraged his worst tendencies – in particular, the tendency towards facile sonority. For him, though, the need to draw some large-scale map of what he idly thought of as 'the modern consciousness' became a thoroughly disabling obsession. He worked on his high-sounding but impossibly obscure long poem for five tormented, drunken years, and after it finally appeared, in 1930, to lukewarm reviews, he took off for Mexico, where, for two years, he rampaged and sulked. Short of money, hooked on alcohol, and feeling himself burnt out and unappreciated as a poet, he began to talk incessantly of suicide. In 1932, heading back to the United States by sea, he jumped overboard and drowned. He was thirty-three.

Since his death, there have been attempts to mythologize Crane as a victim-genius (see, for example, Robert Lowell's 'Words for Hart Crane'), as a superior spirit destroyed by the indifference of the age. No doubt Crane himself would have concurred in such descriptions. He is also remembered as a failure – a 'magnificent failure' is the usual formulation – and in a sense he was. But the victim myth and the triumphant-failure myth, together with the dated obscurity and pretentiousness that surely mar the work he put most faith in, have all led to a situation in which his truest gifts have been forgotten, or seem likely to be permanently set aside. Nowadays, when people talk about Crane, they are likely to discuss his youthful suicide, or the failed 'epic' that he toiled on for so many years. When a poet is turned into a failure myth, as Crane has been, there is a disposition to ignore that poet's lower-key successes.

Thus, Crane's early pre-*Bridge* lyrics tend to be sidelined or overlooked. It is here, though, that his best voice can be heard, a voice that had nothing in it of ecstasy or bombast and was not afraid of clarity:

> There are no stars tonight
> But those of memory.
> Yet how much room for memory there is
> In the loose girdle of soft rain.
>
> There is even room enough
> For the letters of my mother's mother,
> Elizabeth,
> That have been pressed so long
> Into a corner of the roof
> That they are brown and soft,
> And liable to melt as snow.

This, too, is a poem about bridges, one could say, but the bridges it attempts to build are personal and heartfelt, and not at all to do with the manufacturing of giant myths.

My Grandmother's Love Letters

There are no stars tonight
But those of memory.
Yet how much room for memory there is
In the loose girdle of soft rain.

There is even room enough
For the letters of my mother's mother,
Elizabeth,
That have been pressed so long
Into a corner of the roof
That they are brown and soft,
And liable to melt as snow.

Over the greatness of such space
Steps must be gentle.
It is all hung by an invisible white hair.
It trembles as birch limbs webbing the air.

And I ask myself:

'Are your fingers long enough to play
Old keys that are but echoes:
Is the silence strong enough
To carry back the music to its source
And back to you again
As though to her?'

Yet I would lead my grandmother by the hand
Through much of what she would not understand;
And so I stumble. And the rain continues on the roof
With such a sound of gently pitying laughter.

Garden Abstract

The apple on its bough is her desire, –
Shining suspension, mimic of the sun.
The bough has caught her breath up, and her voice,
Dumbly articulate in the slant and rise
Of branch on branch above her, blurs her eyes.
She is prisoner of the tree and its green fingers.

And so she comes to dream herself the tree,
The wind possessing her, weaving her young veins,
Holding her to the sky and its quick blue,
Drowning the fever of her hands in sunlight.
She has no memory, nor fear, nor hope
Beyond the grass and shadows at her feet.

Allen Tate

1899–1979

When Allen Tate died in 1979, Simon and Schuster speedily commissioned a biography, to be written, they announced, by Ned O'Gorman, a poet of some reputation and a friend of two of Tate's three wives. O'Gorman made a conscientious beginning, it would seem, but after a few years was forced to abandon the biography because of 'complications' relating to his subject's love-life. Tate, in his later years, had regularly fallen victim to what O'Gorman calls a 'libidinous fever':

It was a quality in his life that assumed in his marriages a fragmenting power and dealt to his creative life a sundering loss of energy. He lived out a literary 'soap opera'; the tales are infinite, all of them true, most of them scandalous. Many of the ladies with whom Allen slept are alive. Many of them are distinguished, and some of them are celebrities.

Oh really? Who? And this, of course, could be any publicist trying to inject a bit of vigour into a dull literary life. One does recall the stories, though – well, some of them. And it is certainly true that Tate's entanglements were a source of some amusement to his literary friends, and particularly to those who had experienced the lash of his highmindedness. In many American literary biographies or collections of letters, Tate appears in clownishly satyric aspect: the comedy sometimes sharpened by comments on his physical appearance (he had a strangely bulbous head and as a child was reckoned to be hydrocephalic), his intense and platitudinous solemnity, his late-won and unsmiling Roman Catholicism. Tate once said that all his poems sprang from the suffering that comes from disbelief, and perhaps his love pursuits were similarly energized.

But then Tate, post-1940, had become a pronouncing, self-important literary figure, full of vanity and strictness but no longer driven by the programmatic zeal that marked his early years. There were indeed two Tates: the Agrarian Tate, vehement and visionary, and the post-Agrarian Tate, professorial and libidinous. It is the younger Tate who continues to attract attention – albeit as a regionalist phenomenon rather than as a poet of distinction. It was at Nashville's Vanderbilt University that Tate made his first outings as a literary personage, and his stance from the beginning was aggressively cocksure. He linked up with – or took over – a 'discussion group' of local poets, who called themselves the Fugitives and spent much of their time plotting a Deep South 'revival': in other words, or so it sometimes seemed, they wanted their parochial verses and short stories to be praised by New York critics. Happily, such praise was soon forthcoming – the Fugitives included future eminences such as John Crowe Ransom and Robert Penn Warren in addition to the usual line-up of duffers – and the group's magazine, the *Fugitive*, was widely welcomed as the voice of a significant new literary movement. This was a period when every new movement was deemed to be significant. Even T. S. Eliot in London in the 1920s heard about the Fugitives and indicated his approval.

A turning point for Tate, as for so many other American poets of the 1920s, was his reading of *The Waste Land*. Tate was entranced by the poem's self-assured obscurity and by what he could deduce of its prescriptive urgency. His poems at once assumed a clotted bookishness that thoroughly repelled the more old-fashioned of his co-Fugitives, and he took to describing himself as modernism's gift to the Old South. Already he could perceive links between *The Waste Land*'s anti-materialism and his own developing contempt for urban-industrial encroachments from the North. The path ahead seemed clear: he would not allow the rural South to be turned into a spiritual waste land.

In the meantime, though, Tate needed to strengthen his own cultural prestige, and this meant heading north. In 1925, he left Nashville for New York, and there linked up with the Greenwich Village/*Dial* set. In 1928, along with others of the Village crowd, he transferred to Europe. In London, Tate paid homage to Eliot, who had for him by now the status of a demi-god; in Paris, he fell in with all the usual Steins and Hemingways – who met, the lot of them, with his fierce disapproval. After two years abroad, he returned to the United States, eager to take upon himself the Americanist role which Eliot, for all his wondrous merits, had – in Tate's view – made it his business to avoid.

Tate's intelligence was thoroughly didactic. It would not have been enough for him to set up as an Americanist writer in the William Carlos Williams mould, using the shape and language of his poetry to declare a cultural allegiance, or responsibility. The language of Tate's poems was unvaryingly sonorous/poetic, the 'skill' a trifle narcissistic, and his verse persona tended always to the bardic/anonymous:

> Turn your eyes to the immoderate past,
> Turn to the inscrutable infantry rising
> Demons out of the earth – they will not last.
> Stonewall, Stonewall, and the sunken fields of hemp,
> Shiloh, Antietam, Malvern Hill, Bull Run.

Back in Tennessee by 1930, the Tates took up residence in an antebellum mansion, with eighty-five acre estate attached, that had been bought for them by one of Tate's brothers, who had made a lot of northern money out of coal. This evocative location made it possible for him to resume his senior position with the Fugitives. When he had left for New York, some of the more hard-line

Nashvillites had accused him of desertion. Now he had returned, cosmopolitan and modernistic, to occupy a Tennessean mansion. It was time to hoist – re-hoist – the flag.

Over the next few years, Tate devoted most of his time and energy to promoting 'the principles of Agrarianism' – the first such principle being to ensure, somehow, that 'the South should avoid becoming a replica of the industrial North'. The South, it was averred, was spiritual; the North was brutishly commercial. The South stood for Nature; the North for the Machine. In essay upon essay, the predictable antitheses were trotted out: farm v. factory; traditional values v. dollar-hungry opportunism; individual v. mass, and so on. A symposium, *I'll Take My Stand*, appeared in 1930, with contributions from Tate, Warren, Ransom and Donald Davidson, and this was followed in 1938 by *Who Owns America?*

By then, Tate had come to realize that the Agrarian fantasy, or 'culture of the soil', had led him into some dark and difficult terrain. In order to promote Agrarianism, which he continued to see as an American offshoot of literary modernism, 'a reaffirmation of the humane tradition', he entered into an alliance with a blatantly fascistic periodical, the *American Review*. Later on, he would try to play down this connection; at the time, though, he was more than pleased to have a platform for his southern sermons. And anyway, at heart, he was in sympathy with much of what the paper stood for; and so, too, was Eliot (although Eliot's *Criterion* did draw the line at some of Tate's polemics). Bit by bit, during the 1930s, the threat of 'northern industrialism' became, for the Agrarians, almost identical with the more immediately pressing threat of 'international Communism'. Despite his later protestations, Tate and his co-Agrarians were more than ready at the time to overlook the anti-Semitism and pro-Hitlerism of the *American Review* in order to promote their 'spiritual' defence of the Deep South's traditions. And when leftist New York critics pointed out that those traditions included slavery and lynching, Tate was snootily untroubled by their scorn:

I belong to the white race, therefore I intend to support white rule.
Lynching is a symptom of weak, inefficient rule; but you can't destroy
lynching by *fiat* or social agitation; lynching will disappear when the
white race is satisfied that its supremacy will not be questioned in social
crises.

Mr Pope

When Alexander Pope strolled in the city
Strict was the glint of pearl and gold sedans.
Ladies leaned out more out of fear than pity
For Pope's tight back was rather a goat's than man's.

Often one thinks the urn should have more bones
Than skeletons provide for speedy dust,
The urn gets hollow, cobwebs brittle as stones
Weave to the funeral shell a frivolous rust.

And he who dribbled couplets like a snake
Coiled to a lithe precision in the sun
Is missing. The jar is empty; you may break
It only to find that Mr Pope is gone.

What requisitions of a verity
Prompted the wit and rage between his teeth
One cannot say. Around a crooked tree
A moral climbs whose name should be a wreath.

Stevie Smith

1902–1971

Stevie Smith was frequently praised for belonging to no school or tradition. Certainly, none of the obvious pigeon-holes can be stretched to accommodate her: she wrote and published throughout four decades but cannot truthfully be said to have 'belonged' to any of them. Unsusceptible to prevailing trends in verse, she was also fairly unresponsive to upheavals in the world at large. A reader working through her oeuvre unaided by a bibliography would be hard pressed to put a date to individual poems. What many poets might have regarded as subject matter, Smith tended to view as just another instance of the transience of things. She stood back and watched the world go by, preferring to make that (the watching not the world) her kind of subject. Unplaceable, she knew her place.

    In biographical terms, this could hardly have been truer. Born in Hull in 1902, Stevie Smith moved with her family to Palmers Green, London, when she was three – and stayed there, in the same house, for the rest of her life. Moving somewhere else was a possibility too exotic even to be contemplated. Similarly, she stayed in the same job (as secretary to a magazine publisher) for almost twenty years, and only gave it up so that she could devote all her time to looking after a much-grumbled-about invalid aunt (who also lived in that house in Palmers Green). During the last years of her life, Smith took pleasure in bemoaning the drabness of her suburb, its absurd inaccessibility, its inert and often ludicrous inhabitants. All of it had, no doubt, been sent to try her: who was she to choose her burdens?

In her work, of course, rather more resistance could be found. She always had an incisive, wide-eyed way of sneering at suburbia's low-grade pomposities, and many of the lives she satirized (sometimes with a surprising venom) were of the small and settled type – lives rather like her own. But her obsessions were ontological, not social: her most absorbing quarrels were with God and His (almost identical) twin, Death. A cemetery-going taste for the macabre was often a feature of her work, and she enjoyed being on George Herbert-ish terms with the eternal verities ('Well God, it's all very well to talk like this/And I dare say it's all very fine . . .'), but every so often she would go through the motions of objecting to the way things are. But her defiance is of one who can't escape Belief. In other words, it tends towards the glum.

There was always a little-girl-lost air to Smith's verse-persona, and it could be very charming. Her blasphemies were always a shade infantile, somewhat dressed up to be indulged: 'Who makes a God? Who shows him thus?/ It is the Christian religion does/ Oh, oh, have none of it/ Blow it away, have done with it!' Did she mean this? The faint air of girlish tantrum not only makes it hard for us to know; it also ensures that we won't press the question very hard. Stevie Smith would rarely risk not seeming loveable.

Smith's religious conflicts may well have been large and vivid in her life and one can easily see why critics have provided earnestly complicated accounts of her efforts to replace the God of her High Anglican upbringing with a simpler, more just, less dogma-ridden presence. Her verse-persona, though, does have the effect of seeming to miniaturize conflict, to reduce spiritual waverings to the level of mere moody inconsistency. Smith's naïve style of utterance has much to do with this, and so too have her pat personifications, her plonking rhymes and generally offhand versification. It is often as if she has surprised herself by what she has done, an air of 'Goodness me, a poem!':

> My life is vile
> I hate it so.
>
> I'll wait a while
> And then I'll go
>
> Why wait at all?
> Hope springs alive,
> Good may befall
> I yet may thrive.
>
> It is because I can't make up my mind
> If God is good, impotent or unkind.

   Towards the end of her life, Smith's charm found a new outlet at poetry readings. Her performances were as one might expect: girlish, lost, winning, and extremely expert, in terms of pace and timing. She loved it; so did her audiences. To hear them chuckling over her cute spiritual despairs was a fine bonus for her old age, and she took particular pleasure in upstaging beatniks at the avant-garde poetry rallies she for some reason kept getting invited to throughout the 1960s. But then perhaps she was always much further out than we thought, and not drowning but waving.

Not Waving but Drowning

Nobody heard him, the dead man,
But still he lay moaning:
I was much further out than you thought
And not waving but drowning.

Poor chap, he always loved larking
And now he's dead
It must have been too cold for him his heart gave way,
They said.

Oh, no no no, it was too cold always
(Still the dead one lay moaning)
I was much too far out all my life
And not waving but drowning.

Tenuous and Precarious

Tenuous and Precarious
Were my guardians,
Precarious and Tenuous,
Two Romans.

My father was Hazardous,
Hazardous,
Dear old man,
Three Romans.

There was my brother Spurious,
Spurious Posthumous,
Spurious was Spurious
Was four Romans.

My husband was Perfidious,
He was Perfidious,
Five Romans.

Surreptitious, our son,
Was Surreptitious,
He was six Romans.

Our cat Tedious
Still lives,
Count not Tedious
Yet.

My name is Finis,
Finis, Finis,
I am Finis,
Six, five, four, three, two,
One Roman,
Finis.

Norman Cameron

1905–1953

Norman Cameron is almost better known for his poetic friendships than he is for his own, often admirable, poems. He crops up frequently in biographies of Robert Graves and Dylan Thomas. In Graves biographies, he tends to appear as a long-suffering acolyte; in Thomas biographies as an anonymous factotum. Cameron used to look after Thomas when he paid boozy visits to London in the 1940s, and although there were aspects of Thomas that repelled him (see Cameron's poem 'The Dirty Little Accuser'), he was also attracted to the Welshman's bohemian excesses. Cameron, a Scottish vicar's son, was himself a fairly heavy drinker, but he had little of Thomas's wild-man sociability. He may have matched Thomas drink for drink, for all we know, but if he did nobody noticed: he was never drunk enough, it seems, to quite forget himself. Nor did he lose his sense of the ridiculous, by all accounts. While others made a song and dance, he liked to keep watch from the sidelines, smilingly.

And this appears to have been more or less the case with his career as a poet. Born in 1905, Cameron attended school in Scotland and went on to Oriel College, Oxford, where – somewhat surprisingly –

he was active on the student literary scene. He knew Auden as an undergraduate but was never part of the Auden set, and he appeared in *Oxford Poetry* (alongside Auden, it so happens). And then, in the 1930s, he was taken up by Geoffrey Grigson, who printed several of his poems in his ferocious little magazine, *New Verse*. Grigson approved of almost nobody but seems to have been drawn to Cameron's detached, appraising manner, and to have perhaps suspected that this intelligent, non-pushy writer was not quite as well-adjusted as he seemed:

> When you confess your sins before a parson,
> You find it no great effort to disclose
> Your crimes of murder, bigamy and arson,
> But can you tell him that you pick your nose?
>
> If after death you pay for your misdeeds,
> Surely the direst and most just requital
> Would be to listen while an angel reads
> Before a crowd your endless, mean recital:
>
> Golf scorecards faked, thefts from your mother's purse . . .
> But why should Doomsday bother with such stuff?
> This is the Hell that you already nurse
> Within you. You've had punishment enough.

Cameron was pale and shy and hugely tall and could seem bumbling and apologetic. But, non-pushy though he was, he could not easily be pushed around. Grigson, one suspects, encouraged Cameron's contempt for the metropolitan literary racket. It was Cameron who described Stephen Spender as 'the Rupert Brooke of the Depression' – a jest that Grigson treasured, and repeated as often as he could.

Geoffrey Grigson detected something sharp-edged and original in Norman Cameron. Others, though, were happy to pigeon-hole him as a rather drab supporting act. Dylan Thomas called him 'Normal Cameron' and another of his friends exclaimed: 'How one envies Norman's life – no detail at all.' When Cameron was summoned to Majorca by Robert Graves and Laura Riding, they were happy to lap up his admiration, but it is not at all certain that they paid much heed to Cameron's own verse, or to his hidden personality. Although Graves contributed a friendly enough preface to Cameron's *Collected Poems*, this was some years after the poet's death and has a dutiful ring to it.

But even so, the Graves influence – or, rather, the Graves/ Riding influence – was crucial. Cameron met Graves and his formidable consort when the two of them were guests at the Oxford English Club in 1927. Cameron was then an undergraduate and seems to have at once fallen for their trenchant and uncompromising double act. When Cameron left Oxford, he lived near the London house that had become the base for Graves' and Riding's critical assault on the poetry establishment – the house, indeed, at which Riding staged her famously botched suicide attempt. Cameron, it so happened, donated a significant part of his not-very-large inheritance to help pay for the several months that Riding had to spend in hospital after her jump – 'Goodbye, chaps' was her cry – from one of the house's upper windows.

And this outlay left him needing to find work. Cameron signed up as an education officer in Nigeria, a job he never liked. He stuck it out for two years, though, and during this time sent monthly despatches to Laura Riding, despatches in which he was always ready to confide his current sexual problems. Riding liked to hear about other people's sexual problems. She also liked to organize solutions. And Cameron (whose stutter, it is said, was more pronounced than usual when he spoke to Riding) was remarkably susceptible to her intrusions. His first two marriages would, more or less, be fixed by Riding.

After Nigeria, Cameron was recruited by Graves/Riding to serve as one of their full-time acolytes or aides. This meant moving to Majorca, where the couple were now based. There Cameron assisted with the running of the Seizin Press and was persuaded to invest money in a real-estate venture – organized, it seems, by Riding. He also worked on a rewriting of *The Pickwick Papers*, to parallel Graves's *The Real David Copperfield* (i.e., the Dickens novel shorn of what Graves described as 'padding'). Bit by bit, and understandably, Cameron grew tired of his Majorcan labours (he also developed 'a kind of horror' of Laura Riding), and by 1936, he was more than ready to escape. On the way back to England, he allowed himself one final gesture of obedience: he got married to a Riding nominee, who later died. In London, he took work as an advertising copywriter, and in this role he invented a malady called 'Night Starvation', which could only be cured by the consumption of a nightly mug of Horlicks.

During the war – which Cameron saw as a 'sordid interruption of one's personal life' – he worked as a writer on various propaganda projects: radio dialogues, newspaper columns, documentary films. The war years for Cameron were also marked by bouts of heavy drinking and depression, and in 1953 he died, at forty-seven, of a cerebral haemorrhage. After his death, obituarists had a hard time assembling a biography. There was indeed a lack of detail. Since then, however, a few facts have emerged. It turns out that Cameron suffered from congenital hypertension, and – perhaps he knew this – was surely destined for an early death. He was married three times, to a German, an Austrian and a Russian, but not much is known about his wives. He appeared to have no fixed address.

Touchingly forgetful but well-mannered, good-humoured but depressed, Cameron was a strange combination of bohemian fecklessness and Calvinistic self-control, and at some stage in his later life, this conflict – or antithesis – seems to have driven him to breaking point. There are reports that he suffered nervous breakdowns and that he destroyed manuscripts of poems which he considered were not up to scratch. Certainly, postwar, he gave up writing verse and made a kind of living translating from French. At some point in the early 1950s, he underwent an operation called a 'sympathectomy', in which some part of his brain was surgically interfered with. After this operation, Cameron – according to his friends – was 'never quite the same again'. There are stories also that, just before the end, he converted to Roman Catholicism.

As a poet, Cameron clearly learned a lot from Auden and from

Robert Graves – one can point to his traditionally 'formal' rigour as well as to his fondness for epigrammatic summings-up – but he never succumbed to either influence. Oddly, the poet he most resembles is Philip Larkin, whose work he almost certainly never read. There is a slightly theatrical diffidence in Cameron, and an attachment to the gloomy joys of common sense, that do seem to prefigure Larkin's tone. He also has something of Larkin's ability to accommodate the rhythms of ordinary speech within a tightly metred structure. And in this he resembles also some other so-called Movement poets of the 1950s, poets like Kingsley Amis and John Wain, who made their marks some years after Cameron had died. Did they read him? If so, they didn't say so. But if they did, they would surely have seen him as a kindred spirit (although Larkin, oddly, did not include anything by Cameron in his 1973 selection, *The Oxford Book of Twentieth Century English Verse*). Cameron more than once expressed a determination to avoid what he called 'hysteria': in poetry, in politics, and in personal relationships. In spite of what we hear of his uneven deportment, he always aimed to strike a 'neutral tone' (as Donald Davie put it in his manifesto-piece, 'Remembering the Thirties'). In short, then, it could be said that Norman Cameron did not so much miss the boat – the 1950s boat, that is – as simply fail to be there when it finally floated into view.

Green, Green is El Aghir

Sprawled on the crates and sacks in the rear of the truck,
I was gummy-mouthed from the sun and the dust of the track,
And the two Arab soldiers I'd taken on as hitch-hikers
At a torrid petrol-dump, had been there on their hunkers
Since early morning. I said, in a kind of French
'On m'a dit, qu'il y a une belle source d'eau fraîche,
Plus loin, à El Aghir' . . .

                    It was eighty more kilometres
Until round a corner we heard a splashing of waters,
And there, in a green, dark street, was a fountain with two faces
Discharging both ways, from full-throated faucets
Into basins, thence into troughs and thence into brooks.
Our negro corporal driver slammed his brakes,
And we yelped and leapt from the truck and went at the double
To fill our bidons and bottles and drink and dabble.
Then, swollen with water, we went to an inn for wine.
The Arabs came, too, though their faith might have stood between.
'After all,' they said, 'it's a boisson,' without contrition.
Green, green is El Aghir. It has a railway-station,
And the wealth of its soil has borne many another fruit,
A mairie, a school and an elegant Salle de Fêtes.
Such blessings, as I remarked, in effect, to the waiter,
Are added unto them that have plenty of water.

Punishment Enough

    They say that women, in a bombing-raid,
    Retire to sleep in brand-new underwear
    Lest they be tumbled out of doors, displayed
    In shabby garments to the public stare.

You've often seen a house, sliced like a cheese,
Displaying its poor secrets – peeling walls
And warping cupboards. Of such tragedies
It is the petty scale that most appals.

When you confess your sins before a parson,
You find it no great effort to disclose
Your crimes of murder, bigamy and arson,
But can you tell him that you pick your nose?

If after death you pay for your misdeeds,
Surely the direst and most just requital
Would be to listen while an angel reads
Before a crowd your endless, mean recital:

Golf scorecards faked, thefts from your mother's purse . . .
But why should Doomsday bother with such stuff?
This is the Hell that you already nurse
Within you. You've had punishment enough.

William Empson

1906–1984

During his lifetime, William Empson was better known for his dense and complicated criticism than for his dense and complicated poems, and this continues to be the case. Empson, born in Yorkshire in 1906, was a lifelong academic, teaching in Japan and China for long stretches in the 1930s and 1950s. In 1953, he took a professorship at Sheffield University, and remained in this job until his retirement in 1971. Knighted in 1979, he died in 1984.

Most of the best-known Empson stories centre on his youth – the story about him getting into trouble at Cambridge when contraceptives were found in his room has often done the rounds, but usually the tales are to do with his remarkable precocity. Empson was only twenty-four when he published a 'grammatico-critical' treatise called *Seven Types of Ambiguity*, in which he argued that 'the phenomenon of compression' was at the 'very roots of poetry'. The book was greeted with admiring incredulity: how could one so young have staged a critical performance of such dashing subtlety? The rumour was that parts of *Seven Types* had been written as undergraduate essays – and so they had.

It was also known that most of Empson's student career at

Magdalene College had been spent studying Mathematics, not English (the year he spent on English was under the direction of I. A. Richards). Here indeed was a wide-ranging brilliance. Empson had the gifts, it seemed, to effect a marriage between Art and Science: a marriage much discussed – indeed, much yearned for – at the time. He approached literary texts rather as an engineer might inspect some complex mechanical contrivance. Or, to put it in his words, he was in favour of 'a great deal of exposition, in which the business of the critic is simply to show how the machine is meant to work, and therefore to show all its working parts in turn'.

This approach was highly welcome at a time (the 1920s) when literature was seeking a firm foothold in the university curriculum. Also, in the literary world at large, the notion of 'difficulty' was central to the post-Eliot critical orthodoxy. It was smart to be obscure, and Empson's own poems were reputed to be even more difficult than Eliot's. F. R. Leavis, according to one story, had to get Wittgenstein to tell him what was meant by Empson works like 'Legal Fiction' and 'To an Old Lady'.

Although *Seven Types of Ambiguity* made Empson's name in literary-academic circles, it did not sell well and as a result publishers shrank somewhat from issuing a volume of his verse. Empson, it could be said, did not assist his own cause when he declared that poetry like his really did need to be printed with explanatory comments from the author. He envisaged the 'poem with notes' as a plausible new literary form. To an interested publisher, he wrote in 1930:

If I publish a volume with notes longer than the text, as I want to do, will that be a prose book or a verse one? I ask out of curiosity, you understand . . .

When Empson's poems did finally appear in book form (in 1935, and then a second book in 1940), they were noteless – and, as a result, not easy to decipher. By this time, though, the vogue for obscurity had been supplanted by a vogue for urgent-sounding political engagement. Empson's teasing out of arcane intellectual 'conflicts' was felt to be narcissistic and irrelevant (and it did not help that one of his few lucid pieces was called 'Just a Smack at Auden'). It was not until the 1950s, when intelligence and formal ingenuity were back in fashion, that Empson's verse was once again regarded as exemplary.

The 1950s Movement school acknowledged Empson as a guiding spirit, and in 1955 his *Collected Poems* was greeted with much homage. Eighty-nine poems with thirty pages of most useful foot-notes: almost the book that Empson had wished for two decades earlier. The 1950s Empson vogue soon tailed off, though, and shortly afterwards the poet himself stopped writing poems. When he was knighted in 1979, it was generally understood that the honour was directed chiefly at his criticism (since *Seven Types*, he had gone on to produce impressive works like *Milton's God* and *The Structure of Complex Words*). By the time of his death, the poems seemed to be heading for oblivion.

There were other admirers, though, who came at Empson's verse from a direction that he probably would not have favoured. Such readers took the view that, for all his intellectual dandyism, he was – or, at his best, could be – a rather moving and plain-speaking lyric poet. Works like 'Missing Dates', 'Aubade' and 'Let It Go' were cited as evidence of a sombre, heartfelt clarity which somehow had got buried underneath the puzzle-setting intellectual 'brilliance':

> It is the poems you have lost, the ills
> From missing dates, at which the heart expires.
> Slowly the poison the whole blood stream fills.
> The waste remains, the waste remains and kills.

This perhaps sentimental view of Empson was to some extent supported by a new edition of Empson's collected poems, in 2000. John Haffenden, the book's editor, was also Empson's authorized biographer, and many of his notes did serve to underline a sense that Empson often used his poetry as a kind of code: if you knew the personal background you could tap into the personal distress.

Otherwise you would have to settle for the surface cleverness, of which there was always a plentiful supply. Haffenden's volume would have delighted Empson: 100 pages of verse supported by 300 pages of prose explication – even the six-line 'Let It Go', surely the most direct and accessible of Empson's poems, is accompanied by more than fifty lines of notes. And these notes are, one has to say, most usefully supportive of the text.

Missing Dates

Slowly the poison the whole blood stream fills.
It is not the effort nor the failure tires.
The waste remains, the waste remains and kills.

It is not your system or clear sight that mills
Down small to the consequence a life requires;
Slowly the poison the whole blood stream fills.

They bled an old dog dry yet the exchange rills
Of young dog blood gave but a month's desires;
The waste remains, the waste remains and kills.

It is the Chinese tombs and the slag hills
Usurp the soil, and not the soil retires.
Slowly the poison the whole blood stream fills.

Not to have fire is to be a skin that shrills.
The complete fire is death. From partial fires
The waste remains, the waste remains and kills.

It is the poems you have lost, the ills
From missing dates, at which the heart expires.
Slowly the poison the whole blood stream fills.
The waste remains, the waste remains and kills.

Let It Go

It is this deep blankness is the real thing strange.
   The more things happen to you the more you can't
      Tell or remember even what they were.

The contradictions cover such a range.
   The talk would talk and go so far aslant.
      You don't want madhouse and the whole thing there.

John Betjeman

1906–1984

In the Spring 1959 issue of a magazine called *Listen*, Philip Larkin caused a minor stir in poetry circles by hailing, straightfacedly, the literary achievement of John Betjeman, a poet who, said Larkin, 'has changed our idea of what is beautiful'. This praise, coming as it did from the most admired of Britain's younger poets (Larkin was then in his mid-thirties), was taken by some as the mark of an emerging philistinism – an 'anti-arty' style of posturing which had already shown itself in *Lucky Jim* and in the no-nonsense rationalism of the so-called Movement school of poets, of which Larkin was thought to be a leading member. And the praise came at a time when Betjeman's middle-brow renown was at its peak: his *Collected Poems* had just sold more than 30,000 copies and was shaping to sell many more, helped in large measure by the poet's cuddlesome TV appearances – Betjeman was well on the way to becoming a 'much-loved' national celebrity, known not just for his metrical, sad-funny but accessible performances in verse, but also for his love of teddy bears and Victorian church architecture and his loathing of standardized suburban living. 'Come, friendly bombs, and fall on Slough' was one of his famous wartime lines, and its ingratiating flipness (callous flipness, if you lived in Slough) was altogether typical: Betjeman knew how to catch the eye.

Philip Larkin was susceptible to most aspects of the Betjeman self-presentation, but what he really liked about this very English poet was that he wrote as if modernists like Pound and Eliot had never left America, and as if literary criticism had never been invented:

The chief significance of Betjeman as a poet is that he is a writer of talent and intelligence for whom the modern poetic revolution has simply not taken place. For him there has been no symbolism, no objective correlative, no T. S. Eliot or Ezra Pound, no rediscovery of myth or language as gesture, no *Seven Types* or *Some Versions*, no works of criticism with titles like Communication as Discipline and Implicit and Explicit Image-Obliquity in Sir Lewis Morris.

In his *Listen* article, Larkin was full of praise for Betjeman's eye for local, English detail and for middle-class social affectations. He stressed too the poet's occasional bouts of melancholia, his fear of death, and so on – as if to remind us, or assure us, that this bard was no comedian. What he wanted most of all to recommend, though, was Betjeman's readability, his knack of turning out shrewd, witty, undemanding verses which quite a lot of people liked to read: his whole enterprise ran counter, healthily, to modernism's cult of the obscure – its cult, indeed, of the 'demanding'.

This *Listen* piece on Betjeman could easily be taken as Philip Larkin's own poetic manifesto: certainly, it was tied in with the mid-1950s effort to locate a distinctively 'English line' in modern verse, a line that ran back to Hardy and beyond but which, thanks to mid-Atlantic modernism, had become repugnantly obscured. The 'English line' – clear, metrical and unpretentious – needed a mid-century English hero. That hero would, of course, be Philip Larkin, but he was not to know it at the time: in the meantime, he would have us turn our gaze to Betjeman. Even in 1959, though, it was pretty clear that Larkin's own work had the edge on Betjeman's, and in ways that Larkin's article did not encompass.

Against Oblivion

Yes, Betjeman was accessible and shrewd and funny – but why did he always seem so trippingly theatrical, so eagerly lightweight, so keen to please? Why did he always seem so *expert* – even in his command of topographical nostalgia, his eye for vanished snobberies? Betjeman had the equipment for manufacturing slick, sociological light verse, but whenever he attempts to engage our sympathies beyond the point of mere smiling acquiescence, he finds it impossible to adapt – or should one say escape? – an ingrained showmanship, a look-at-me predictability. And this, of course, is not assisted by his habitually metronomic rhythms. Betjeman has an ear for metre and for dotty turns of speech, but his rhythms are essentially mechanical, in rather the way that modernists had derided long ago. For us to be persuaded that the 'English line' still had some vigour and direction, we had to wait for Philip Larkin to demonstrate that the rhythms of ordinary speech need not fall victim to a metred discipline. Betjeman's verses serve to remind us that inheritance too often comes served up as hit-me-please obedience:

> The sort of girl I like to see
> Smiles down from her great height at me.
> She stands in strong, athletic pose
> And wrinkles her *retroussé* nose.
> Is it distaste that makes her frown,
> So furious and freckled, down
> On an unhealthy worm like me?
> Or am I what she likes to see?

John Betjeman was born in London's Highgate in 1906, the son of a small businessman, but 'as early as I can remember,' he wrote in 1950, 'I wanted to be a poet'. At Highgate Junior School, where he was briefly taught by T. S. Eliot (then known as 'The American Master'), and later at the Dragon School in Oxford, he began printing his precocious juvenilia, evincing an early potential for sleek doggerel, and he continued to do so as an undergraduate at Oxford, where he was a contemporary of Auden (whom he saw as 'oracular') but was never quite recruited to the Auden set. According to his own account, Betjeman was drawn rather to the company of aesthetes – 'trivial, baroque, incense-loving'. Wystan's gang were too long-faced and political.

After Oxford, Betjeman, like so many other beginning poets of the day, took teaching jobs at various prep schools before setting up in London as a freelance writer. He worked for the *Architectural Review*, wrote film reviews for the London *Evening Standard*, and, when the war came, joined the Ministry of Information. Postwar, he took employment with the British Council, and during the late 1940s served time with the Oxford Preservation Trust. It was not really until this period that he began to build much public recognition as a poet: his first book had appeared in the late 1930s but was not much noticed. Attention began to grow with *New Bats in Old Belfries* in 1945, and continued two years later with *Slick But Not Streamlined*, an American selection of his work which was assembled by a maybe-homesick Auden. An English *Selected Poems* followed in 1948. At this point in his career he was viewed indulgently as belonging to the kingdom of Light Verse.

This view began to alter in the 1950s – a period in which lightly worn fedupness was the English norm. Betjeman was suddenly spoken of as rather weighty – and not just by Philip Larkin (dons like John Sparrow and Maurice Bowra also spoke up on his behalf). It was during the 1960s, though, that Betjeman emerged as a national figure. During this decade, he was something of a fixture on TV: 'Betjeman's London', 'Journey to Bethlehem', 'The Englishman's House', 'Railways for Ever'. Betjeman was loveable old-school, hired to speak up on behalf of the England that TV culture would soon enough be ready to destroy: he was knighted in 1969, and in 1972 became the Poet Laureate. In 1976 came his autobiography – in verse and on TV – a work both tedious and twee called *Summoned by Bells*. Betjeman died in 1984.

A Subaltern's Love-song

Miss J. Hunter Dunn, Miss J. Hunter Dunn,
Furnish'd and burnish'd by Aldershot sun,
What strenuous singles we played after tea,
We in the tournament – you against me!

Love-thirty, love-forty, oh! weakness of joy,
The speed of a swallow, the grace of a boy,
With carefullest carelessness, gaily you won,
I am weak from your loveliness, Joan Hunter Dunn.

Miss Joan Hunter Dunn, Miss Joan Hunter Dunn,
How mad I am, sad I am, glad that you won.
The warm-handled racket is back in its press,
But my shock-headed victor, she loves me no less.

Her father's euonymus shines as we walk,
And swing past the summer-house, buried in talk,
And cool the verandah that welcomes us in
To the six-o'clock news and a lime-juice and gin.

The scent of the conifers, sound of the bath,
The view from my bedroom of moss-dappled path,
As I struggle with double-end evening tie,
For we dance at the Golf Club, my victor and I.

On the floor of her bedroom lie blazer and shorts
And the cream-coloured walls are be-trophied with sports,
And westering, questioning settles the sun
On your low-leaded window, Miss Joan Hunter Dunn.

The Hillman is waiting, the light's in the hall,
The pictures of Egypt are bright on the wall,
My sweet, I am standing beside the oak stair
And there on the landing's the light on your hair.

By roads 'not adopted', by woodlanded ways,
She drove to the club in the late summer haze,
Into nine-o'clock Camberley, heavy with bells
And mushroomy, pine-woody, evergreen smells.

Miss Joan Hunter Dunn, Miss Joan Hunter Dunn,
I can hear from the car park the dance has begun,
Oh! Surrey twilight! importunate band!
Oh! strongly adorable tennis-girl's hand!

Around us are Rovers and Austins afar,
Above us the intimate roof of the car,
And here on my right is the girl of my choice,
With the tilt of her nose and the chime of her voice.

And the scent of her wrap, and the words never said,
And the ominous, ominous dancing ahead.
We sat in the car park till twenty to one
And now I'm engaged to Miss Joan Hunter Dunn.

Louis MacNeice

1907–1963

'He cannot be a politician and he will not be a reactionary' was
Geoffrey Grigson's verdict on Louis MacNeice. Grigson was, of
course, comparing him to Auden – Grigson compared everyone to
Auden – and criticizing what he saw as MacNeice's tendency to
indecisive self-absorption. This tendency was present, to be sure, and
MacNeice was well aware of it. Even in a vivid documentary work
like the famous *Autumn Journal* (a long work written during the
Munich crisis), there are disabling bouts of self-interrogation: what
kind of human being should I be? Is the quest for personal integrity
in fact a cover-up for never quite knowing what to do? In a few early
poems, like 'Bagpipe Music' and 'Les Sylphides', MacNeice's satiric
verve was undisturbed by autobiographical head-scratching:

> Life in a day: he took his girl to the ballet;
> Being shortsighted himself could hardly see it –
>   The white skirts in the grey
>   Glade and the swell of the music
>   Lifting the white sails.

Calyx upon calyx, canterbury bells in the breeze
The flowers on the left mirror to the flowers on the right
   And the naked arms above
   The powdered faces moving
   Like seaweed in a pool.

Now, he thought, we are floating – ageless, oarless –
Now there is no separation, from now on
   You will be wearing white
   Satin and a red sash
   Under the waltzing trees.

A similar directness can be found in several of MacNeice's shorter love poems. All in all, one is led to wonder what kind of 1930s poet he might have become if he'd been, well, less conscientious, less intelligently troubled.

In life, MacNeice was generally found to be aloof and mysterious – in spite of his pub-dwelling habits and his interest in girls. People knew that his childhood had been shaped by the mental illness, and then the early death, of his mother (she, who had been the mainstay of the family, competent and bright, was suddenly removed to an institution when MacNeice was five, leaving him in the care of his sorrowingly prayerful father, a Church of England vicar), but MacNeice was never one to go on about his most intimate obsessions – except, sometimes, on the page:

When I was five the black dreams came
Nothing after was quite the same.

Born in Belfast in 1907, MacNeice eventually went on to Merton College, Oxford, and from there became a Classics lecturer at Birmingham University. In 1941, having earned a reputation as one of the four most noticeable 1930s poets (a quartet lampooned by Roy Campbell as MacSpaunday: MacNeice, Spender, Auden and Day-Lewis), he joined the BBC's then-celebrated features department, and remained there until his death in 1963. During the war he wrote propaganda; postwar he wrote verse-plays.

These facts were known, but people who had social dealings with MacNeice tended, when asked about him by biographers, to scratch their heads and recollect not very much. And MacNeice's own unfinished autobiography, *The Strings Are False*, discouragingly opened with the phrase 'So what?' Friends recalled him as a 'dark horse' and mentioned his seeming lack of warmth, his silences, his impenetrable moods. He was constantly in the pub, they'd say, but never really *of* the pub. He kept himself not just to himself but for himself. That's to say, for the poems – poems that were too often overburdened with self-scrutiny.

It has also been observed, though, that MacNeice's aloofness did carry over into the way he proceeded as a poet. He was always to one side of the fashionable tendency, even during the 1930s – he was of the swim, it might be said, but never in it. Thus he was a Sitwellian sparkler in the 1920s but, being Irish and dark-visioned, could never settle for the merely jewelled phrase. At Oxford he was an apprentice dandy but too 'irredeemably heterosexual' to connect with the main action (this was the view of his ex-Marlborough schoolfriend Anthony Blunt). In the 1930s, he tried to turn himself into a socially conscious poet but was too riven by self-doubt, by the awareness that 'If it were not for Lit. Hum. I might be climbing/ A ladder with a hod'. Postwar, he wanted to be a fire-tongued sage and seer, like his BBC colleague Dylan Thomas. MacNeice worshipped Thomas and did not, we trust, live to read Dylan's description of his work as 'thin and conventionally minded, lacking imagination and not sound in the ear'.

MacNeice may not have known for certain that this was how his hero rated him (Thomas also described MacNeice as 'a very good chap'), but he possibly sensed it, and may not have disagreed. Being MacNeice, he may have feared that hard work could never compensate for an essential absence in his make-up, a lack of that creative magic which poets like Dylan Thomas assumed they were full of, head to toe. MacNeice did not know that he would die of pneumonia at fifty-five, but his last poems read as if he did:

in them, laborious self-appraisal has deepened into horrified self-knowledge:

> . . . the day of course is fine
> And a grown-up voice cries Play! The mallet slowly swings,
> Then crack, a great gong booms from the dog-dark hall and the ball
> Skims forward through the hoop and then through the next and then
>
> Through hoops where no hoops were and each dissolves in turn
> And the grass has grown head-high and an angry voice cries Play!
> But the ball is lost and the mallet slipped long since from the hands
> Under the running tap that are not the hands of a child.

When MacNeice assembled what turned out to be his final book, *The Burning Perch*, he was 'taken aback', he said, by the 'fear and resentment' it evinced, 'by the high proportion of sombre pieces, ranging from bleak observation to thumbnail nightmares . . . I am not sure why this should be so'. He may not have been sure, but he must have had a pretty good idea. After a lifetime of asking himself large, convoluted questions, he was beginning to come up with a few crisp replies.

Les Sylphides

Life in a day: he took his girl to the ballet;
Being shortsighted himself could hardly see it –
    The white skirts in the grey
    Glade and the swell of the music
    Lifting the white sails.

Calyx upon calyx, canterbury bells in the breeze
The flowers on the left mirror to the flowers on the right
    And the naked arms above
    The powdered faces moving
    Like seaweed in a pool.

Now, he thought, we are floating – ageless, oarless –
Now there is no separation, from now on
    You will be wearing white
    Satin and a red sash
    Under the waltzing trees.

But the music stopped, the dancers took their curtain,
The river had come to a lock – a shuffle of programmes –
    And we cannot continue down-
    Stream unless we are ready
    To enter the lock and drop.

So they were married – to be the more together –
And found they were never again so much together,
    Divided by the morning tea,
    By the evening paper,
    By children and tradesmen's bills.

Waking at times in the night she found assurance
In his regular breathing but wondered whether
   It was really worth it and where
   The river had flowed away
   And where were the white flowers.

Bagpipe Music

It's no go the merrygoround, it's no go the rickshaw,
All we want is a limousine and a ticket for the peepshow.
Their knickers are made of crêpe-de-chine, their shoes are made
    of python,
Their halls are lined with tiger rugs and their walls with heads of
    bison.

John MacDonald found a corpse, put it under the sofa,
Waited till it came to life and hit it with a poker,
Sold its eyes for souvenirs, sold its blood for whisky,
Kept its bones for dumb-bells to use when he was fifty.

It's no go the Yogi-Man, it's no go Blavatsky,
All we want is a bank balance and a bit of skirt in a taxi.

Annie MacDougall went to milk, caught her foot in the heather,
Woke to hear a dance record playing of Old Vienna.
It's no go your maidenheads, it's no go your culture,
All we want is a Dunlop tyre and the devil mend the puncture.

The Laird o' Phelps spent Hogmanay declaring he was sober,
Counted his feet to prove the fact and found he had one foot over.
Mrs Carmichael had her fifth, looked at the job with repulsion,
Said to the midwife 'Take it away; I'm through with
    over-production.'

It's no go the gossip column, it's no go the ceilidh,
All we want is a mother's help and a sugar-stick for the baby.

Willie Murray cut his thumb, couldn't count the damage,
Took the hide of an Ayrshire cow and used it for a bandage.
His brother caught three hundred cran when the seas were lavish,
Threw the bleeders back in the sea and went upon the parish.

It's no go the Herring Board, it's no go the Bible,
All we want is a packet of fags when our hands are idle.

It's no go the picture palace, it's no go the stadium,
It's no go the country cot with a pot of pink geraniums,
It's no go the Government grants, it's no go the elections,
Sit on your arse for fifty years and hang your hat on a pension.

It's no go my honey love, it's no go my poppet;
Work your hands from day to day, the winds will blow the profit.
The glass is falling hour by hour, the glass will fall for ever,
But if you break the bloody glass you won't hold up the weather.

Theodore Roethke
1908–1963

I think I've got hold of a really big theme: it's got everything, involves just about every neurosis, obsession, fundamental itch or what have you . . . it may take me five years or longer, but when I get done, Eliot will be nothing: a mere *litterateur*. He ain't much more, anyway. Here's an elegy which should reduce you to tears.

This is Theodore Roethke writing to Kenneth Burke in 1949. Roethke had just turned forty and his second book had been published a year earlier, to moderate acclaim. Moderate acclaim, though, would never be enough for Roethke: he wanted nothing less than global homage. And his pursuit of such homage would cost him dearly, not just in terms of sleepless nights. Over the years, he fell victim to a sort of creeping megalomania. His best gift as a poet was for touching, small-scale lyricism (see 'Elegy for Jane', 'My Papa's Waltz'). More and more, though, he was drawn towards what he believed to be the 'major' themes: Man and God, Eternity, the Universe, and so on. Spiritual afflatus took over from direct experience; inspiration was supplanted by ambition. In this sense, Roethke was a typical mid-century case study.

Like so many other American poets of his generation, Roethke was a heavy drinker and susceptible to bouts of mental illness. During such bouts, his careerist braggadocio went haywire: 'I've got old Cal [Lowell] beat, but really', 'I can write rings around some of those punks on [Eliot's] list', and so on. A hulking six-footer, Roethke liked to boast of his Capone-like past (which he'd invented), and in polite literary circles he was always likely to project an air of menace. Rival poets were mown down like Chicago hoods. At the same time, though, as a career academic, Roethke was constantly beset by anxieties about security of tenure. Luckily for him, he functioned at a time when universities indulged unstable poets, and Roethke, for all his belligerence, knew how to charm an audience.

He also had a sentimental streak. Sometimes this redeemed his big-shot affectations. Sometimes, in his poems, it was cloying:

> I knew a woman, lovely in her bones;
> When small birds sighed, she would sigh back at them.

Roethke, in his lighter moods, could be a fluent versifier – he wrote poetry for children – and from time to time he made mock of his own fluency. He was also a compulsive pasticheur: for a period during the mid-1950s he was enslaved by Yeats's rhythms (and also, one suspects, by Yeats's elevated posturing). Roethke tried to make a virtue out of this enslavement – 'I take this cadence from a man called Yeats' – and, being Roethke, imitation was also a form of battery, or competitive aggression: 'I'm damned if I haven't outdone him in the personal and love lyric.'

Early on, the chief influence was Auden. Later, via Dylan Thomas and Hopkins, Roethke turned to Whitman – who, in many ways, turned out to be his most companionable model, if only because he seems to have directed Roethke back to the intent scrutiny of nature that marked his early, so-called 'greenhouse' poems. Born in 1908, in Saginaw, Michigan, Roethke was the son of a German

market–gardener and spent many months of his childhood pottering
about in his family's gigantic greenhouse, which became for him, he
said, 'my symbol for the whole of life, a womb, a heaven–on–earth'.
Plants and flowers, roots and stems were Roethke's boyhood friends
and there were times when he felt himself to be more plant-like
than boy-like: 'I could say hello to things':

> I can hear, underground, that sucking and sobbing,
> In my veins, in my bones I feel it, –
> The small waters seeping upward,
> The tight grains parting at last.
> When sprouts break out,
> Slippery as fish,
> I quail, lean to beginnings, sheath-wet.

   In Roethke's second book, *The Lost Son* (1948), there are several
of these greenhouse poems and they are among the best things he
wrote: convincing and exact, and rich in loamy detail. In his last
book, *The Far Field* (1965), the views are more spacious, but there
is a similar vivacity of observation, a similar self-confidence –
although it is weighted, at this stage, by adult sadness:

> In the vaporous gray of early morning,
> Over the thin, feathery ripples breaking lightly against
>   the irregular shoreline –
> Feathers of the long swell, burnished, almost oily –
> A single wave comes in like the neck of a great swan
> Swimming slowly, its back ruffled by the light cross-winds,
> To a tree lying flat, its crown half-broken.
>
> I remember a stone breaking the envying current,
> Neither white nor red, in the dead middle way,
> Where impulse no longer dictates, nor the darkening shadow,
> A vulnerable place,
> Surrounded by sand, broken shells, the wreckage of water.

For most of his adult life, Theodore Roethke taught in universities (mostly at the University of Washington, in Seattle). Early on
he struggled to get academic jobs, and at least some of his lust for
self-advancement as a poet had to do with the need to impress his
academic paymasters; he always had one eye on his next CV. In
later years, when he was famous (and during the late 1950s and
early 1960s he was highly esteemed, both in America and Britain),
Roethke became a regular on the poetry-reading circuits. He liked
to see himself as both teacher and entertainer and he enjoyed
nothing more than to cavort on public platforms – presenting
himself, quite often, as a cuddlesome, inebriated dancing bear (in
middle age, his bulk got bulkier): he didn't just read his poems –
he liked to sing and dance them, too. Audiences loved him, and he
lapped up their applause, even if, later on, he would go back to
wondering how his reputation now compared with those of Yeats
and Eliot. Caught between the platform and the page, his predicament was shared by many poets of the period and it did little to
protect his fragile but, when left alone, authentic gift. Roethke died
in 1963, having suffered a coronary thrombosis while swimming in
a neighbour's pool.

Frau Bauman, Frau Schmidt, and Frau Schwartze

Gone the three ancient ladies
Who creaked on the greenhouse ladders,
Reaching up white strings
To wind, to wind
The sweet-pea tendrils, the smilax,
Nasturtiums, the climbing
Roses, to straighten
Carnations, red
Chrysanthemums; the stiff
Stems, jointed like corn,
They tied and tucked, –
These nurses of nobody else.
Quicker than birds, they dipped
Up and sifted the dirt;
They sprinkled and shook;
They stood astride pipes,
Their skirts billowing out wide into tents,
Their hands twinkling with wet;
Like witches they flew along rows
Keeping creation at ease;
With a tendril for needle
They sewed up the air with a stem;
They teased out the seed that the cold kept asleep, –
All the coils, loops, and whorls.
They trellised the sun; they plotted for more than themselves.
I remember how they picked me up, a spindly kid,
Pinching and poking my thin ribs
Till I lay in their laps, laughing,
Weak as a whiffet;
Now, when I'm alone and cold in my bed,
They still hover over me,

These ancient leathery crones,
With their bandannas stiffened with sweat,
And their thorn-bitten wrists,
And their snuff-laden breath blowing lightly over me in my
    first sleep.

Elegy for Jane

(My Student, Thrown by a Horse)

I remember the neckcurls, limp and damp as tendrils;
And her quick look, a sidelong pickerel smile;
And how, once startled into talk, the light syllables leaped
    for her,
And she balanced in the delight of her thought,
A wren, happy, tail into the wind,
Her song trembling the twigs and small branches.
The shade sang with her;
The leaves, their whispers turned to kissing;
And the mould sang in the bleached valleys under the rose.

Oh, when she was sad, she cast herself down into such a pure
    depth,
Even a father could not find her:
Scraping her cheek against straw;
Stirring the clearest water.

My sparrow, you are not here,
Waiting like a fern, making a spiny shadow.
The sides of wet stones cannot console me,
Nor the moss, wound with the last light.

If only I could nudge you from this sleep,
My maimed darling, my skittery pigeon.
Over this damp grave I speak the words of my love:
I, with no rights in this matter,
Neither father nor lover.

Stephen Spender

1909–1995

Throughout his long career – he died in 1995, aged eighty-six – Stephen Spender gave rise to several varieties of puzzlement. A saint or a schemer? A victim of fashion or a skilful self-advancer? A talent neglected or a small gift made too much of? These are the familiar questions. Everyone asks them, but no one seems to know quite where they came from. The answer is: they came from him. In his numerous volumes of poetry, fiction, autobiography, diaries and letters, Spender had one predominating subject: Who am I? To which, in each book, there was usually but one reply: I wish I knew. If Spender is now to be viewed as something of an enigma, this is not because he showed us too little of himself. On the contrary, he gave us more than we could easily digest – a surfeit of self-exploration.

And, some would say, a surfeit of self-love, plus a disabling weakness for personal publicity. This weakness Stephen traced back to his father, Harold Spender, a well-known liberal journalist and would-be politician. When Harold stood for Parliament in 1922, he recruited his two sons – the fourteen-year-old Stephen and his younger brother – to act as his campaign aides, and this experience instilled in Stephen a sharp and enduring appetite for popular attention. In his autobiography, *World Within World*, Spender confessed that 'It often disgusts me to read a newspaper in which there is no mention of my name.'

Even at fourteen, Stephen judged himself to be more sensitive than his father, and by the time he went to Oxford, in 1928, he had decided to pursue fame as a poet. When, in years to come, Spender told T. S. Eliot that he wanted to 'be a poet', Eliot responded, 'I can understand your wanting to write poems, but I don't quite know what you mean by "being a poet".' Nor, at twenty, did Spender. The affectation was what mattered and, for this, Oxford in the 1920s was the place to be. The so-called Brideshead generation had moved on by the time Spender enrolled at University College, but much of its legacy remained. People still painted their rooms pink, wore monogrammed silk shirts and threw outrageous parties: lobster Newburg served in dustbins, blood-coloured soup, and so on.

In this context, Spender made his mark by announcing himself to be 'a pacifist and a socialist, a genius'. He wore a red tie, hung reproductions of paintings by Gauguin, Van Gogh and Paul Klee on his walls, and 'on fine days, I used to take a cushion into the quadrangle, and sitting down on it read poetry'. This was enough, it seems, to bring him to the attention of W. H. Auden, who had already achieved legendary status in the university by promoting an alternative to the old Brideshead styles of affectation. Where the standard Oxford aesthete of the 1920s had been showily dissipated, full of wild talk about decadence and beauty, Auden was preaching a new gospel of icy austerity and self-control. Spender, who had been shaping up as an apprentice Blake or Shelley, was entranced. It was not that he wanted to write poetry like Auden's – he already suspected that he couldn't – but he did want to join his gang. When Auden eventually gave him a qualified thumbs-up, he was elated.

To be a fully accepted member of the Auden gang, you had to be a homosexual. Spender was fairly certain that he qualified for membership – but, as with most things, he could not be sure. Throughout the 1930s, he agonized about his sexuality, and in spite of one or two fulfilling trips to Isherwood's Berlin, he was reluctant to abandon what he called 'a normal way of life'. He resented being forced to choose, he said. As with sex, so with politics. Again, there was much public searching of the Spender conscience. Was he a poet or a political activist? Could the quest for personal fulfilment be reconciled with a commitment to the public good? And how Left was he, really? Not Left enough to make a lasting commitment to the Party, but Left enough to want to go to Spain – which Spender did, somewhat bumblingly, on more than one occasion.

Some of this political self-questioning got into Spender's poems, and during the 1930s he was widely praised for adding a dimension of soulfulness and passion to Auden's cold-eyed admonitions. Apart from the odd pylon or express train, Spender's 1930s poems were thoroughly old-fashioned, much given to archaic diction, confused syntax and fervent apostrophes to Time, History and Freedom. But somehow all this seemed to boost his standing. Auden, after all, was often forbiddingly cryptic and oblique. And Spender was a busy presence, also, on the 1930s social scene, enjoying invitations to the Woolfs and gleeful visits to Ottoline Morrell's salons. He was well liked by the pacifists, monarchists and aesthetes who controlled the London literary world. They found him engagingly impulsive and muddle-headed.

Spender solved his sexual problem, so he hoped, by marrying one Inez Pearn in 1936. This marriage was greeted with astonishment by Spender's male assiciates and, unsurprisingly, it didn't last. By 1939, with the outbreak of war, many of the delusions of the 1930s lay in ruins. When Auden and Isherwood fled to the United States, Spender stayed put in London – wifeless and companionless and, in the eyes of many, a symbol of the decade's follies. During the war, he enlisted in the London Fire Service and helped Cyril Connolly to start the magazine *Horizon*. In 1941, he got married for a second time, to the pianist Natasha Litvin, and this union remained intact until his death.

After the war, Spender joined Unesco and this marked a new phase of his celebrity: a twenty-year-long stint as a kind of globe-trotting cultural emissary. During the late fifties and throughout the sixties, he was perpetually on the move, sometimes as troubled

ambassador for Western values, for the Congress for Cultural Freedom, for International PEN, or for the British Council, and sometimes as hard-up literary journeyman, lecturing on modern poetry at
various American universities, and taking on various book projects,
such as *Love-Hate Relations*, a study of Anglo-American literary
relationships, and *The Year of the Young Rebels*, an indulgent account
of the 1968 upheavals in Paris, Prague, New York and West Berlin.
He also co-edited the magazine *Encounter*, but resigned in 1967
after discovering that the journal had for many years been paid for
by the CIA. In 1970, he was appointed to a professorship at
University College, London – not bad going, he would say, for
one who called himself 'ineducable'.

Spender published relatively little poetry in his later years and
was inclined to see himself as a neglected figure: 'I imagine the
young reading nothing of me but the bad notices to other young
critics.' He felt himself to be locked into his ranking as a thirties
phenomenon – famous for period pieces which everybody knew
but nobody took very seriously: 'The Pylons', 'The Landscape near
an Aerodrome', 'I Think Continually of Those Who Were Truly
Great'. He was not consoled by the enthusiasm that greeted his
Journals 1939–83 when they appeared in 1985, nor by the respectful
attention that was paid to his last book, *The Dolphins* (1994). On
this, the verdict seemed to be that, by lowering his sights, he had
achieved a decent competence, and that his later poems shared with
his *Journals* and his autobiographical writings a gift for portraiture
and elegy. The language, pared down, purged of the old luridness,
still failed to sparkle and the rhythms too often were inert, but
Spender seemed at last to have a sensible measure of his gifts. This
famous explorer of the self turned out to be at his most effective
when exploring his memories of other people; in the end, the
prophet's best insights came from looking back.

Elegy for Margaret

Poor girl, inhabitant of a strange land
Where death stares through your gaze,
As though a distant moon
Shone through midsummer days
With the skull-like glitter of night:

Poor child, you wear your summer dress
And your shoes striped with gold
As the earth wears a variegated cover
Of grass and flowers
Covering caverns of destruction over
Where hollow deaths are told.

I look into your sunk eyes,
Shafts of wells to both our hearts,
Which cannot take part in the lies
Of acting these gay parts.
Under our lips, our minds
Become one with the weeping
Of the mortality
Which through sleep is unsleeping.

Of what use is my weeping?
It does not carry a surgeon's knife
To cut the wrongly multiplying cells
At the root of your life.
It can only prove
That extremes of love
Stretch beyond the flesh to hideous bone
Howling in hyena dark alone.

Oh, but my grief is thought, a dream,
Tomorrow's gale will sweep away.
It does not wake every day
To the facts which are and do not only seem:
The granite facts around your bed,
Poverty-stricken hopeless ugliness
Of the fact that you will soon be dead.

Elizabeth Bishop

1911–1979

For most of her writing life, Elizabeth Bishop was known for not wanting to be known. Where other poets muscled their careers to centre stage, she hovered in the wings. Where others importuned their audience with news of their most private sorrows, she remained tight-lipped. A near-contemporary of the so-called confessional poets, poets such as Robert Lowell and John Berryman, she once said of them: 'You just wish they'd keep some of these things to themselves.'

Bishop died in 1979, aged sixty-eight, prize-laden and greatly respected by her fellow poets. 'A poet's poet's poet' was James Merrill's well-known tag. And yet she was still thought of as somehow marginal to the action. Austere and almost fiddlingly skilful, more interested in places than in people, detached almost to the point of authorial invisibility, she was there to be invoked as a cool, neo-classical alternative to the various slacknesses and excesses of the moment: excessive avant-gardism, excessive self-exposure, excessive political engagement, and so on. There was nothing excessive about Bishop, so it seemed. For her, there was an active virtue to be found in self-forgetfulness, in saying 'look at that' instead of 'look at me'.

The year 1994 saw the publication of Bishop's *Letters*, and of two biographies – together, they revealed a life that had been filled almost to ruination by excess: drink, sexual passion, sickness, suicides. Suddenly it was possible to read the Bishop oeuvre in a different way: to find in its low-key formality a painful yearning for the non-excessive, the repetitive, the stable. Take the poem called 'One Art':

> I lost my mother's watch. And look! my last, or
> next-to-last, of three loved houses went.
> The art of losing isn't hard to master.
>
> I lost two cities, lovely ones. And, vaster,
> Some realms I owned, two rivers, a continent.
> I miss them, but it wasn't a disaster.

Thanks to biography, we now know that this poem was written in delayed response to a catastrophe, a major turning-point in Bishop's life: the suicide of Lota de Macedo Soares, with whom she had lived in South America for fifteen years. Knowing this, we can work out what Bishop means by 'two cities', 'three loved houses', 'a continent'. And the line about her mother's watch assumes a new forcefulness when we know about the poet's childhood. Bishop's father died when she was a baby. When she was five, her mother was removed to an insane asylum. Brought up by her grandparents, Bishop never saw her mother again (she died in 1934, when Bishop was twenty-three).

At the start of Bishop's writing life, the joys and skills of simple observation seemed sufficient, almost therapeutic. Her first literary mentor was Marianne Moore, herself famous (in Moore's words) as 'one of those who despise clamor about substance'. Bishop and Moore met in the substance-full 1930s, and each found an enjoyable delinquency in concentrating on the local, the miniature, the recondite. In a period dominated by large-scale vehemence and theory, they liked to cultivate an art of the curious-particular. They liked to keep smiling, or half-smiling, while everyone around them sported solemn masks of doom. Marianne Moore, though, was a natural eccentric: she really did prefer pelicans to people. Bishop's quirkiness, not in the least fake but maybe somewhat worked up for Moore's benefit, was not central to her personality. Bishop was more of a dreamer, a worrier. And – at the time of her Moore involvement – she was very young, and more ambitious for literary advancement than she made out; more, perhaps, than she knew. Her manners and her aspirations could not for long be fashioned to Moore's model. And neither could her poems. Perhaps she came to feel that Moore's influence imprisoned her in habits of detachment. But how to close the gap between the seer and the seen?

By the time Bishop settled in Florida in 1938 (she stayed there for nine years), the personality that she was accustomed to excluding from her poems had shaped itself in ways that Moore would not have found appealing. Bishop knew she was lesbian and she knew too that Moore was contemptuous of 'sodomites'. She knew that she was alcoholic and that her drinking was sometimes the talk of New York literary gatherings – there had been several drunken scenes. She had to get out of the city, not just for the sake of her reputation but also for health reasons. Bishop suffered wretchedly from asthma and needed to be in the sun. This last was a condition that she *was* able to disclose to Moore.

After Florida, Brazil. Bishop's fifteen years with Lota Soares were the best years of her life. The letters that she wrote from Brazil after settling there in 1951 are as vivacious as anything she wrote in verse. Lota was a forceful protector: she had money, owned the house that she and Bishop lived in, and had even built her poet-friend a study. She was heavily involved in local politics but in the early years she saw it as her chief role to keep Bishop focused on her writing, to safeguard the poet's health and to restrain her from the bottle. According to a mutual friend, Lota believed that Bishop needed 'the affectionate protection of a home, a sense of belonging, the orderly consolations of habit and dailiness, the will to stay put.

They became lovers, even if Lota more often acted the mother to Elizabeth the child.'

In her Brazil location, Bishop also felt ready to recall episodes from her strange, puzzled childhood, episodes which for years she had kept at a distance. Much of Bishop's 'Brazil book', *Questions of Travel*, which appeared in 1965, was set in Nova Scotia, her birthplace. Nova Scotia now seemed like the opposite of where she was – and not just in terms of climate and geography. Bishop's childhood home had never felt like home. She had been shunted from one set of grandparents to another; she was always a guest in other people's houses. Now that she had found a home, she could afford to ask herself some leading questions: had she inherited her mother's madness? Why was she unable to give up drink, even with Lota to watch over her?

In the 1960s, the Brazil idyll began to fall apart as Bishop and Lota became increasingly involved in their separate careers – Lota became bossier, Bishop more mouse-like and aggrieved, in spite of her increasing reputation as a poet. After Lota's death, she was appalled to find that some of her much-prized Brazilian friends had not been friends at all – some of them blamed her for Lota's suicide. Bishop's final port was Harvard, where, despite the ministrations of a small coterie of worshipful disciples, she felt herself to be neglected. In her sixties, the woman who cherished domesticity found herself lodging in cramped, dingy rooms in a student dormitory. By day, she steeled herself to teach 'Advanced Verse Writing' to what she called 'the usual nuts and freaks'.

In Bishop's last, short book, *Geographies III*, there are hints that, had she lived, she might have attempted to follow the instructions of 'One Art', simply to '*Write* it'. Poems like 'Crusoe in England', 'In the Waiting Room' and 'The Moose' seem melancholy worlds away from the 'mere observation' poems of her youth. It seems doubtful, though, that she would ever have wished to break out, Lowell-style, into full-blooded candour. Even the one or two late pieces of hers that have been called 'confessional' are essentially well-guarded, wry, rueful, and impressively resigned. 'What's wrong about self-pity, anyway?' she asked, towards the end, and the question is answered by her work.

Sandpiper

The roaring alongside he takes for granted,
and that every so often the world is bound to shake.
He runs, he runs to the south, finical, awkward,
in a state of controlled panic, a student of Blake.

The beach hisses like fat. On his left, a sheet
of interrupting water comes and goes
and glazes over his dark and brittle feet.
He runs, he runs straight through it, watching his toes.

– Watching, rather, the spaces of sand between them,
where (no detail too small) the Atlantic drains
rapidly backwards and downwards. As he runs,
he stares at the dragging grains.

The world is a mist. And then the world is
minute and vast and clear. The tide
is higher or lower. He couldn't tell you which.
His beak is focussed; he is preoccupied,

looking for something, something, something.
Poor bird, he is obsessed!
The millions of grains are black, white, tan, and gray,
mixed with quartz grains, rose and amethyst.

One Art

The art of losing isn't hard to master;
so many things seem filled with the intent
to be lost that their loss is no disaster.

Lose something every day. Accept the fluster
of lost door keys, the hour badly spent.
The art of losing isn't hard to master.

Then practice losing farther, losing faster:
places, and names, and where it was you meant
to travel. None of these will bring disaster.

I lost my mother's watch. And look! my last, or
next-to-last, of three loved houses went.
The art of losing isn't hard to master.

I lost two cities, lovely ones. And, vaster,
some realms I owned, two rivers, a continent.
I miss them, but it wasn't a disaster.

– Even losing you (the joking voice, a gesture
I love) I shan't have lied. It's evident
the art of losing's not too hard to master
though it may look like (*Write* it!) like disaster.

Roy Fuller

1912–1991

Roy Fuller used to date the beginning of his 'poetic life' from a meeting with the critic John Davenport in 1930. Davenport introduced him to the youthful work of Auden and Spender, and from then on Fuller was a would-be Thirties Poet. Aged eighteen in 1930, he had already contributed a poem (in 1928) to the celebrated Poet's Corner of the *Sunday Referee*, where Dylan Thomas and Pamela Hansford Johnson discovered each other, and he had composed more than one unpublished volume in the style of Humbert Wolfe. Pre-Auden, he had also begun to explore Pound and Eliot and to realize that modern poetry had more to offer than his school librarian had ever dreamed of. This new Thirties work, though, from poets of near his own generation, chimed in more excitingly with his awakening political enthusiasm.

In 1930, Fuller was already articled to a solicitor in Blackpool (he was born near Oldham). He had attended a genteel, unambitious school in Blackpool (his novel *The Ruined Boys* was based on it) and the question of his going on from there to university was never raised – pupils became solicitors, chartered accountants or, more usually, they went into their fathers' businesses. Fuller's own father, who had worked his way up to become a director of a rubber-proofing firm and prospered supplying groundsheets to the Army in the 1914–18 War, had died young, when Fuller was eight. It was therefore a toss-up between accountancy and law, and he chose law. (From these beginnings, he would rise to become solicitor to the Woolwich Building Society and a member of the Law Society's working party on conveyancing.) At the age of sixteen, Fuller was articled; he passed his finals at twenty-one, and at twenty-two he was managing a local branch office.

In his early twenties, Fuller was writing just like Auden and was happily caught up in the activities of local left-wing groups. For him, he would later attest, this was the one brief period of his life when poetry really did seem usefully bound up with day-to-day political affairs. Unable subsequently to recapture this rare fusion, he never stopped wondering what had happened to it, and never stopped insisting that poetry ought to have such relevance. A frequent persona in his post-1930s verse was that of an artist-figure mocked by a crippling alienation from the 'unteachable mass' he yearned to teach.

After moving from Blackpool to Ashford, Kent, in 1935, Fuller's political activities began to peter out. He remained, though, 'absolutely sympathetic to Marxist ideas'. His deepening conviction during the 1930s (he was, he once confessed, 'too timid' for Spain) was that 'history had caught up with one so it didn't matter too much what one did', that 'one was entering into a period of Caesarism, that civilization would end'. In 1941 he was called up and, he said, 'opted for the Navy, influenced by a friend, and thinking woolily that any hostilities in which I might be involved would be conducted at a genteel distance'. He was posted to Africa as a radar mechanic in 1942, spent most of 1943 in Nairobi, 'idling time away or repairing radar sets', and returned to England in 1944 to a commission and a desk at the Admiralty. Apart from a bout of malaria, nothing very hazardous had happened to him.

He had, though, written two books which rank with the best 'war poetry' of 1939–45 – *The Middle of a War* and *A Lost Season*. The subjects of Fuller's war poems are the familiar ones – transit-camp boredom, awed response to foreign climes, separation from loved ones, ludicrousness of army life, pervading sense of doom, and so on – but in attempting to break away from Auden's generalizing habit into something more sharply autobiographical, he struck an original and moving vein. His style in these poems, though it runs easily to the loose and rhetorical, works as a kind of bridge between two epochs: the public, admonitory manner of the 1930s attempting to accommodate the personal suffering it had so icily predicted. It is a style that works unevenly, but at its best it generates a curiously formal manner of despair which, in its stiff, bleak, rather stilted way, can be quite powerful:

> My photograph already looks historic.
> The promising youthful face, the matelot's collar,
> Say 'This one is remembered for a lyric.
> His place and period – nothing could be duller.'
>
> Its position is already indicated –
> The son or brother in the album; pained
> The expression and the garments dated,
> His fate so obviously preordained.

After the war, Fuller was prolific in both prose and verse and, until illness obliged him to adopt more relaxed habits, he would regularly rise in the early hours and work at his writing until it was time for a full day of legal chores – England's answer to Wallace Stevens, some have said. Books of verse, novels, detective stories, children's books, reviews and articles: an impressive output for a spare-time writer. He also paid the penalty of middle-aged eminence in terms of committee work, prize panels and the like. He was elected Oxford Professor of Poetry in 1968 and in the 1970s was a governor of the BBC. He died in 1991.

It would be untrue to say that Fuller's writing during his busy postwar years did not bear signs of haste, but there was no serious default from standards of intelligence and honesty, from what he called 'the criterion of success in poetry: brain power allied at least to a dogged alertness and integrity'.

In Memory of My Cat Domino: 1951–1966

Rising at dawn to pee, I thought I saw you
Curved in a chair, with head raised to look at me,
As you did at such hours. But the next moment,
More used to the gloom, there was only a jar
And a face-cloth. Time enough, nonetheless,
For love's responsibilities to return
To me.

             The unique character of the dead
Is the source of our sense of mourning and loss;
So, back in bed, I avoided calling up
What I know is intact in my mind, your life,
Entirely possessed as it was by my care.

I could conceive you not as dead but merely
Gone before me to a world that sends to us
Decreasing intimations of its beings –
No doubt because they find us in the end
Pathetic, worthy, but of small importance.

So long had we been together it never
Occurred to me I might fall somewhat behind.
Even when, familiar fur in my hands,
The sickly wave of barbiturate rose up,
I thought it was I who was journeying on –
But looking back there is only emptiness,
Your dusty medicaments and my portrait
Taken with you: sad mode of life you've outpaced.

The Middle of a War

My photograph already looks historic.
The promising youthful face, the matelot's collar,
Say 'This one is remembered for a lyric.
His place and period – nothing could be duller.'

Its position is already indicated –
The son or brother in the album; pained
The expression and the garments dated,
His fate so obviously preordained.

The original turns away: as horrible thoughts,
Loud fluttering aircraft slope above his head
At dusk. The ridiculous empires break like biscuits.
Ah, life has been abandoned by the boats –
Only the trodden island and the dead
Remain, and the once inestimable caskets.

R. S. Thomas

1913–2000

R. S. Thomas's four autobiographies (four memoir-essays, really) were written in Welsh, and the most substantial of the four was titled *Neb*, which means 'nobody' – as in 'a nobody' or 'nobody very special'. And this fits well with how Thomas was regarded in his lifetime. Was he too humble or too proud? Was he to be admired for self-effacement or chastised for self-absorption? Over the years, Thomas asked himself such questions many times, and his replies were no more definite than those of his reviewers.

According to Thomas's biographer, Justin Wintle, a complete tally of the R. S. Thomas oeuvre would add up to some 1,200 poems, not all of which appear in the 500-page *Collected Poems*. These figures still seem surprising: Thomas, after all, was never thought of as abundant. Nor was he. The truth is that for long stretches he wrote the same poem over again, several times. First, there were the startlingly sour Iago Prytherch poems, then the Welsh Nationalist poems, then the 'deus absconditus' prayer-poems, then the vague musings about God as cosmic scientist, then the poems about paintings, and so on. More than with most poets, Thomas's work can be divided into chapters. The drift throughout, though, was away from the carefully wrought individual poem towards a kind of open-ended ruminative jotting.

In Thomas's *Collected Poems*, there are very few star items. The impact is by way of dogged, impervious accumulation. The words come at us in clumps and yet they somehow don't seem meant for us. With Thomas, the reader doesn't read: he listens in. As with their author, the poems are proffered as nothing very much. Spare, colourless and repetitive, Thomas's work makes up for its lack of vigour by the unembarrassed steadiness with which it focuses on this or that obsession, for as long as the obsession lasts. Here is an art that simply goes about its business. The business is humble, sometimes dismal, but somebody (a nobody-somebody) has to do it.

But then again, perhaps somebody didn't have to do it. Thomas's attitude to his own verse-making, as to several other features of his life and personality, and to most aspects of the modern world, was rarely other than reproving. This much could be gathered from his verses but there is a powerful strain of misanthropy in his memoirs, especially those written in the third person, with Thomas referred to as 'R. S.' or 'the rector' or 'the vicar'. If these memoirs had been fictions, the author would probably have been reproached for his ungenerous and superficial treatment of his central character. Does this poor 'rector' have to be so dreary and resentful, so hard on himself? After all, the rector did go through the Sunday motions and fulfilled the most important of his pastoral responsibilities: did it matter that he had scant patience with church ritual and abhorred the hymns? Did it matter that he disliked – and was disliked by – many of his flock (or flocks, since Thomas changed parishes several times, ostensibly in search of a Welsh-speaking berth)? It didn't matter much to Thomas that he was not loved by his low-grade parishioners – his yokels, squires, weekenders, and the like: he painted his church pews black, drove slowly in the middle of the road, upbraided any locals caught ordering their groceries in English. Reading Thomas's biography, we often get the feeling that for him the only good church was an empty one.

Thomas was born in Cardiff in 1913, son of two non-Welsh

speakers. His father was a merchant seaman; his mother, as depicted in his memoirs, was an overbearing shrew who failed to teach little R. S. Welsh (R. S. stands for Ronald Stewart), but instead enrolled him in a theological college and thus set in motion his life's miseries. He served as an English-speaking priest until his retirement in 1978. He died in 2000.

Thomas's inability to write poetry in Welsh was for him a constant discomfiture – a source, sometimes, of shame. And, sure enough, we can detect a grudgingness in his deployment of the English tongue – the tongue, as he would say, of his oppressor. And yet this grudgingness did serve the poet well: the bare simplicity of Thomas's poetic speech was one of his great strengths. For him, though, 'bare and simple' was as close as he could get, in English, to honouring his anti-Englishness. Even the faintest tremor of luxuriance might have given his compatriots the wrong idea. Over the years, Thomas's language-guilt had a central, and perhaps debilitating influence on his career – or, rather, his careers: as poet, as Welsh patriot, as priest. In poetry-career terms, certainly, he staked out a kind of no man's land, or call it a nobody's land. He felt obliged, it seems, to stand aloof from his 'in English' contemporaries, as if he might be tainted, further tainted, by their anthology-companionship, by their co-poets' sympathy for his predicament. He was famously frosty and austere, and remained that way until the end.

In politics, although Thomas was vehement in his attacks on the loathed English, he never quite won over the most hardline of his nationalist comrades. OK, some of those would say, he has to write his poetry in English, but why did he accept so many English honours – not least the Queen's Gold Medal? Why did he seem to nurture his English reputation with appearances on radio and TV, and in English periodicals? Why, when he spoke English, did he sound so thoroughly non-Welsh? Why did he choose to educate his son at English schools? And why, if the Welsh language meant so much to him, did he not spend more time translating the great English poets into Welsh – or, come to that, the great Welsh poets into English?

Thomas was, of course, well aware of such reproaches. Sometimes he levelled them against himself. The trouble was, though, that although Thomas loved Wales and its language, he found it hard to scrape up much affection for the Welsh. The Welsh, Thomas believed, bore a large slice of the blame for their own subjugation. From Prytherch onwards, he found it hard to disguise his contempt for Welsh stupidity and feebleness, as evidenced by his parishioners. Thomas acknowledged his own bookishness and did his best, he said, to warm to other people. But these compatriots of his, whose souls were in his charge, got on his nerves. Even if Thomas had written his poems in Welsh, who would have read them? Most days, rather than preach to oafish Welshmen, Thomas preferred to go bird-watching, or to whisper imprecations to an absent God.

Here

I am a man now.
Pass your hand over my brow,
You can feel the place where the brains grow.

I am like a tree,
From my top boughs I can see
The footprints that led up to me.

There is blood in my veins
That has run clear of the stain
Contracted in so many loins.

Why, then, are my hands red
With the blood of so many dead?
Is this where I was misled?

Why are my hands this way
That they will not do as I say?
Does no God hear when I pray?

I have nowhere to go.
The swift satellites show
The clock of my whole being is slow.

It is too late to start
For destinations not of the heart.
I must stay here with my hurt.

The Country Clergy

I see them working in old rectories
By the sun's light, by candlelight,
Venerable men, their black cloth
A little dusty, a little green
With holy mildew. And yet their skulls,
Ripening over so many prayers,
Toppled into the same grave
With oafs and yokels. They left no books,
Memorial to their lonely thought
In grey parishes; rather they wrote
On men's hearts and in the minds
Of young children sublime words
Too soon forgotten. God in his time
Or out of time will correct this.

Randall Jarrell

1914–1965

In April 1965, Randall Jarrell's just-published book of verse, *The Lost World*, was reviewed in the *New York Times Book Review* by Joseph Bennett. Bennett admired four poems in the book. The rest of them, he said, were:

> taken up with Jarrell's familiar, clanging vulgarity, corny clichés, cutenesses, and the intolerable self-indulgence of his tear-jerking bourgeois sentimentality . . . His work is thoroughly dated; prodigiousness encouraged by an indulgent and sentimental Mama-ism; its overriding feature is doddering infantilism.

A few days after reading this, Jarrell cut his left wrist in a suicide attempt. He had been in a depressed state for several weeks and a year earlier had had some kind of nervous breakdown. According to his widow, this Bennett onslaught was the final straw. The review was nastily phrased, but did Jarrell the acerbic poet-critic fear that it was not entirely off the mark? Six months later, Jarrell was dead – hit by a car when out walking, after dark, on a North Carolina highway. Accident or suicide? On this question, there is still much argument, and the evidence is inconclusive. At the time, though, it was agreed by Jarrell's friends that for the past two years (Jarrell turned fifty in 1964) this imperiously vital arbiter of America's poetic taste had lost his taste for living. 'Don't make mountains out of mole hills,' Jarrell's Mama had advised him in 1964. And he had answered: 'When you are depressed, there are no mole hills.'

In the early 1940s, to be on the receiving end of one of Jarrell's sizzling assassinations was to put oneself in line for immortality. Who would nowadays remember Oscar Williams's verses if Jarrell had not said that they seemed to have been written on a typewriter by a typewriter? Williams at that time was a powerful anthologist, and in career terms it was bad policy to mock him. Jarrell, though, seemed not to care about careers – indeed, the very word 'career' would certainly have set his teeth on edge. Although he spent his whole life teaching in universities – apart from war service, a year on *The Nation* as literary editor, and a stint as poetry consultant at the Library of Congress – he repeatedly let it be known that he did not belong on campus. In his letters from academia, he casts himself as a highly superior misfit, and his wearyingly witty 'novel', *Pictures from an Institution* (1954), is mostly a celebration of this stance.

Maybe the university jobs came to Jarrell too easily, or too early. A full-of-himself student at Vanderbilt University in Nashville in the 1930s, he was taken up by Allen Tate and John Crowe Ransom, and most of his later academic appointments could easily be traced back to this connection. Not that Jarrell ever felt inclined to gratitude: another of his most famous and most joyous thrusts as a reviewer was aimed at the vitals of his early Agrarian mentors – 'To expect Tate's and Warren's poems to be most influenced by Ransom's is like expecting two nightmares to be influenced by a daydream.'

When Jarrell's friends heard of his breakdown in the early 1960s, they responded with bewilderment. For Randall to go mad was the last thing they envisaged, and yet at the same time they found that they were less surprised than they would have expected to be. Overridingly at first there was a feeling that Randall was too clever to go mad. There had always seemed to be something impregnable about his sense of his own worth. 'When I'm right, I'm right,' he used to say. He played tennis all the time, he kept himself in shape, he had in 1952 – and with stunningly abrupt efficiency – exchanged an insufficiently worshipful first wife for one who was prepared to dedicate herself to Randall's adoration.

And his poetry was nothing if not sane. Indeed, it was quite often distended by an excess of common sense (and not unlike his own version of late Auden: 'too conscious, too thin, too merely rational'). As a poet, Jarrell aimed to speak for ordinary people, in ordinary speech. He was fond of the dramatic monologue. But Jarrell's people, though meant as individual cases, are too dampened by their ordinariness, their function as instructive symptoms (symptoms, mostly, of society's impersonal, abstracting deadliness), ever to fire more than a merely dutiful kind of sympathy. His language, too, although meant to sound straight from the heart, pleads spontaneity by means of pace and accumulation, by capturing not just the hasty cadences of actual speech but also its meanderings, its parentheses, its second thoughts, its dots and dashes, and so on:

> Today, in a German dictionary, I saw *elend*
> And the heart in my breast turned over, it was –
>
> It was a word one translates *wretched*.
>
> It is as if someone remembered saying:
> 'This is an antimacassar that I grew from seed,'
> And this were true.
> And, truly,
> One could not wish for anything more strange –
> For anything more. And yet it wasn't *interesting* . . .
> – It was worse than impossible, it was a joke.
>
> And yet when it was, I *was* –

During wartime, Jarrell as ordinary joe found it particularly difficult to eliminate all traces of his own superior intelligence.

Most of Jarrell's poems are far too long – they don't know when or how to stop – and in his wartime verses the attempt to replicate the 'ordinary speech' of his new army buddies gave him, it would seem, a special licence to go on and on. It is ironic, therefore, that Jarrell's best-known war poem, 'The Death of the Ball Turret Gunner', should be one that verges on the epigrammatic.

The critic John Thompson once opined that it was Jarrell's sense of his own 'precariousness' that caused him to keep his distance from the 'mad' poets of his generation – and particularly from Robert Lowell, who admired him greatly. Thompson knew both Lowell and Jarrell at Kenyon College in the late 1930s, and even in those early days Randall was looked on as an oddball. He was brilliantly erudite and talkative but insufferably arrogant as well. And this arrogance fed into his mystique. He was pampered and indulged by Tate and Ransom, although even the benign Ransom took exception to Jarrell's 'untactful manners', and altogether found him trying. Tate in later years would call Jarrell a 'self-adulating little twerp'. Even so, they did encourage this 'strange boy'. Jarrell's derivative verses – sub-Crane followed by sub-Auden followed by sub-Frost – were printed in the *Southern Review* and the *Kenyon Review*, and before long his famous arrogance was let loose on the review pages of the *New Republic*. Jarrell was twenty-one when he published his first major axe-job, and most of his best work as a critic was written before he had turned forty.

Jarrell's essays were always more vivacious and convincing than his poems, more springily intense. As admiring readers of those essays, we can be grateful that he exercised his inspiration in a genre for which, finally, he had not much respect. For Jarrell, as he once testified, being a great poetry critic was a paltry sort of thing, involving a measure of self-relegation which, in the end, he maybe found impossible to bear.

The Woman at the Washington Zoo

The saris go by me from the embassies.

Cloth from the moon. Cloth from another planet.
They look back at the leopard like the leopard.

And I . . .
            this print of mine, that has kept its color
Alive through so many cleanings; this dull null
Navy I wear to work, and wear from work, and so
To my bed, so to my grave, with no
Complaints, no comment: neither from my chief,
The Deputy Chief Assistant, nor his chief –
Only I complain . . . this serviceable
Body that no sunlight dyes, no hand suffuses
But, dome-shadowed, withering among columns,
Wavy beneath fountains – small, far-off, shining
In the eyes of animals, these beings trapped
As I am trapped but not, themselves, the trap,
Aging, but without knowledge of their age,
Kept safe here, knowing not of death, for death –
Oh, bars of my own body, open, open!

The world goes by my cage and never sees me.
And there come not to me, as come to these,
The wild beasts, sparrows pecking the llamas' grain,
Pigeons settling on the bears' bread, buzzards
Tearing the meat the flies have clouded . . .
                                          Vulture,
When you come for the white rat that the foxes left,
Take off the red helmet of your head, the black
Wings that have shadowed me, and step to me as man:
The wild brother at whose feet the white wolves fawn,

To whose hand of power the great lioness
Stalks, purring . . .
                         You know what I was,
You see what I am: change me, change me!

The Death of the Ball Turret Gunner

From my mother's sleep I fell into the State,
And I hunched in its belly till my wet fur froze.
Six miles from the earth, loosed from its dream of life,
I woke to black flak and the nightmare fighters.
When I died they washed me out of the turret with a hose.

Weldon Kees

1914–1955?

In July 1955, Weldon Kees's car was found abandoned in a parking lot near the Golden Gate Bridge in San Francisco. There was no trace of Kees – no body, no suicide note – and to this day the mystery remains unsolved. Some people believe that Kees is still alive. They remind us that, not long before his disappearance, he was urging a friend to join him in a flight to Mexico. And since 1955 there have been rumours of Kees sightings.

Officially, though, the verdict seems to be that he committed suicide and that his suicide had more than a little to do with his low standing as a poet, a low standing he had good reason to resent. According to Donald Justice, who edited the posthumous *Collected Poems*, Kees was intensely serious about his verse, and also ferociously ambitious for acclaim, even though he wrote and published little and went in for lots of other quasi-creative occupations: at various times Kees functioned as a painter, a photographer, a film-maker and a jazz musician. He spent most of his time in the company of artists of one sort or another. His poetry, though, was what really mattered to him, and in this field he was never greatly honoured in his lifetime.

Born in Nebraska in 1914, Weldon Kees was just over forty when he died. A dangerous age, and especially so for writers, or so Malcolm Cowley would have us believe:

That's the time when writers have to face up to what they've been doing. They are halfway through their artistic careers and perhaps they've made a little success, but not the sort they were hoping for, and now the future begins to look like the past and not so interesting.

Donald Justice quotes these words of Cowley's and quotes also Scott Fitzgerald's famous dictum about writers having only 'so large an account to draw on, and once you've drawn on it, that's all there is'. Apparently Kees liked to repeat this theory of Fitzgerald's.

According to Alfred Kazin, who knew him, Weldon Kees's ambition as a poet knew no bounds. He 'desperately wanted to be famous', says Kazin, 'to be "up there", as he used to say, with Eliot, Pound and other stars in our firmament'. This being so, one has to wonder why Weldon was not more of a hustler on his own behalf. So far as we know, he seems to have done very little in the way of careerist self-advancement – although, to judge from photographs, he was by no means short of vanity. Arrogant, embittered and melancholic, he waited for acclaim to come to him, but none of the three books he published in his lifetime made much of a mark. (One commentator has suggested that Kees sold maybe a thousand copies of his work – a thousand copies altogether – before he disappeared.)

Kees was also unlucky in the sense that his poems did not fit with any of the then-prevailing vogues. He was not an experimentalist, but on the other hand he could scarcely be thought of as a natural conservative. Technically, he veered between tight forms and a sort of prosy, flat, free verse. Most important of all, perhaps, was the fact that he began publishing in the 1930s. Although Kees dabbled in politically conscious satire and nurtured a deep loathing of America's consumer culture, he was always too blackly self-absorbed to throw himself into any movement for political or social change. He mistrusted the large gesture. And in any case, so far as he was concerned, the American dream – by which he meant the Whitman-optimistic dream – was well and truly over. In his view, civilization was terminally botched.

Just before he disappeared, Kees wrote a magazine article in which he lamented 'our present atmosphere of distrust, violence and irrationality, with so many human beings murdering themselves – either literally or symbolically'. This article appeared in the *New Republic* on the day that Kees's abandoned car was found and is now cited as a possible explanation of his suicide, if suicide it was. Kees, some people like to think, died a symbolic death, and can now be hailed as one of Poetry's martyrs. Less sentimental critics, though, are more inclined to think that Kees might have been saved by one or two enthusiastic reviews, that he had simply had enough of being overlooked by critics and anthologists, and in any case had possibly run out of inspiration. 'I don't know what happened to my muse,' Kees wrote in a letter not long before the end, 'but along the poetic front things are quiet, very very quiet. Just not much of an impulse. Usual reaction to those I have is: "I've been over this ground before."'

When a poet is regularly fed with praise, he tends not to mind repeating himself. When he is ignored, the feeling often is: why bother? And if poetry no longer actively occupies the centre of a poet's life, what does? Still, if Weldon Kees really is alive and well in Mexico (he would now be in his eighties, let us not forget), he could very well be smiling. Thanks to his interesting disappearance, he now enjoys far more esteem than ever came his way when he was still around. In recent years, there has been an exhibition of his paintings, the publication of a once-rejected novel, and even a Weldon Kees Day in his home town of Beatrice, Nebraska. But mainstream literary recognition of the sort he coveted continues to elude him: he rarely figures in surveys and anthologies, except as a biographical conundrum. This is a pity because, at his best, Kees has a lot to offer. There is an offputting bleakness in his work, and sometimes this borders on self-pity, but there is also a stoical-sardonic vein that can be more attractively engaging than, perhaps, it means to be.

There is also an impressively quick eye for social detail, the kind
of detail that you might look for in a novel or short story. And the
character called 'Robinson' who crops up in certain poems, a sort
of professional-class Prufrock, has an almost loveable forbearance
as he goes about his routine daily business – business which is not,
of course, in any heartfelt sense *his* business. But then again: what
is?

> Robinson walking in the Park, admiring the elephant.
> Robinson buying the *Tribune*, Robinson buying the *Times*.
> Robinson
> Saying, 'Hello. Yes, this is Robinson. Sunday
> At five? I'd love to. Pretty well. And you?'

Robinson, we might say, seems always to be with us, but in truth
he is always somewhere else. He takes life as it comes but this does
not mean that he enjoys what comes, or wants much more of it.
The point about Robinson, however, is that he puts up with his
predicament. He bears it because, well, it's bearable. He knows
himself to be a man apart, a man afflicted by dissociation – but
dissociation to what purpose? So far as he can see, he has no choice
but to continue living, or to stop. Or has he, actually, already
stopped – died without quite noticing that his circumstances have
undergone a major change? Certainly, it's difficult to imagine the
mildly rueful, deeply passive Robinson stirring himself so far as to
jump off a bridge.

Aspects of Robinson

Robinson at cards at the Algonquin; a thin
Blue light comes down once more outside the blinds.
Gray men in overcoats are ghosts blown past the door.
The taxis streak the avenues with yellow, orange, and red.
This is Grand Central, Mr Robinson.

Robinson on a roof above the Heights; the boats
Mourn like the lost. Water is slate, far down.
Through sounds of ice cubes dropped in glass, an osteopath,
Dressed for the links, describes an old Intourist tour.
– Here's where old Gibbons jumped from, Robinson.

Robinson walking in the Park, admiring the elephant.
Robinson buying the *Tribune*, Robinson buying the *Times*.
  Robinson
Saying, 'Hello. Yes, this is Robinson. Sunday
At five? I'd love to. Pretty well. And you?'
Robinson alone at Longchamps, staring at the wall.

Robinson afraid, drunk, sobbing Robinson
In bed with a Mrs Morse. Robinson at home;
Decisions: Toynbee or luminol? Where the sun
Shines, Robinson in flowered trunks, eyes toward
The breakers. Where the night ends, Robinson in East Side
    bars.

Robinson in Glen plaid jacket, Scotch-grain shoes,
Black four-in-hand and Oxford button-down,
The jeweled and silent watch that winds itself, the brief-
Case, covert topcoat, clothes for spring, all covering
His sad and usual heart, dry as a winter leaf.

Relating to Robinson

Somewhere in Chelsea, early summer;
And, walking in the twilight toward the docks,
I thought I made out Robinson ahead of me.

From an uncurtained second-story room, a radio
Was playing *There's a Small Hotel*; a kite
Twisted above dark rooftops and slow drifting birds.
We were alone there, he and I,
Inhabiting the empty street.

Under a sign for Natural Bloom Cigars,
While lights clicked softly in the dusk from red to green,
He stopped and gazed into a window
Where a plaster Venus, modeling a truss,
Looked out at Eastbound traffic. (But Robinson,
I knew, was out of town: he summers at a place in Maine,
Sometimes on Fire Island, sometimes the Cape,
Leaves town in June and comes back after Labor Day.)
And yet, I almost called out, 'Robinson!'

There was no chance. Just as I passed,
Turning my head to search his face,
His own head turned with mine
And fixed me with dilated, terrifying eyes
That stopped my blood. His voice
Came at me like an echo in the dark.

'I thought I saw the whirlpool opening.
Kicked all night at a bolted door.
You must have followed me from Astor Place.
An empty paper floats down at the last.

And then a day as huge as yesterday in pairs
Unrolled its horror on my face
Until it blocked —' Running in sweat
To reach the docks, I turned back
For a second glance. I had no certainty,
There in the dark, that it was Robinson
Or someone else.
                    The block was bare. The Venus,
Bathed in blue fluorescent light,
Stared toward the river. As I hurried West,
The lights across the bay were coming on.
The boats moved silently and the low whistles blew.

Henry Reed

1914–1986

Most poets have one or two recognized 'anthology pieces' – works which are time and again offered as representative or typical of their life's work. And most poets eventually resent the work they are best known by: why don't these editors print X or Y – why is it always A or B? Sometimes this resentment can turn into self-contempt: maybe there's something *wrong* with A and B that they should be so popular.

And what goes for the poet can go for readers too. Few committed Yeatsians would name 'The Lake Isle of Innisfree' as their Master's greatest work; few Larkinists would name 'This Be the Verse'. With Henry Reed, though, there is rarely any disagreement. Reed, it is universally acknowledged, wrote one poem of distinction. The rest of his work, although intelligent and competent, belongs to a much lower rank. Certainly, no anthologist wishing to represent Reed's work would choose a sample other than the one, the only one, by which this poet is now known.

'Naming of Parts' is section one of a five-section sequence called *The Lessons of War*, and it can claim, without much fear of contradiction, to be *the* poem of the Second World War – the cleverest and, by some distance, the most likeable: good-humoured, funny, sexy and resigned, it captures perfectly the period's strange mix of tedium and fear. Reed's parade-ground protagonist is being taught how to handle weapons but his mind is elsewhere: he is thinking about sex, he is thinking about spring, about renewal. He is thinking, in other words, about life, the life that wartime now prohibits and that he himself, the soldier-poet, is being taught how to destroy:

> Today we have naming of parts. Yesterday,
> We had daily cleaning. And tomorrow morning,
> We shall have what to do after firing. But today,
> Today we have naming of parts. Japonica
> Glistens like coral in all of the neighbouring gardens,
>   And today we have naming of parts.

The second section of *The Lessons of War*, called 'Judging Distances', is less ingenious and oblique than 'Naming of Parts' and much more explicit in its setting-up of the war–life opposition, but this very explicitness permits the sounding of a richer, more distressful note – a note of anguished but teethgritting wistfulness:

> A barn is not called a barn, to put it more plainly,
> Or a field in the distance, where sheep may be safely grazing.
> You must never be over-sure. You must say, when reporting:
> At five o'clock in the central sector is a dozen
> Of what appear to be animals; whatever you do,
>   Don't call the bleeders *sheep*.

> I am sure that's quite clear; and suppose, for the sake of example,
> The one at the end, asleep, endeavours to tell us
> What he sees over there to the west, and how far away,
> After first having come to attention. There to the west,
> On the fields of summer the sun and the shadows bestow
>   Vestments of purple and gold.

The still white dwellings are like a mirage in the heat,
And under the swaying elms a man and a woman
Lie gently together. Which is, perhaps, only to say
That there is a row of houses to the left of arc,
And that under some poplars a pair of what appear to be humans
    Appear to be loving.

(The poplars/elm joke will not be clear from this quotation. In the poem's second stanza, not quoted here, the recruit is told that, in army-speak, there are 'three kinds of tree, three only, the fir and the poplar/ And those which have bushy tops to'.)

Later on, Reed would add three more lessons to the sequence, but none of these quite lived up to lessons one and two. But then living up to lessons one and two became, for Reed, a lifetime's burden, and he would soon enough come to resent these wartime favourites. Reed was much influenced by later Eliot and would have wished to have attention focused on some of his more lofty-sounding pieces, like 'Tintagel' or 'Triptych', but readers who encountered Reed in this, his more portentous mode, tended to mix him up with Herbert Read – another cross he had to bear throughout his literary life.

Henry Reed was born in Birmingham in 1914. His father was a bricklayer who liked reading; his mother was illiterate but knew many fairy stories. Reed read Classics at Birmingham University (where he met Louis MacNeice). His early adult years followed a fairly routine 1930s pattern: he discovered that he was homosexual and became a teacher. Conscripted into the Army in 1941, he was soon afterwards transferred to Intelligence at Bletchley, where he learned Japanese and published his first poems in the *Listener* and *New Statesman*. In 1941, he earned himself some minor fame by winning a *New Statesman* competition with a parody of T. S. Eliot's *Four Quartets* ('As we get older we do not get any younger'). After the war, Reed joined the BBC and made an early mark there with his radio-dramatic version of *Moby Dick*. By the 1950s he was regarded – along with Louis MacNeice – as an important exponent of verse-drama (a genre much in fashion at the time). This was probably the most settled and successful stretch of Reed's career. He even managed to turn to good account his well-known ambition to write a biography of Thomas Hardy (a task which he had toiled on conscientiously for many years but had somehow never managed to complete): he incorporated the fruit of his researches – and of his frustrations – into a sequence of successful verse-plays, two of which, *A Very Great Man Indeed* and *Hilda Tablet*, are regularly spoken of as reasons for regretting the demise of the Third Programme.

Reed, though, always viewed himself as something of a failure: a one-poem poet, a biographer who never delivered, a homosexual whose one important love affair had come to ruin in the early 1950s. Alcohol became a problem, and the last decades of Reed's life turned into something of a downward slide: in the bar of his much-frequented Savile Club he was for years a Man to be Avoided. He continued to write for radio (although the vogue for verse-drama went into terminal decline during the 1960s), and in 1964 he was delighted to be given a teaching post at the University of Washington, in Seattle. This part-time job sustained him for three years, and during the early 1970s he published a number of admired translations, from French and Italian dramas, some of which were staged or broadcast. It was also rumoured at this time that he would shortly be publishing a second book of verse (his first and only book, *A Map of Verona*, had appeared in 1946). The drinking got much worse, though, and Reed's final years were something of a horror tale, by all accounts. Reclusiveness and self-neglect took hold, and by the end even his close friends seem to have had trouble keeping track of him. He died in 1986. In 1991, Jon Stallworthy edited Reed's *Collected Poems*, and included a number of 'uncollected' pieces, among them 'Psychological Warfare' – a sixth section, it would seem, of *Lessons of War*, and thoroughly in the manner of that sequence: witty, rueful, heartfelt. Elsewhere in the book, there is an excess of portentousness and self-importance, and it is easy to conclude that, yes, Reed really was a single-poem poet. Somebody once tried to cheer him, in the Savile Club bar, with the proposition that surely it was better to have written one fine poem than to have written none at all. It took Reed a few moments to control his fury. Then he said: 'I'm not so sure.'

Naming of Parts

Today we have naming of parts. Yesterday,
We had daily cleaning. And tomorrow morning,
We shall have what to do after firing. But today,
Today we have naming of parts. Japonica
Glistens like coral in all of the neighbouring gardens,
    And today we have naming of parts.

This is the lower sling swivel. And this
Is the upper sling swivel, whose use you will see,
When you are given your slings. And this is the piling swivel,
Which in your case you have not got. The branches
Hold in the gardens their silent, eloquent gestures,
    Which in our case we have not got.

This is the safety-catch, which is always released
With an easy flick of the thumb. And please do not let me
See anyone using his finger. You can do it quite easy
If you have any strength in your thumb. The blossoms
Are fragile and motionless, never letting anyone see
    Any of them using their finger.

And this you can see is the bolt. The purpose of this
Is to open the breech, as you see. We can slide it
Rapidly backwards and forwards: we call this
Easing the spring. And rapidly backwards and forwards
The early bees are assaulting and fumbling the flowers:
    They call it easing the Spring.

They call it easing the Spring: it is perfectly easy
If you have any strength in your thumb: like the bolt,
And the breech, and the cocking-piece, and the point of
    balance,

Which in our case we have not got; and the almond-blossom
Silent in all of the gardens and the bees going backwards and
    forwards,
    For today we have naming of parts.

Judging Distances

Not only how far away, but the way that you say it
Is very important. Perhaps you may never get
The knack of judging a distance, but at least you know
How to report on a landscape: the central sector,
The right of arc and that, which we had last Tuesday,
    And at least you know

That maps are of time, not place, so far as the army
Happens to be concerned – the reason being,
Is one which need not delay us. Again, you know
There are three kinds of tree, three only, the fir and the poplar,
And those which have bushy tops to; and lastly
    That things only seem to be things.

A barn is not called a barn, to put it more plainly,
Or a field in the distance, where sheep may be safely grazing.
You must never be over-sure. You must say, when reporting:
At five o'clock in the central sector is a dozen
Of what appear to be animals; whatever you do,
    Don't call the bleeders *sheep*.

I am sure that's quite clear; and suppose, for the sake of example,
The one at the end, asleep, endeavours to tell us
What he sees over there to the west, and how far away,
After first having come to attention. There to the west,
On the fields of summer the sun and the shadows bestow
    Vestments of purple and gold.

The still white dwellings are like a mirage in the heat,
And under the swaying elms a man and a woman
Lie gently together. Which is, perhaps, only to say
That there is a row of houses to the left of arc,
And that under some poplars a pair of what appear to be humans
  Appear to be loving.

Well that, for an answer, is what we might rightly call
Moderately satisfactory only, the reason being,
Is that two things have been omitted, and those are important.
The human beings, now: in what direction are they,
And how far away, would you say? And do not forget
  There may be dead ground in between.

There may be dead ground in between; and I may not have got
The knack of judging a distance; I will only venture
A guess that perhaps between me and the apparent lovers,
(Who, incidentally, appear by now to have finished,)
At seven o'clock from the houses, is roughly a distance
  Of about one year and a half.

John Berryman

1914—1972

John Berryman once said: 'The artist is extremely lucky who is presented with the worst possible ordeal that will not actually kill him. At that point he's in business.' The phrase 'in business' was well chosen. Berryman was essentially a poet of the sixties, and it was indeed good business then for an artist to present himself as a voyager into dangerous psychological terrain. The theory was that in an epoch haunted by recollections of the Holocaust and faced with the near-certain prospect of nuclear extinction, the serious poet should seek to explore the 'sources' of these global nightmares – and to explore them not just in poems but in person: a high-risk undertaking, with madness, alcoholism and suicide the more-than-likely side-effects. 'Poetry is a terminal activity, taking place out near the end of things' was another of Berryman's pronouncements.

John Berryman's real name was John Smith. Born in 1914, he was the son of John Allyn Smith, an unsuccessful banker who shot himself when Berryman was twelve. The poet was brought up by his schoolteacher mother, a formidably possessive woman who had literary ambitions of her own, and who followed John's career tenaciously. After her husband's suicide, she married again, to John

Berryman Senior, but her ruling interest was her son. Early on, she encouraged him through college – Columbia and then Cambridge University – and encouraged him also to believe that creativity was wondrously akin to madness. In addition, she was a big drinker – bigger even than John Junior, who endured many years of alcoholism before his own suicide, in 1972.

After Berryman's death, one of the crueller rumours was that he had left a note for his great rival, Robert Lowell, saying 'Your move, Cal.' With Berryman, the confusion between psychic despair and tortured vanity was never easy to sort out; indeed, some of his distinctiveness as a poet seems to have depended on this confusion being kept intact. From the beginning, thanks in part to Mother, he was inclined to view his private turbulence as a sure mark of literary giftedness. Although his earliest poems (published in the 1940s, when he was a struggling academic) are markedly Audenesque in diction and subject, there is little in them of the master's impersonal severity. Berryman's compassion for suffering humanity, for those whose 'happiness runs out like water', was usually accompanied by a perhaps more deeply felt despair that he, the artist, could do nothing to alleviate the general woe: not because art cannot heal but because artists, poetic artists, are not listened to.

By the time of *Homage to Mistress Bradstreet* (1959), Berryman's preoccupation with the role, or non-role, of the artist had developed into an obsession. And by then he had begun almost to revel in his own inaccessibility: as if to say, You like poetry? Well, come and prove it. Luckily, with *Bradstreet*, he found a subject and a style that could accommodate his edginess and self-absorption and yet at the same time could seem to be fathoming a cultural malaise, a specifically American cultural malaise. *Homage to Mistress Bradstreet* sets itself to re-create that point in history when America first tried to tame its poets – to tame them in order to be able to neglect them. In seventeenth-century Puritan New England, Anne Bradstreet (*c.* 1612–72) composed verse that was orderly and dutiful. She was afraid to give voice to her deepest, most unruly instincts – or so it is assumed by the twentieth-century John Berryman, who addresses

her both as a fellow poet ('We are on each other's hands / Who
care. Both of our worlds unhanded us') and as Anne's longed-for
and appalling lover, the one who will unlock and liberate her, the
one who will encourage her to speak.

   When Anne does speak, it is in a most peculiar idiom: antique,
jagged and obscure but almost hysterically urgent. With difficulty,
we learn of her early life in America, her marriage at sixteen to
'so-much-older-Simon', her 'shamefast, chaste, laborious' subservi-
ence to wifely tasks, her first childbirth, her homesickness. Made
articulate at last by Berryman, her vehemence collides with his
in an extraordinary dialogue / duet, 'a sort of extended witch-
seductress and demon-lover bit', as Berryman − the real-life
Berryman − would later describe it. It is this vivid, hectic moment
in Berryman's poetry that sets the tone of his best-known later
work:

> I see the cruel spread Wings black with saints!
> Silky my breasts not his, mine, mine to withhold,
> or tender, tender.
> I am sifting, nervous and bold.
> The light is changing. Surrender this loveliness
> You cannot make me do. *But* I will. Yes.
> What horror, down stormy air,
> warps towards me? My
>   threatening promise faints
> torture me, Father, lest I be not thine!

   Before finishing *Bradstreet* (a poem which in fact secured for its
author the heavyweight recognition he so craved), Berryman had
begun to write the loosely rhymed, three-stanza 'songs' that would
become his catch-all for the next few years. By infiltrating the
artificial Bradstreet diction with tough-colloquial American
speech–rhythms and vocabulary, Berryman found himself in possession of a seductive and highly novel manner. Nobody else, from
this point, sounded like John Berryman:

> I wish the barker would come.
>> There seems to be to eat
> Nothing. I am unusually tired.
> I'm alone too.
> If only the strange one with so
>> few legs would come.

As a sequence, the *Dream Songs* are as directionless as the life of their hero, one Henry (a writer of 'mad books' who is 'at odds wif de world and its god' and is here 'pried open for all the world to see'), and as uneven: the majority of them are so obliquely rendered and so privately whimsical that it scarcely seems worth our while trying to decipher them. Berryman simply doesn't give us enough clues. He uses the songs pretty much as the mood takes him, drunk or sober: as diary entries, messages to friends, snapshots of foreign parts, notes for current or further reading, memos, jokes and prayers. Henry is to be found in bars and movie theatres, on campuses giving lectures or in mental hospitals drying out.

Over 400 pages, the *Dream Songs* make for an exhausting and sometimes irritating read, but are likely to be valued long after the more hospitable and prose-like *Love and Fame* has been sidelined. The poem's novel idiom can run to incoherence, and there is something deeply self-indulgent in the entire *Dream Songs* operation. But fragments of it are hard to forget – especially the more comic, hard-boiled pieces in which Henry is nagged and cajoled by a vaudeville coon character called Mr Bones. Berryman was perhaps the unhappiest of his unhappy generation, but he was also the only one who could make us chuckle even as he (almost) broke our hearts.

He Resigns

Age, and the deaths, and the ghosts.
Her having gone away
in spirit from me. Hosts
of regrets come & find me empty.

I don't feel this will change.
I don't want any thing
or person, familiar or strange.
I don't think I will sing

any more just now,
or ever. I must start
to sit with a blind brow
above an empty heart.

Dream Song 29

There sat down, once, a thing on Henry's heart
so heavy, if he had a hundred years
& more, & weeping, sleepless, in all them time
Henry could not make good.
Starts again always in Henry's ears
the little cough somewhere, an odour, a chime.

And there is another thing he has in mind
like a grave Sienese face a thousand years
would fail to blur the still profiled reproach of. Ghastly,
with open eyes, he attends, blind.
All the bells say: too late. This is not for tears;
thinking.

But never did Henry, as he thought he did,
end anyone and hacks her body up
and hide the pieces, where they may be found.
He knows: he went over everyone, & nobody's missing.
Often he reckons, in the dawn, them up.
Nobody is ever missing.

Dylan Thomas

1914–1953

In the *Norton Anthology of Modern Poetry*, the editors print Dylan Thomas's sonnet-sequence *Altarwise by Owl-Light*, and add footnotes to the text. The title-sonnet boasts seventeen footnotes to its fourteen lines:

> Altarwise[1] by owl-light[2] in the half-way house[3]
> The gentleman[4] lay graveward[5] with his furies;
> Abaddon[6] in the hangnail cracked from Adam,[7]
> And, from his fork,[8] a dog among the fairies,
> The atlas-eater[9] with a jaw for news,
> Bit out the mandrake[10] with tomorrow's scream.[11]

And so it continues for the entire sequence – the text offputtingly peppered with numerals and, down below, the solemn explanations: '1. Facing East, that is, towards the light. 2. A paradoxical term for the dark. 3. Womb. 4. The foetus 5. Pointed towards life, but also towards death . . .'

Well, thank you, might be our response to this assistance. The truth is, though, that even with such help – if help it is – the poem continues to seem difficult, if not impossible, to fathom. Sex and death are in there, to be sure, but to what purpose? The poem's sense, such as it is, seems to have been determined by linguistic momentum, or by linguistic chain-reaction rather than by any central, organizing sensibility, or author. And Thomas used to 'explain' his poems in these terms. They were mysteriously self-engendering, he'd say. The poet would think up 'one image' and then:

let it breed another, let that image contradict the first, make, out of the third image bred out of the other two together, a fourth contradictory image, and let them all, within my imposed formal limits, conflict. Each image holds within it the seed of its own destruction . . .

Our confident suspicion, though, is that Thomas, when sufficiently drunk or sufficiently fired up with chapel *hwyl*, was usually more interested in how a poem sounded than in what it said, provided that it sounded grand and deep. He loved to give poetry readings and his readings would always aim for booming, actorly magnificence. Pictures of Thomas tend to portray him as a slightly bewildered-looking cherub and his self-presentation carried with it the suggestion that verbal splendour was, for him, mysteriously heaven-sent. Thomas projected himself as ebulliently Welsh but he could not speak the Welsh language, which is maybe just as well, and was glad to have escaped the 'smug darkness' of his Swansea birthplace. His appeal was to an English audience which, for almost half a century, had been starved of high-sounding music-ality. Not since the 1890s had a poet postured so self-consciously as Thomas did. After Eliot and Auden, and in the middle of the war to end all wars, it was natural enough for there to be an appetite for the apocalyptic, and Thomas was more than ready to reclaim the poet's bardic robes. In doing so, he inaugurated that wave of fire-tongued pretentiousness which we now think of as typically 1940s, but he cannot be blamed – or can he? – for the sins of his disciples.

Born in 1914, Thomas was sixteen when he left Swansea Gram-mar School (where his father was the English teacher), and had no wish to go to college. He wanted to be a poet, and after a few precocious magazine successes he published his first volume, *18 Poems*, at the age of twenty. In 1934, the influence of Auden was paramount and most young poets aimed to be political and clever, and tuned in to current world events. Few would have claimed to be 'inspired'. In this context, Thomas's murky incantations seemed refreshingly in touch with the eternal verities: assuredly they were not newspaper-poems and seemed to demand little from their readers beyond a willing ear for their sonority.

After the success of *18 Poems*, Thomas moved to London, where he was taken up by Edith Sitwell, she of the 'dark vowels', and Stephen Spender, a poet who was himself always straining to restore to poetry that 'spiritual' ingredient which the early Auden had expunged. In 1937, Thomas got married to Caitlin Macnamara, a volcanic Irishwoman, and began to consolidate his reputation as a hard-drinking sub-bohemian. During the war years Thomas worked as a broadcaster and scriptwriter and this work, it could be said, encouraged in his verse a new lucidity. With Thomas, lucidity tended to expose a certain simple-mindedness (see poems like 'The Hand that Signed the Paper'), but for the first time it was possible to work out what his poems were supposed to be about, and even – with 'Fern Hill' and 'Should Lanterns Shine', for instance – to succumb to his sonority without having to trade in one's whole intelligence:

> All the sun long it was running, it was lovely, the hay
> Fields high as the house, the tunes from the chimneys, it was air
> > And playing, lovely and watery
> > > And fire green as grass.
> > > And nightly under the simple stars
> > As I rode to sleep the owls were bearing the farm away,
> All the moon long I heard, blessed among the stables, the night-jars
> > > Flying with the ricks, and the horses
> > > > Flashing into the dark.

Also, in these later poems, there were signs of Thomas taking an interest in nature and in other people – not altogether convincingly, but providing none the less relief from his oppressive narcissism. 'If I look at the exterior world,' Thomas once confessed, 'I see nothing or me.' Although he was never short of acolytes and hangers-on, Thomas seems not to have had many friends, and those he did have were exploited to the full (see his *Letters to Vernon Watkins*). A good two-thirds of Thomas's *Collected Letters* begin with an apology – for missing an appointment, for not replying earlier, for failing to repay a debt, for having caused some drunken scene – and in several instances the apology turns into a request: for money, usually. Rarely does one get the sense that personal relations mattered very much to him, except as negotiable procedures which, if handled with verbal aplomb, could usually be made to yield cash or applause, or both. Thomas was a skilled, seductive rhetorician and he stretched this unattractive talent to the limit, both in art and life.

The final years of Thomas's short life have been heavily documented: the drink-drenched reading tours of the United States (described in detail by John Malcolm Brinnin in his bestselling *Dylan Thomas in America*), the pitiable death in a New York hotel in 1953. Thomas's last work, the unexpectedly amusing radio play *Under Milk Wood*, was completed just months before his death, and he had lately begun work on a libretto for Stravinsky. The tendency, it seems, was in the direction of performance. Thomas's general popularity, and the posthumous 'legend' it turned into, owe much to radio, and when he died, it has been said, he was *en route* for Hollywood. Had Thomas survived, he would almost certainly have claimed a role in the impending triumph of pop culture. All too easily one can imagine him on platforms in the 1960s. And television, it seems certain, would have reckoned him to be a natural.

Fern Hill

Now as I was young and easy under the apple boughs
About the lilting house and happy as the grass was green,
    The night above the dingle starry,
      Time let me hail and climb
     Golden in the heydays of his eyes,
And honoured among wagons I was prince of the apple towns
And once below a time I lordly had the trees and leaves
     Trail with daisies and barley
    Down the rivers of the windfall light.

And as I was green and carefree, famous among the barns
About the happy yard and singing as the farm was home,
    In the sun that is young once only,
      Time let me play and be
     Golden in the mercy of his means,
And green and golden I was huntsman and herdsman, the calves
Sang to my horn, the foxes on the hills barked clear and cold,
     And the sabbath rang slowly
    In the pebbles of the holy streams.

All the sun long it was running, it was lovely, the hay
Fields high as the house, the tunes from the chimneys, it was air
    And playing, lovely and watery
      And fire green as grass.
     And nightly under the simple stars
As I rode to sleep the owls were bearing the farm away,
All the moon long I heard, blessed among stables, the night-jars
     Flying with the ricks, and the horses
       Flashing into the dark.

And then to awake, and the farm, like a wanderer white
With the dew, come back, the cock on his shoulder: it was all

Shining, it was Adam and maiden,
    The sky gathered again
And the sun grew round that very day.
So it must have been after the birth of the simple light
In the first, spinning place, the spellbound horses walking warm
    Out of the whinnying green stable
      On to the fields of praise.

And honoured among foxes and pheasants by the gay house
Under the new made clouds and happy as the heart was long,
    In the sun born over and over,
      I ran my heedless ways,
    My wishes raced through the house high hay
And nothing I cared, at my sky blue trades, that time allows
In all his tuneful turning so few and such morning songs
    Before the children green and golden
      Follow him out of grace,

Nothing I cared, in the lamb white days, that time would take me
Up to the swallow thronged loft by the shadow of my hand,
    In the moon that is always rising,
      Nor that riding to sleep
    I should hear him fly with the high fields
And wake to the farm forever fled from the childless land.
Oh as I was young and easy in the mercy of his means,
      Time held me green and dying
    Though I sang in my chains like the sea.

Alun Lewis

1915–1944

It is now more than fifty years since Alun Lewis died, but his ranking as a modern poet still seems insecure. He routinely gets grouped with poets of World War Two (along with Keith Douglas and Sidney Keyes), but he is by no means an automatic choice for non-specialized anthologies – not in the way that Douglas is, for instance, although Douglas's posthumous reputation got off to a slower start.

The reason could be that it is difficult, even for his admirers, to decide on a Lewis poem that 'works' all the way through. There is an unfinished look to almost everything he did: half a dozen haunting lines, a couple of inspired stanzas, and then the thing begins to wobble into awkwardness or over-emphasis. In his first book, *Raider's Dawn*, the tilt is towards wildness and excess; in his second, *Ha! Ha! Among the Trumpets*, there is an almost opposite tendency, towards an overmellifluous rhetoric of general wisdom.

There are those who believe that Lewis's future as a writer would have been in prose, and it is certainly true that stories like 'The Last Inspection' and 'The Orange Grove' have a consistency and self-assurance that cannot often be discovered in the verse. But

Lewis's ambition was for poetry, and his sensibility was too. This sensibility had a reflective, almost preachy cast, however, and maybe it could only have found its best expression if Lewis's war-nerves had been allowed to heal.

Alun Lewis was no warrior. His background was in education and socialist good works. Born in a South Wales mining town in 1915, he was not from a mining family – his parents were both teachers – but many of his boyhood friends had fathers who toiled underground. Lewis was both of the miners and above them – the 'above' in his case meaning that he felt a peculiar obligation to care for their plight and to speak out on their behalf.

The Depression (plus a high-minded literary mother) shaped the essentials of Lewis's always-pressing sense of duty. From early on, though, he had trouble reconciling his dreamy, introverted personality with the ruder practicalities of public service. And the war brought this conflict to a head. On the one hand, Lewis wanted to serve, to fight for what he saw as a just cause, and he wanted also to experience real kinship with his fellow soldiers. On the other hand, he approached the war as a romantic personal quest, or test. He would not kill, he said, at the outbreak of war, but he was ready 'to be killed, instead':

> I have begun to die.
> For now at last I know
> That there is no escape
> From Night.

This is Lewis on sentry duty. In army camps in England, this earnest, doomed young poet was torn between an educationalist zeal to improve the hearts and minds of the soldiers placed under his command (Lewis took a commission with misgivings and later regretted having done so) and the alienated stance of the romantic artist. He organized debating societies, lectures on world affairs, he wanted to start a weekly magazine. At the same time, he was writing poems like 'All Day It Has Rained' and 'After Dunkirk', in which the fastidious author is painfully distanced from his cultureless

comrades: 'But leisurely my fellow soldiers stroll among the trees/
The cheapest dance-song utters all they feel':

> And next, the rough immediate life of camp
> And barracks where the phallic bugle rules
> The regimented orchestra of love;
> The subterfuge of democracy, the stench
> Of breath in crowded tents, the grousing queues,
> And bawdy songs incessantly resung
> And dull relaxing in the dirty bar;
> The difficult tolerance of all that is
> Mere rigid brute routine; the odd
> Sardonic scorn of desolate self-pity.
> The pathetic contempt of the lonely for the crowd;
> And, as the crystal slowly forms,
> A growing self-detachment making man
> Less home-sick, fearful, proud,
> But less a man.

In India, where Lewis was posted in 1943, the same conflict was at work but with more subtlety and depth. Lewis was both appalled and thrilled by India. The humanitarian individualist was shocked by poverty and backwardness on a scale that paralysed goodwill. The fated poet was stirred by the sufferers' benign acceptance of their lot. All the old reforming decencies were made to seem puny and irrelevant. The questing self was invited to ruminate on absolutes:

> The bamboos creak like an uneasy house;
> The night is shrill with crickets, cold with space.
> And if the mute pads on the sand should lift
> Annihilating paws and strike us down
> Then would some unimportant death resound
> With the imprisoned music of the soul?
> And we become the world we could not change?
> Or does the will's long struggle end
> With the last kindness of a foe or friend?

For nearly three years, Lewis served in the Army without making any sort of contact with the enemy. The longer he waited, the more excited and exalted he became, so it is said. The Indian jungle, he believed, would be his battlefield and he began to see its lush, intoxicating silences as promising some spiritual apotheosis: 'a showdown with fate', he called it. At last within killing distance of the foe, Lewis one morning was found dead: shot through the head by his own revolver. The official Army verdict was Accidental Death, but there was no one in Lewis's regiment who did not believe that it was suicide.

The Sentry

I have begun to die.
For now at last I know
That there is no escape
From Night. Not any dream
Nor breathless images of sleep
Touch my bat's-eyes. I hang
Leathery-arid from the hidden roof
Of Night, and sleeplessly
I watch within Sleep's province.
I have left
The lovely bodies of the boy and girl
Deep in each other's placid arms;
And I have left
The beautiful lanes of sleep
That barefoot lovers follow to this last
Cold shore of thought I guard.
I have begun to die
And the guns' implacable silence
Is my black interim, my youth and age,
In the flower of fury, the folded poppy,
Night.

Dawn on the East Coast

From Orford Ness to Shingle Street
The grey disturbance spreads
Washing the icy seas on Deben Head.

Cock pheasants scratch the frozen fields,
Gulls lift thin horny legs and step
Fastidiously among the rusted mines.

The soldier leaning on the sandbagged wall
Hears in the combers' curling rush and crash
His single self-centred monotonous wish;

And time is a froth of such transparency
His drowning eyes see what they wish to see;
A girl laying his table with a white cloth.

.   .   .   .

The light assails him from a flank,
Two carbons touching in his brain
Crumple the cellophane lanterns of his dream.

And then the day, grown feminine and kind,
Stoops with the gulfing motion of the tide
And pours his ashes in a tiny urn.

From Orford Ness to Shingle Street
The grey disturbance lifts its head
And one by one, reluctantly,
The living come back slowly from the dead.

Robert Lowell

1917–1977

More perhaps than any other poet since Yeats, Robert Lowell invested his life and work with an unflagging sense of the momentous. Nothing insignificant happened to this author, or so he believed. In Lowell's case, the idea of having been elected to some high creative duty was perhaps congenital: as a Boston Lowell (albeit from a minor branch of that distinguished line), he harboured from the start aristocratic, or imperial delusions. As a child, he revered Napoleon, at school his classmates called him Caligula, during psychotic episodes he identified with Hitler, and so on.

Lowell's earliest poems were driven by a lofty rage: rage, chiefly, against Boston – for not being what it thought it was, and should have been. Born in 1917, the son of a humbly land-locked naval officer and a domineering, snobbish and possessive mother, little Cal exhibited early signs of the manic-depressive disposition that would torment his later years. He quarrelled violently with his parents, whom he saw as smug and mediocre, and unfit to bear the Lowell name, and this rage carried over into his first poems, which were mostly intended to outrage his Boston associates. He converted to Roman Catholicism, he married the Catholic novelist

Jean Stafford, and in his verse he unleashed a battery of loftily aggressive rhetoric against the so-called 'spirit of New England'. In his first two books, *Land of Unlikeness* and *Lord Weary's Castle*, Lowell imagines Calvinist Boston as a hell on earth: its streets are 'hell-fire streets', its adulterers grow snake-like scales, its waters are fouled with sailors who gave their lives in service of New England profiteering. The literary echoes were of Melville, the cries for help were Roman, but the rhetoric itself came straight from Cotton Mather.

In other words, the rhetoric of Lowell's early verse forever bordered on the uncontainable. A densely alliterative iambic line, a thrusting enjambement half-blocked by thudding rhymes: the overall effect was of strait-jacketed hysteria. Sometimes there was an agitated grandeur in this driven eloquence, and certainly there was nothing to compare it with in mid-century American poetry. Its energy and oddity, together with its air of scholarly allusiveness, were greeted with somewhat bewildered plaudits and Lowell began to be spoken of as the most promising new poet of the day. Prizes were showered on him, as they would be for the rest of his career, and he secured the influential backing of critics like Tate and Jarrell. In his third book, *Mills of the Kavanaughs* – a response to the break-up of his marriage to Jean Stafford – Lowell employed narrative as a means of steadying his headlong eloquence, but it was not until *Life Studies* (1959) that he achieved true equilibrium. This he managed, to some extent, by setting himself to work from a prose text – his own autobiography-in-progress – and by studying the ways in which William Carlos Williams had jettisoned tight metres in the interest of colloquial directness of expression. Lowell's free verse was more supple and stately than Williams would have readily approved, but the real impact of *Life Studies* was less to do with technique than with the book's extraordinary candour – intimate family details were assessed without a flicker of inhibition or reserve (after all, to be a Lowell was, for a New Englander, to be half-public), and so too were incidents from the poet's generally unstable life so far.

In his early work, Lowell had seemed almost maniacally

possessed. In *Life Studies*, he counts the cost of that intensity. At the same time, he uses his own family history to reassess his feelings about Boston – what it used to be and what it has become. By 1959, Lowell's personal life had undergone numerous upheavals since *Lord Weary's Castle*: he had renounced Roman Catholicism, married again (to Elizabeth Hardwick), served time in prison as a conscientious objector and had been hospitalized several times for mental illness. During his breakdowns, he tended to leave a trail of chaos in his wake. When recovered, he was usually stricken with remorse, and *Life Studies*, one could say, is a remorseful book, a book which, as Lowell half-confessed, offered a 'tranquillized' respite from the exalted horrors of derangement.

With his next two volumes, *For the Union Dead* (1963) and *Near the Ocean* (1967), Lowell found a way of recapturing some of his old energy and intensity without having to resort to hell-fire rhetoric. In the 1963 volume, his command of free verse seems even more subtle and assured than in *Life Studies*, and his so-called 'confessional' intimacy of address makes itself hospitable to public themes: in particular, the threat of nuclear extinction – a vividly felt probability at that time. There is also a new tightness of construction, with Lowell setting up intricate patterns of interlocking images whilst at the same time sounding urgent and impassioned. The personal anguish, the sense of an impending horror, that runs through these poems of the 1960s is never merely personal. Lowell somehow manages to seem both apprehensive and imperious – his pain is global pain:

> No weekends for the gods now. Wars
> flicker, earth licks its open sores,
> fresh breakage, fresh promotions, chance
> assassinations, no advance.
> Only man thinning out his kind
> sounds through the Sabbath noon, the blind
> swipe of the pruner and his knife
> busy about the tree of life . . .

> Pity the planet, all joy gone
> from this sweet volcanic cone;
> peace to our children when they fall
> in small war on the heels of small
> war – until the end of time
> to police the earth, a ghost
> orbiting forever lost
> in our monotonous sublime.

Lowell's impulse to speak out on public themes got somewhat out of hand in the ensuing years. A grandiosity began to show itself, and this was accompanied by a slackening of intensity and technical control. Stirred by the example of John Berryman's *Dream Songs*, Lowell began to assemble a day-by-day journal of slack, sonnet-shaped responses to whatever happened to attract his fancy: politics, personalities, newspaper incidents, books he was reading, and so on. During the late 1960s, Lowell composed hundreds of these 'sonnets' and eventually collected them in two huge volumes, *History* and *Notebook*, each of them prosily slapdash and monotonous – ingestive rather than creative. Lowell's gift was not for large-scale structures.

In 1970, with these two unapplauded books behind him, Lowell quit America for England, divorced Elizabeth Hardwick and soon after married the Anglo-Irish writer Caroline Blackwood. This upheaval coincided with one of his manic breakdowns and, as with earlier illnesses, friends assumed that Lowell would soon break free of his latest attachment, and return to the United States. For a few years, though, in the early 1970s, Lowell seemed to have achieved a true contentedness with Blackwood. A new book, *Dolphin*, hymned this happiness, but unfortunately Lowell was not ready to abandon his stiff sonneteering habits. And not long afterwards, the Blackwood marriage began to show signs of collapse. For a few years, Lowell shuttled between England and America, unable to decide where he should settle. The Hardwick attachment was still powerful and Blackwood was unable to cope with Lowell's instability. The poet himself was fearful and bewildered. Much of this turbulence is reflected in his last two books, the notorious *For Lizzie and Harriet* (notorious because Lowell sonnetized certain of Hardwick's private, and impassioned, letters), and the happily sonnet-free *Day by Day*. Lowell died of a heart attack in 1977, aged sixty.

Home After Three Months Away

Gone now the baby's nurse,
a lioness who ruled the roost
and made the Mother cry.
She used to tie
gobbets of porkrind in bowknots of gauze –
three months they hung like soggy toast
on our eight foot magnolia tree,
and helped the English sparrows
weather a Boston winter.

Three months, three months!
Is Richard now himself again?
Dimpled with exaltation,
my daughter holds her levee in the tub.
Our noses rub,
each of us pats a stringy lock of hair –
they tell me nothing's gone.
Though I am forty-one,
not forty now, the time I put away
was child's-play. After thirteen weeks
my child still dabs her cheeks
to start me shaving. When
we dress her in her sky-blue corduroy,
she changes to a boy,
and floats my shaving brush
and washcloth in the flush . . .
Dearest, I cannot loiter here
in lather like a polar bear.

Recuperating, I neither spin nor toil.
Three stories down below,
a choreman tends our coffin's length of soil,

and seven horizontal tulips blow.
Just twelve months ago,
these flowers were pedigreed
imported Dutchmen, now no one need
distinguish them from weed.
Bushed by the late spring snow,
they cannot meet
another year's snowballing enervation.

I keep no rank nor station.
Cured, I am frizzled, stale and small.

For the Union Dead

'Relinquunt Omnia Servare Rem Publicam.'

The old South Boston Aquarium stands
in a Sahara of snow now. Its broken windows are boarded.
The bronze weathervane cod has lost half its scales.
The airy tanks are dry.

Once my nose crawled like a snail on the glass;
my hand tingled
to burst the bubbles
drifting from the noses of the cowed compliant fish.

My hand draws back. I often sigh still
for the dark downward and vegetating kingdom
of the fish and reptile. One morning last March,
I pressed against the new barbed and galvanized

fence on the Boston Common. Behind their cage,
yellow dinosaur steamshovels were grunting
as they cropped up tons of mush and grass
to gouge their underworld garage.

Parking spaces luxuriate like civic
sandpiles in the heart of Boston.
A girdle of orange, Puritan-pumpkin colored girders
braces the tingling Statehouse,

shaking over the excavations, as it faces Colonel Shaw
and his bell-cheeked Negro infantry
on St Gaudens' shaking Civil War relief,
propped by a plank splint against the garage's earthquake.

Two months after marching through Boston,
half the regiment was dead;
at the dedication,
William James could almost hear the bronze Negroes breathe.

Their monument sticks like a fishbone
in the city's throat.
Its Colonel is as lean
as a compass-needle.

He has an angry wrenlike vigilance,
a greyhound's gentle tautness;
he seems to wince at pleasure,
and suffocate for privacy.

He is out of bounds now. He rejoices in man's lovely,
peculiar power to choose life and die –
when he leads his black soldiers to death,
he cannot bend his back.

On a thousand small town New England greens,
the old white churches hold their air
of sparse, sincere rebellion; frayed flags
quilt the graveyards of the Grand Army of the Republic.

The stone statues of the abstract Union Soldier
grow slimmer and younger each year –
wasp-waisted, they doze over muskets
and muse through their sideburns . . .

Shaw's father wanted no monument
except the ditch,
where his son's body was thrown
and lost with his 'niggers'.

The ditch is nearer.
There are no statues for the last war here;
on Boyleston Street, a commercial photograph
shows Hiroshima boiling

over a Mosler Safe, the 'Rock of Ages'
that survived the blast. Space is nearer.
When I crouch to my television set,
the drained faces of Negro school-children rise like balloons.

Colonel Shaw
is riding on his bubble,
he waits
for the blessèd break.

The Aquarium is gone. Everywhere,
giant finned cars nose forward like fish;
a savage servility
slides by on grease.

Keith Douglas

1920–1944

Keith Douglas was twenty-four when he was killed in action, in 1944, and although quite a few of his poems had by then appeared in anthologies and magazines, he was not generally thought of as a significant 'war poet'. But then, who was? 'Where are the war poets?' was a familiar journalistic cry from 1939 to 1945, and few answers were forthcoming. There were two main poetic fashions on offer at the time: worn-out Audenesque or a torrid neo-Romanticism that had Dylan Thomas as its vaguely guiding force. Keith Douglas had no particular allegiance to either camp, although he was closer to Auden than to Thomas and had had a poem published in *New Verse* when he was still at school. But he was also represented in *Eight Oxford Poets*, a supposedly key selection of the day, in which one of the editors (Sidney Keyes) apologized for the 'over-floridity' of his contributors, explaining that 'we have on the whole little sympathy with the Audenian school of poets'. Douglas, it should be said, was pretty scathing about the anthology, when he saw it: 'Some of the decade's worst printed verse.'

On the whole, Douglas kept his distance from literary company, allowing friends like Edmund Blunden and J. C. Hall to push his

work, and when successes came his way, he tended to respond to
them with a theatrical offhandedness. Edmund Blunden at one
point sent a batch of Douglas's work to T. S. Eliot at Faber and
Faber and Eliot was encouraging. Douglas's reaction was to wonder
how much he could get for Eliot's autograph. Some of this was
tough-guy affectation but a substantial part of it was genuinely felt.
Douglas wanted to write poems but he had no wish to be regarded as
a cissy poet. He had a soldierly distaste for emotional display and
always had one eye on his 'cynical' or common-sensical self-
presentation. And this sometimes made things difficult for his
admirers. Douglas soaked up their praise as if it meant not very much,
got ratty when his work was criticized on technical grounds or found
to be insufficiently 'poetic', and altogether made a point of seeming
to be quite indifferent to the ins and outs of poetry politics.

In 1939, with war declared and all verse-warnings utterly
unheeded, it was a rare versifier who did not feel himself to be
somewhat redundant. And yet poetry continued to be written. For
poets of the Audenesque persuasion, there was a quasi-documentary
function: describing how it felt to be in the Army, what olive
groves looked like, how peculiar life seemed to be in Africa or
Burma. For Thomasites, on the other hand, there was the dark
unconscious, the 'surreal' rendering of soon-to-be-blitzed inner
territories, along with a defiant assertion of individual personality
in the face of mass-manipulation. The typical war poet came across
as gawky misfit or loopy narcissist.

Keith Douglas was determined not to qualify for either of these
categories. He saw himself as well prepared for army life – his father
had won an MC at Gallipoli and Douglas had been brought up on
stories of military valour. At the age of six he was to be found
dressed up in combat gear and standing guard at his front door;
visitors to the Douglas household had to get past little Keith.
Douglas's relations with his war-hero father were probably central
to the shaping of his personality. Daddy Douglas, having indoctrin-
ated his child in martial lore, left home when Keith was eight, and
was never seen again (he ran off with the domestic help). Keith
afterwards refused to speak his father's name, and makes no mention

of him in his letters, post-1928. His mother, on the other hand, was his chief confidante: she was sickly and impoverished but staunchly genteel, and impressively resourceful in her efforts on behalf of her entirely worshipped only child. And Keith in turn saw himself as both dependant and mainstay, as stand-in for his absent and unmentionable dad. Much of his 'cynical' attitudinizing can be traced back to his father, or to the absence of his father.

At Christ's Hospital, the old school of Coleridge, Hunt and Edmund Blunden, Douglas was a king-pin of the cadet corps. Although rebellious when faced with schoolmasterly authority, he changed his tune as soon as he put on a uniform. He seemed to enjoy polishing his footwear and keeping his equipment in good, sparkling nick. From him, then, there would be no wartime tales of boot-camp inconvenience. Nor would there be any sensitive recoiling from the vulgarities of his co-Tommies. Douglas always assumed that he would be granted a commission. He knew too that his military know-how would gain him the immediate respect of his comrades, and that he would probably not find these comrades vulgar.

So much for the awkward-recruit approach to army life. Although Douglas in his later work would style himself as a reporter, he had little patience for the deary-me astonishment that marked and undermined the work of so many soldier-documentarists. And he had even less patience for those (largely civilian) poets who argued for high-toned explorations of the Self. When J. C. Hall once dared to suggest that Douglas's work might aim for more sonority or 'lyricism', he was ferociously rebuffed:

I am surprised you should still expect me to produce musical verse. A lyric form and a lyric approach will do even less good than a journalese approach to the subjects we have to discuss now. I don't know if you have come across the word Bullshit – it is an army word and signifies humbug and unnecessary detail. It symbolizes what I think must be got rid of – the mass of irrelevancies, of 'attitudes', 'approaches', propaganda, ivory towers, etc . . . To be sentimental or emotional now is dangerous to oneself and to others.

Keith Douglas was wounded in the Desert War and could easily have opted out of further active service. He insisted on rejoining his regiment at D-Day and was killed in Normandy. The poems we are left with are on the whole more cynical than lyrical, although some of the early poems – poems of premonition like 'Canoe' – are softish at the centre, one could say. But cynical is not really the word. What separates Douglas's combat-poems from those of his contemporaries (and remarkably few World War Two poems were actually to do with combat) is the neutrality of their approach. 'Think of them as waxworks,' he writes of dead bodies on a battlefield, 'or think they're struck with a dumb, immobile spell.' His dead are nearly always seen as statuesque, as figures in a land-scape. And when it came to his own attitudes, Douglas always seemed less interested in deploring the idea of combat than in celebrating the daft, heroic gallantry of his military colleagues:

> Peter was unfortunately killed by an 88;
> it took his leg off, he died in the ambulance.
> When I saw him crawling, he said
> It's most unfair, they've shot my foot off.

In another poem, we are called upon to admire the 'scarlet and tall/ Leisurely fellows' who 'stroll with royal slow motion' to their doom: 'a gentle/ obsolescent band of heroes'. Although Douglas served in the desert as a tank commander, he had originally trained for the cavalry, and so too had most of his comrades. They rode their Shermans into battle, so to speak, as though they were still hunting in the shires, and Douglas was thrilled and impressed. This war poet felt much closer to his fellow warriors than to his fellow poets.

The Prisoner

Today, Cheng, I touched your face
with two fingers, as a gesture of love;
for I can never prove enough
by sight or sense your strange grace,

but mothwise my hands return
to your fair cheek, as luminous
as a lamp in a paper house,
and touch, to teach love and learn.

I think a hundred hours are gone
that so, like gods, we'd occupy.
But alas, Cheng, I cannot tell why,
today I touched a mask stretched on the stone

person of death. There was the urge
to break the bright flesh and emerge
of the ambitious cruel bone.

Syria

The grasses, ancient enemies
waiting at the edge of towns
conceal a movement of live stones,
the lizards with hooded eyes
of hostile miraculous age.

It is not snow on the green space
of hilltops, only towns of white
whose trees are populous with fruit

and girls whose velvet beauty is
handed down to them, gentle ornaments.

Here I am a stranger clothed
in the separative glass cloak
of strangeness. The dark eyes, the bright-mouthed
smiles, glance on the glass and break
falling like fine strange insects.

But from the grass, the inexorable lizard,
the dart of hatred for all strangers finds
in this armour, proof only against friends
breach after breach, and like the gnat is busy
wounding the skin, leaving poison there.

Philip Larkin

1922–1985

When Philip Larkin died in 1985, at sixty-three, the obituaries were full of warmth; there was much talk in the London papers of our 'nation's loss'. Larkin was known to have gone a bit funny in his final years, falling in love with Mrs Thatcher and giving out with some reactionary comment, but all this was reckoned to be amiably bufferish, a bit of a self-parody, and thoroughly in line with the poignantly expressed outsiderism that ran through some of his most haunting verse. Only a few people knew that there was nothing at all funny about the way Larkin had gone funny, or that his conservatism was tinged with the same vehemence that had come to mark his ever-deepening self-hatred and despair. There was also, in these final years, a serious drink problem – a port-for-breakfast kind of problem. Since the death of his mother in 1977, Larkin had stopped writing poetry, or stopped expecting to write poetry, and when he did take up his pen it was either from duty or from rage – and it was not always easy to tell which was which.

When Larkin's *Collected Poems* appeared, three years after his death, the book's editor was criticized for certain policy decisions, but nobody complained that he had left out late, unpublished pieces like 'Prison for strikers/ Bring back the cat/ Kick out the niggers/

What about that'. Some readers, though, did wonder about the inclusion of a startling poem called 'Love Again', which had been discovered among Larkin's papers:

> Love again: wanking at ten-past-three
> (Surely he's taken her home by now?),
> The bedroom hot as a bakery,
> The drink gone dead . . .
>
> Someone else feeling her breasts and cunt,
> Someone else drowned in that lash-wide stare,
> And me supposed to be ignorant,
> Or find it funny, or not to care,
> Even . . . but why put it into words?

Larkin was known for his settled, near-boastful sense of sexual resignation. He had memorably hymned the joys and sorrows of the solitary life. There had been an immense sadness in his work but also a determined self-reliance. This poem was quite different, though (which is maybe why he never printed it). None of Larkin's earlier unburdenings, however disconsolate and self-reproachful, had had anything like the same unmerciful ferocity, the same screaming-point force of attack. There is no 'Larkinesque' effort here to mitigate the poem's central horror, no wry acknowledgement that 'how we live measures our own nature'. The poem's concluding lines are closer to self-pity than any of Larkin's published or self-published work, however blankly miserable, was ever quite allowed to be:

> Isolate rather this element
>
> That spreads through other lives like a tree
> And sways them on in a sort of sense
> And say why it never worked for me.
> Something to do with violence
> A long way back, and wrong rewards,
> And arrogant eternity.

If Larkin had lived, he probably would not have printed 'Love Again'. On the other hand, one's guess is that he badly wanted us to see it. We knew that he was 'fucked up' by his mum and dad, because he'd told us so, but the Larkin we had come to know really was 'supposed to find it funny or not to care' when love-relationships went wrong – or at any rate to have the gift of transmuting daily glooms into rich, beautifully crafted, lyric statements about love and death – our loves and deaths as well as his. In 'Love Again', the unhappiness strictly belongs to him. Our share in it is that of the pitying, appalled spectator.

Larkin from the start believed, or said he did, in his own 'genius', but even as an adolescent he seems to have spent more time worrying about how to make it as a writer than he did enjoying the satisfactions of a job well done – or, come to that, making sure the job *was* well done. His early poems were sub-Auden, then sub-Yeats, and it was not until 1949, when he read Hardy, that he began to evince signs of a distinctive voice. As a young aspirant, Larkin fancied himself as, first of all, a novelist (his two fictions, *Jill* and *A Girl in Winter* were highly competent, if somewhat effortful and strained), and when he finally conceded that fiction was beyond him, he also had to concede that – unlike Kingsley Amis, his close college friend and lifelong rival – he would never be able to 'live as a writer'. He became a university librarian – at Leicester, then Belfast and then (from 1955 until his death) at Hull. The toad work would squat on him for keeps. He grumbled about its dullness but he was known to be almost pedantically efficient.

When Larkin abandoned fiction for poetry, out came the cycle clips (see 'Church Going'). In *The Less Deceived*, there is much defeated jeering at the so-called Emotional Life (at 'Sex, yes, but what is sex?'), ranking it along with God and Art as just another tarnished absolute, a snare of affectation. To be wary of extreme emotion is, for Larkin, to be 'undeceived' and thus superior to the dumb herd. Superior but in the end impoverished. The typical strategy of an early Larkin poem is to project, with wry, contented resignation, a 'grown-up' social stance – unemotional, excluded, undeceived – and then, culminatingly, to introduce a tinge of cosmic horror. The self-sufficient persona is rebuked by the love-hungry poet. The social posturing, though wittily expressed, is shown to be grotesquely self-defeating.

In Larkin's early poems – post-1949, pre-1964 – this strategy can get to seem a little pat. As his writing gains in subtlety, however, it makes for a transfixing inner tension. Although Larkin continues to be caustic at the expense of that 'much-mentioned brilliance, love', his portrait of the loveless Mr Bleaney is anything but abstract. Bleaney's tragedy is that he probably *can* be summed up by his flowered curtains, his saucer-souvenir, his four aways, and all the other desolating paraphernalia with which Larkin kits him out. But the poet, having amassed the well-observed minutiae of self-sufficiency, can't help but ask:

> But if he stood and watched the frigid wind
> Tousling the clouds, lay on the fusty bed
> Telling himself that this was home, and grinned,
> And shivered, without shaking off the dread
>
> That how we live measures our own nature,
> And at his age having no more to show
> Than one hired box should make him pretty sure
> He warranted no better, I don't know.

(Two rhymed stanzas, one sentence – or, rather, one giant sub-clause leading up to that suspended 'I don't know': nowhere more impressively does Larkin demonstrate his gift for accommodating real speech into metre without even the faintest hint of toil and strain.) But how, one might respond, could Bleaney have improved his situation? Not, we deduce from other Larkin poems, by reading, travel or marriage. Money, perhaps? We never learn, in Larkin's 'The Whitsun Weddings', if having the real thing instead of 'jewellery-substitutes' would have redeemed those sorry brides. In 'Faith Healing', there seems to be no getting away from that 'much-mentioned brilliance':

> In everyone there sleeps
> A sense of life lived according to love.
> To some it means the difference they could make
> By loving others, but across most it sweeps
> As all they might have done had they been loved.

On the one hand, there is 'everybody making love and going shares', love that is organized into the drudgery of marriage, that cheats and disappoints and is undone by time. On the other, there is the isolation and unhappiness of those who have never had it or who have expected too much from it, seeking it romantically as an 'enormous yes'. The closing lines of 'The Whitsun Weddings' both contain and energize this conflict. The image of the arrow-shower beautifully intertwines those strands of aspiration and defeat that run through Larkin's work:

> and it was nearly done, this frail
> Travelling coincidence; and what it held
> Stood ready to be loosed with all the power
> That being changed can give. We slowed again,
> And as the tightened brakes took hold, there swelled
> A sense of falling, like an arrow-shower
> Sent out of sight, somewhere becoming rain.

Larkin once predicted of himself: 'I believe that when I am old I shall bitterly regret having wasted my life, which I may have done. This is because I shall never attain the absolute — in other words the *continual* ecstasy — because it doesn't exist. Therefore in addition to being afraid of death, I shall feel cheated and angry.' In Larkin's case, as he well knew, a whole lifetime was spent avoiding not just the 'continual ecstasy' that 'doesn't exist' but also the non-continual fragments of near-ecstasy at which most people set their sights — the type of ecstasy that Larkin would habitually describe as expensive, time-wasting and productive of much personal inconvenience. One of the last poems Larkin wrote was about a hedgehog he had accidentally killed. 'We should be careful of each other', he wrote,

'We should be kind/ While there is still time'. An echo here of Hardy's great, remorseful elegies for the dead wife he was rarely very kind to when she lived.

Larkin, of course, never married or had kids (see 'Self's the Man'), but sexual relationships, or an idea of them, are at the centre of his work. Early on, Larkin's sex life was what the poems say it was: all in the head. He had no luck at school in Coventry (where he was born) and not much luck at Oxford (where he met Kingsley Amis, a co-student at St John's). There was plenty of fantasizing, though, and it was in these early years that he developed his life-long interest in pornography. His juvenile fiction tended to be about schoolgirl swishings at St Bride's.

Real women began to enter his life in the early 1940s, when he started work as a librarian. By this time, though, he had already evolved his doctrines of self-sufficiency. His parents' marriage – the father a bookish, imperious Nazi-fancier; the mother a vacuous, slow-drip complainer – instilled in him a determination to stay unattached. His parents' union, he said, had 'left me with two convictions: that human beings should not live together and that children should be taken from their parents at an early age'. When he was twenty-one, and stepping out with his first girl, he was telling his male friends: 'I don't want to take a girl out and spend circa £5 when I can toss myself off in five minutes, free, and have the rest of the evening for myself.'

Larkin's *Letters*, when they appeared in 1992, were filled with such blokish brutalities and made a serious dent in Larkin's Betjemanlike image – and so too did Andrew Motion's 1993 biography, which revealed the complicated love-entanglements of Larkin's final years. The term 'Larkinesque' now stands for all manner of bad things: hating women, being right-wing, saying 'fuck' a lot, and so on. Larkin the poet is no longer the cherished hesitant of 'Church Going' but the sloganizer of 'They fuck you up, your mum and dad' and 'Books are a load of crap'. Larkin once predicted that his 'Lake Isle of Innisfree' would be 'This Be the Verse': 'I fully expect to hear it recited by a thousand Girl Guides before I die.'

Well, he was almost right.

Mr Bleaney

'This was Mr Bleaney's room. He stayed
The whole time he was at the Bodies, till
They moved him.' Flowered curtains, thin and frayed,
Fall to within five inches of the sill,

Whose window shows a strip of building land,
Tussocky, littered. 'Mr Bleaney took
My bit of garden properly in hand.'
Bed, upright chair, sixty-watt bulb, no hook

Behind the door, no room for books or bags –
'I'll take it.' So it happens that I lie
Where Mr Bleaney lay, and stub my fags
On the same saucer-souvenir, and try

Stuffing my ears with cotton-wool, to drown
The jabbering set he egged her on to buy.
I know his habits – what time he came down,
His preference for sauce to gravy, why

He kept on plugging at the four aways –
Likewise their yearly frame: the Frinton folk
Who put him up for summer holidays,
And Christmas at his sister's house in Stoke.

But if he stood and watched the frigid wind
Tousling the clouds, lay on the fusty bed
Telling himself that this was home, and grinned,
And shivered, without shaking off the dread

That how we live measures our own nature,
And at his age having no more to show
Than one hired box should make him pretty sure
He warranted no better, I don't know.

The Whitsun Weddings

That Whitsun, I was late getting away:
    Not till about
One-twenty on the sunlit Saturday
Did my three-quarters-empty train pull out,
All windows down, all cushions hot, all sense
Of being in a hurry gone. We ran
Behind the backs of houses, crossed a street
Of blinding windscreens, smelt the fish-dock; thence
The river's level drifting breadth began,
Where sky and Lincolnshire and water meet.

All afternoon, through the tall heat that slept
    For miles inland,
A slow and stopping curve southwards we kept.
Wide farms went by, short-shadowed cattle, and
Canals with floatings of industrial froth;
A hothouse flashed uniquely: hedges dipped
And rose: and now and then a smell of grass
Displaced the reek of buttoned carriage-cloth
Until the next town, new and nondescript,
Approached with acres of dismantled cars.

At first, I didn't notice what a noise
    The weddings made
Each station that we stopped at: sun destroys
The interest of what's happening in the shade,
And down the long cool platforms whoops and skirls
I took for porters larking with the mails,

And went on reading. Once we started, though,
We passed them, grinning and pomaded, girls
In parodies of fashion, heels and veils,
All posed irresolutely, watching us go,

As if out on the end of an event
   Waving goodbye
To something that survived it. Struck, I leant
More promptly out next time, more curiously,
And saw it all again in different terms:
The fathers with broad belts under their suits
And seamy foreheads; mothers loud and fat;
An uncle shouting smut; and then the perms,
The nylon gloves and jewellery-substitutes,
The lemons, mauves, and olive-ochres that

Marked off the girls unreally from the rest.
   Yes, from cafés
And banquet-halls up yards, and bunting-dressed
Coach-party annexes, the wedding-days
Were coming to an end. All down the line
Fresh couples climbed aboard: the rest stood round;
The last confetti and advice were thrown,
And, as we moved, each face seemed to define
Just what it saw departing: children frowned
At something dull; fathers had never known

Success so huge and wholly farcical;
   The women shared
The secret like a happy funeral;
While girls, gripping their handbags tighter, stared
At a religious wounding. Free at last,
And loaded with the sum of all they saw,
We hurried towards London, shuffling gouts of steam.
Now fields were building-plots, and poplars cast

Long shadows over major roads, and for
Some fifty minutes, that in time would seem

Just long enough to settle hats and say
  I nearly died,
A dozen marriages got under way.
They watched the landscape, sitting side by side
– An Odeon went past, a cooling tower,
And someone running up to bowl – and none
Thought of the others they would never meet
Or how their lives would all contain this hour.
I thought of London spread out in the sun,
Its postal districts packed like squares of wheat:

There we were aimed. And as we raced across
  Bright knots of rail
Past standing Pullmans, walls of blackened moss
Came close, and it was nearly done, this frail
Travelling coincidence; and what it held
Stood ready to be loosed with all the power
That being changed can give. We slowed again,
And as the tightened brakes took hold, there swelled
A sense of falling, like an arrow-shower
Sent out of sight, somewhere becoming rain.

Allen Ginsberg

1926–1997

When Allen Ginsberg's *Collected Poems* appeared in 1984, some people were amused by the 'squareness' of its presentation. The poems themselves were unaltered: on page after apostrophizing page, the son of SuperBlake came 'roaring down' on us 'in a haze of hot cars and garbage – with a mouthful of shit'. This was the Ginsberg we knew about from the 1960s and either worshipped or despised: the drug-crazed lunatic of *Howl*, the lamenting hipster-Jew of *Kaddish*, the woolly-faced prophet of gay promiscuity and oriental godliness, the 'Om'-chanting guru of the flower people.

The joke was in finding that this same creature of inspiration, this friend of flux, had attached to his complete works nearly 100 pages of straight-faced academic explication: notes to the poems, data on obscure co-Beats, snapshots of himself when very young, an Index of Proper Names which – if exclamation marks were added – might easily have passed muster as a Ginsberg poem: 'Apollo! Arafat! Ardinarishvara! Arthat! Artaud!', and so on. And on the book's rear jacket was a photo of the author dressed up as an American college professor: trim of beard, wearing a collar and tie and proudly clutching a bundle of his publications. A faintly lascivious smirk was all that had survived of the famous old 'clock of meat bleakly pining for the sweet immaterial paradise'. There could be little doubt that here was a production aimed squarely at the academic squares. The wild man of yesteryear was offering himself up for college scrutiny.

And this served to remind us that Ginsberg, when he first started out, *was* pretty square. Born in 1926, he was the son of a failed, or unpublicized, poet-father and a psychotic mother who had a thing about taking her clothes off in public (as Allen himself did when he turned into a Beat). Both parents were ardent, change-the-world socialists and for a time they hoped that their son would choose a life in politics. Louis Ginsberg, the father, never admired Allen's verses: no doubt their hysterical pitch seemed far too close to home and in any case he distrusted their background of drug-inspiration. The boy Ginsberg seems to have had little of the self-assurance for which he would later be admired. At first, he was troubled, hesitant and modest. Maybe his father was right: maybe his work was not 'lofty incantation' but 'gibberish', which was rather how his father saw it. Ginsberg was an obedient son and at Columbia University he was taught by Lionel Trilling, by no means a supporter of unreason.

And then came *Howl* (first performed in San Francisco in the mid-1950s). Ginsberg, to do him justice, never really believed that his poem's sorry cast-list represented the 'best minds' of his generation. Nor did he think much of his own 'new method of Poetry. All you got to do is lay down on a couch and think of anything that comes into your head.' It was only when the audience began to yell for more that he was able to suppress the fear that he was more his mother's than his father's son. If he really was his mother's son – well, why not take it all the way? After the huge success of *Howl*, Ginsberg was up for grabs.

Once grabbed, he became a full-time hipster prophet, exhorting his followers to see themselves as exalted disaffiliates. Fired by vanity, a flair for self-promotion, and – incidentally – a gluttonous appetite for homosexual conquest, Ginsberg in the late 1950s became the organizing central figure of the burgeoning Beat Generation. By the 1960s he had added a dash of oriental mysticism to his apocalyptic social wrath. He started dressing up in robes and beads and sported a huge mystic's beard. He connected himself to the pop-music scene ('mass machine-made folk song of one soul' was his ingenious description of Bob Dylan) and became a prominent figure in the peace movement. Even as he edged eerily towards his forties, he never relinquished his gift for flattering the young.

When gay pride came along, Ginsberg was more than ready for it. He had been boasting of his own homosexuality for years ('Sweet Boy, Gimme yr. Ass' is one of his later efforts in this vein). And his prose-poem *Kaddish*, an elegy for his recently dead mother, persuaded quite a few of the more swinging mainstream critics to speak out on behalf of his 'natural', if largely misused, gifts. By the end of the 1960s, Ginsberg was no longer just a raving bard. He had become an American institution.

In this guise he devoted many of his later years of fame to global tours, preaching about the need for peace and love, alternating visits to Himalayan holy men with soulful overtures to world-stage politicians: advising Castro to boost his image by putting on a Beatles concert, offering the Prague Writers Union a poem that confessed 'I lie/ with teenage boys afraid of the red police'. By the 1980s, Beat Studies had become a popular component of many English Literature curricula, and Ginsberg began to take a scholar's interest in the detail of his own career. Much of the early history of the Beats was the history of who did what to whom. Did Jack ever do it to Bill, or Bill to Jack, or Neal to Peter, and so on.

One thing was sure: Allen did it to them all, and he was determined that history should get it right. To this end, says his biographer Barry Miles, he 'kept all the sixty-thousand-plus letters he received throughout his life, and he has saved his manuscripts, journals, notebooks and doodles. Since the 1970s he has frequently taped his lectures, his conversations with relatives and friends and, on occasion, his telephone conversations.' Shortly before Ginsberg's death in 1997, a profilist visited his office on Union Square: 'a proper office with three Apple Macs, a cuttings library, Ginsberg's massive photographic archive, a photocopier and multiple phone lines. It acts as a "servicing organization", helping poets with hand-outs from Ginsberg's Committee on Poetry – a charitable foundation set up in 1965 to avoid paying taxes to a war-mongering government – or for "stuff like fixing their teeth or an emergency of some kind". More than 100 poets have ben-efited from Ginsberg's redistribution of his earnings.'

Maybe Allen was, after all, his father's son. Louis Ginsberg, he would not have forgotten, probably collected more rejection slips than any other poet in America. But Louis never stopped trying, never stopped calling himself 'a poet'; he would have liked the sound of his son's generous Committee.

'Junk Mail'

I received in mail   offer beautiful certificate National Conference
    Synagogue Youth
invites subscriber   Monthly Review   Independent Socialist Mag
Congressman Koch reports on collapse of our cities
Epilepsy Foundation misdelivered for Mr Pantonucci   light
    candle understanding 4 million Americans
Dear Mr Orlovsky put Salvation Army on your Christmas List
    $50 return enclosed envelope
American Friends Service Committee act now meet urgent human
    needs   hungry families   Prisoners
in remote penal institutions   Rehabilitation Vietnam Laos
    Northern Great Plains Indians block land-destruction by
    energy seeking industries   Contact between Israeli Jews &
    Arabs
Psychoenergetics workshops in Vermont   Green Mountain
    Quarterly's Imperialist Ideology in Donald Duck   with a
    new bibliography Sri Aurobindo and the Mother protected
    by Intnl. copyright laws News of Auroville
Dear Friend: we are Michael & Robert Meeropol, sons of Julius &
    Ethel Rosenberg executed by US Government 22 years ago.
Sue the Government for the Files   duplicating fees alone Twenty-
    five Thousand Dollars
Christmas Greetings   Help Hospitalized Veterans   art or craft
    Kit enthused busily working for days   Bob Hope helps.
Fund For Peace if your blood boils   Press accounts CIA   black-
    mail assassination a powerful alternative to World
    Violence   Private Citizens acting Global
Gay Peoples Union NYU faces bankruptcy   Dance Halloween
Boycott Gallo Grapes lettuce United Farmworkers of America
    Our struggle is not over   make checks payable   Si Se Puede
    Cesar E. Chavez   Union Label
Announcing Energy & Evolution Quarterly   how to make harps

lyres & dulcimers   Quantum Theory   Tantra & land reform
    organic gardening
Give Poets & Writers' CODA to a friend   subscribe United
    Nations Children's Fund   severe malnutrition   Starvation
    faces 400 to 500 million children poorer countries. Dwarfism
disease blindness mental retardation stunted growth crop failures
    drought flood   exhausted wheat rice reserves skyrocketing
    fuel costs   fertilizer shortages   Desperately need your help.
Racial motives lead to Innocent Marine's conviction in Georgia
    murder trial   a thick envelope from Southern Poverty Law
    Center Julian Bond
'I didn't mean to harm anyone. I only went into that Police Station
    to see what they were doing to my brother . . .' sd Marine
    Sgt. Roy Patterson
Won't you help millions in desperate need Thanksgiving urgently
    bless Carl's Holiday Food Crusade 'Yes! use my tax deductible
    donation to keep them alive.'
Catholic Peace Fellowship Activist Fund's special appeal help the
    Staff to foster Christian Pacifist Continental Walk   Dis-
    armament & Social Justice
( ) I have no money at present but I wish to remain on the mailing
    list ( ) Please take my name off your mailing list
An important message from Robert Redford about the Environ-
    ment   80 separate legal actions   Dirty air you pay your
    life Aerosol Spray cancer   the National Resources Defense
    Council needs your support
The Continental Walk itself: the Nations spent $4.5 Trillion
    military security since 1946   This year $240 Billion join us
    walk across ⅛ of the Planet's surface Nonviolent resistance
    Unilateral Disarmament
Aum   Sri Ganeshaya   Namah Tantra Non-salacious in tone
    & intent lecturer Dr Thackur   George Washington Hotel
    Lexington Avenue NYC
Dear Friend: the War Resisters International is in a desperate
    financial situation

Nuclear Age pacifist work must advance   leafleting soldiers British
  Withdrawal from Northern Ireland Campaign

We are in need of the kind of Miracle you can bring to pass.
  The huge influx of Russian Immigrants upon Bikur Cholem
  Hospital in the heart of Jerusalem – Don't turn your back on
  the Herculean efforts . . .

First priority reservation on new gold $100 Canadian Olympic
  Coin now available at just $110! for American Express
  Cardmembers –

Ad Hoc Coalition for a New Foreign Policy (formerly Coalition
  to Stop Funding the War) hopes you will join the network by
  filling out the enclosed envelope

Human Rights Amendment, end Vietnam Trade Embargo, cut
  foreign military assistance encourage people to people
  Friendshipments to Vietnam

A literary miracle   843 poems written in 24 hours by Indian Yogi
  Sri Chinmoi   Aum Publications

If you haven't joined the Great Falls Development Corp. now's
  the time to do so

& subscribe to the William Carlos Williams Newsletter. Penmaen
  Press: Two fascinating heretofore unpublished letters written
  in 1956 to Richard Eberhart by Allen Ginsberg . . .

Please won't you help Central America Sub-Saharan Africa and
  the Indian Subcontinent? Give generously to Planned Parent-
  hood–World Population

Confidential – Memo to supporters of Open Housing from Fund
  for Open Society a nonprofit mortgage Co. to advance equal
  housing: fight racial steering

Dear Citizen of the World: First days explosion bomb radioactivity
  starve Ozone layer? Isn't it time we did something?

1) Send cooperators ten addresses w/zip codes 2) Mail friends
  endorsement 3) Write your Congressman President Newspaper editor & Presidential Candidate.

As a final move, the World Authority would destroy all Nuclear
  Weapons.

James Merrill

1926–1995

James Merrill was probably the wealthiest of modern poets – the son of the stockbroker Charles Merrill, who founded the banking firm of Merrill Lynch – and one day, no doubt, somebody will write a study of his work and personality from this perspective. For a time, this poet was better known for his generosity to other poets than he was for his own work.

Born in New York in 1926, Merrill went to Amherst College, served for a year in the US Army, and published his first book in 1946. His earliest poems were decoratively arty, somewhat in the Stevens manner, and it was not until the 1960s that he began to write directly from his own experience, of travel, nature, friends. With *Braving the Elements* (1973), there was a deepening candour, and an effort – so it seemed – to purge his work of the camp-dandyism that was perhaps his most distinctive, and instinctive, idiom:

> Ladder horned against moonlight,
> Window hoisted stealthily –
> That's what I'd steel myself at night
> To see, or sleep to see.

My parents were out partying,
My nurse was old and deaf and slow.
Way off in the servants' wing
Cackled a radio.

On the Lindbergh baby's small
Cold features lay a spell, a swoon.
It seemed entirely plausible
For my turn to come soon.

By the time *Braving the Elements* appeared, Merrill was already at work on the project for which he is most likely to be remembered: a long (560-page) work both dandified and candid. In 1968, Merrill and his long-time companion David Jackson (DJ in the poem) began taking dictation from the Other World. It was a kind of parlour game at first: the two friends would set up the ouija board at their home in Stonington, Connecticut (or at the one in Athens, Greece), and smilingly invite smart-talking spirits down (or is it out?) to play. The summoned immaterials luckily turned out to be chaps rather like themselves: droll, aesthetic types with a taste for whimsical speculation and a quick ear for silly puns. Merrill began taking notes of some of their exchanges and incorporated one or two fragments of spirit-speech into his poems.

It seems to have been in the early 1970s that Merrill recognized the larger possibilities of his ouija evenings: the openings they offered into a limitless new realm of subject matter – or, rather, of subjects without matter. He could, with help from his tea-cup, assemble a cast of 'good-value' wits and seers; he could quiz them and cajole them, receive instructions from them about morality and art, he could invest them with comic, other-worldly traits, he could dream up post-mortal ranks and stations. With the ones he most liked, he could chatter on for pages. Here W. H. Auden speaks in capitals:

We think of Wystan's face runneled and seamed,
Faintly soiled above his Gimli sweatshirt.
MY DEARS IT IS ME MY MINERALS MINED OUT EARLY,
I SPENT SLOW DECADES COVERING THE SCARS
HAD I SUNK SHAFTS INTO MY NATURE OR
UPWARDS TO THE DEAD I WD HAVE FOUND RICH
    VEINS
INSTEAD I LOOKED FOR INSPIRATION TO
RITUAL & DIFFY MORAL STRICTURES
SO WRONG   'The concept Ought would make, I thought,
Our passions philanthropic'? One of my
Touchstone stanzas – please don't run it down.
NOT BAD   BUT OTHER BITS MAKE MY TOES WIGGLE

The ouija ploy also enabled the poet to play around with theology
and science, history and myth, to invent comically unsuitable
reincarnations for the recently dead, and strange 'earlier lives' for the
still-with-us. And Merrill, the author-auditor, could throughout all
this remain this-worldly: wry, shrewd, ironical. The heavens he
listened in on could always be brought down to earth.

Merrill took eight years to complete his epic, and published it in
book form bit by bit. 'The Book of Ephraim' was published in
Divine Comedies in 1976, *Mirabell: Books of Number* in 1978, *Scripts
for a Pageant* in 1980. The whole poem – incorporating these three
books and adding a new 'coda', *The Higher Keys* – was called, in
1982, *The Changing Light at Sandover*. All in all, it is a sprawling,
daunting work of some 17,000 lines, about twice the length of
Paradise Lost. But Merrill's epic was not constructed to any Miltonic
grand design: it simply unfolded, year by year. And it did not
improve as it went on. On the contrary, it became bloated with its
pretensions: the longueurs got longer, the speculation more fanciful,
the comedy more strenuously 'gay'.

This was a pity, because 'Ephraim', the first book, was impressive
in its self-assurance. The book had a vivid central ghost, Ephraim
himself, who was not just a device for instructing us on 'the relation
of the individual to the cosmos'; he was a memorable fictional

character in his own right. And there was a balance in the book between supernatural frivolity and earth-bound woes:

> HL REMEMBERS U
> STILL HEARS THRU U JM A VERNAL MUSIC
> THIS WILL BE YOUR LAST LIFE THANKS TO HIM
> – News that like so much of Ephraim's leaves me
> Of two minds. Do I want it all to end?
> If there's a choice – and what about my friend?
> What about David? Will he too – DJ
> HAS COME ALL THINGS CONSIDERED A LONG WAY
> What things? Well, that his previous thirty-four
> Lives ended either in the cradle or
> By violence, the gallows or the knife.
> Why was this? U DID NOT TAKE TO LIFE
> Now, however, one or two, at most
> Three lives more . . .
>   Stop, oh stop!
> Ephraim, this cannot be borne. We live
> Together. And if you are on the level
> Some consciousness survives – right? Right.
> Now tell me, what conceivable delight
> Lies for either of us in the prospect
> Of an eternity without the other?
> Why not *both* be reborn? . . .
>
> His answer's unrecorded. The cloud passed
> More quickly than the shade it cast,
>
> Foreshadower of nothing, dearest heart,
> But the dim wish of lives to drift apart.

In the later books there are, to be sure, stretches in which this balance is sustained, and Ephraim does make welcome reappearances, but as we read on, the first volume comes more and more to seem correct in scale. It offered a cosmology both touchingly miniature and incongruously social. Once this scale was abandoned, Merrill seems to have felt free to indulge himself, to ramble and inflate, to settle for '. . . this net of loose talk tightening to verse/ And verse once more revolving between two poles/ Gassy expansion and succinct collapse'.

Angel

Above my desk, whirring but self-important
(Though not much larger than a hummingbird)
In finely woven robes, school of Van Eyck,
Hovers an evidently angelic visitor.
He points one index finger out the window
At winter snatching to its heart,
To crystal vacancy, the misty
Exhalations of houses, and of people running home
From the cold sun pounding on the sea;
While with the other hand
He indicates the piano
Where the Sarabande No. 1 lies open
At a passage I shall never master
But which has already, and effortlessly, mastered me.
He drops his jaw as if to say, or sing,
"Between the world God made
And this music of Satie,
Each glimpsed through veils, but whole,
Radiant and willed,
Demanding praise, demanding surrender,
How can you sit there with your notebook?
What do you think you are doing?"
However he says nothing – wisely: I could mention
Flaws in God's world, or Satie's; and for that matter
How did he come by *his* taste for Satie?
Half to tease him, I turn back to my page,
Its phrases thus far clotted, unconnected.
The tiny angel shakes his head.
There is no smile on his round, hairless face.
He does not want even these few lines written.

James Wright

1927–1980

When Donald Hall, in the early 1960s, compiled a Penguin anthology of *Contemporary American Poetry*, he found himself suggesting that the next step for American verse might not involve a choice between sub-Eliot and sub-Williams, between European sophistication and Americanist self-exploration. Hall had, he believed, discerned a possible third way, a way which would assimilate both Eliot and Williams and at the same time push forward to a perhaps potent new alliance – an alliance between the North American pragmatic and the South American fantastical. This alliance would be arrived at via Spain, or – more specifically – via Spanish surrealism, as practised by South Americans like Vallejo, Jimenez or Neruda. In his introduction Hall drew attention to recent work by Robert Bly, Louis Simpson and James Wright, poets associated with a magazine called *The Sixties* (and formerly *The Fifties*), and claimed that in them 'a new kind of imagination seems to be working'. He went on to quote lines by Bly and Simpson and to comment:

The vocabulary is mostly colloquial but the special quality of the lines has nothing to do with an area of diction; it is quality learned neither from

T. S. Eliot nor William Carlos Williams. This imagination is irrational yet the poem is usually quiet and the language simple; there is no straining for apocalypse and no conscious pursuit of the unconscious.

Hall did not mention Latin America, but readers of *The Sixties* would have been familiar with the magazine's vaunting of Spanish-language poets. And such readers might also have known that talk of continental brotherhood was actually a reddish herring. What Bly was looking for was that 'new kind of imagination' that Hall speaks of in his introduction. Bly, along with many other poets of the 1960s, believed that American poetry, by narrowing its choices and by concentrating too academically on the Williams/Eliot split, had taken insufficient notice of other – perhaps vitalizing – models, models which the South Americans had learned from. Surrealism, for example, had made little or no impact on English-language verse. In Spain, though, it had opened doors into strange and thrilling realms of the unconscious: it had indeed offered a 'new kind of imagination'.

The Pound/Eliot school of modernism had always tended to be caustic at the expense of Freud, Jung and their literary disciples (Pound described Surrealism as 'any decayed cabbage cast upon any pale satin sofa'). For Eliot, the unconscious offered a short cut either to God or to insanity. Pound's insistence on precise and accurate observation made it unlikely that he could ever be beguiled by talk of images which had 'freed themselves' from referential duties.

Bly and his followers presented their own work as 'poems written out of laziness and silence', and many of them did seem to have been written in states of semi-wakefulness, states in which metaphor borders on hallucination:

> There is this cave
> In the air behind my body
> That nobody is going to touch:
> A cloister, a silence
> Closing around a blossom of fire.
> When I stand upright in the wind,
> My bones turn to dark emeralds.

These lines are by James Wright, the most gifted of Bly's allies, and they represent him at his self-indulgent worst. Much of Wright's later work involved an effort to inject some worldly substance into the dream-whimsy that suffused most *Sixties* poems. Wright liked to project himself as a dreamy, heavy-drinking seeker of strange visions – bones that turn into emeralds and so on – but he was also the product of a tough Ohioan background and was more convincingly 'political' than any of his *Sixties* colleagues. He wanted, he said, to make his poems 'say something humanly important instead of just showing off with language'. He tried to speak 'of the beauty and again of the ugliness of the poor and neglected'. Many of the social outcasts who populate Wright's work are drawn from memories of his childhood in Ohio, where his father toiled as a steelworker.

Wright's poetic background also made it hard for him to embrace the anti-rational so fervently as Bly did. Born in 1927, Wright was educated at Kenyon College under John Crowe Ransom, and at the University of Washington, Seattle, under Theodore Roethke during Roethke's sub-Yeats phase, and when he began writing poetry his inclinations were traditional and academic. There are hints of Dylan Thomas in *The Green Wall* (1957), his first book, and *Saint Judas*, two years later, is noticeably influenced by Frost and Edgar Lee Masters, but in both volumes the language is literary-antique and the technique laboriously unoriginal.

It was with his third book, *The Branch Will Not Break* (1963), that Bly's influence first showed itself. Abandoning the tight stanzas and artificial diction of his early verse, Wright suddenly began to sound as if he meant what he was writing. The colloquial delivery, the subtle use of interior rhyme, the alternating line lengths: Wright's mastery of free verse was all the more impressive because it seemed to have been at his disposal all along.

In his post-1960s work, Wright developed an attractively plain-speaking manner and purged himself of Bly-like affectation. A university teacher since his graduation (most lengthily at the University of Minnesota and at Hunter College in New York), Wright was none the less a busy traveller, and there are some powerful

'Italian' poems to be found in his last book, *To a Blossoming Pear Tree* (1977). Wright died in 1980 at the age of fifty-three. A posthumous volume, *This Journey*, was published in 1982.

Lying in a Hammock at William Duffy's Farm in Pine Island, Minnesota

Over my head, I see the bronze butterfly,
Asleep on the black trunk,
Blowing like a leaf in green shadow.
Down the ravine behind the empty house,
The cowbells follow one another
Into the distances of the afternoon.
To my right,
In a field of sunlight between two pines,
The droppings of last year's horses
Blaze up into golden stones.
I lean back, as the evening darkens and comes on.
A chicken hawk floats over, looking for home.
I have wasted my life.

Eisenhower's Visit to Franco, 1959

> '. . . we die of cold, and not
> of darkness.'   UNAMUNO

The American hero must triumph over
The forces of darkness.
He has flown through the very light of heaven
And come down in the slow dusk
Of Spain.

Franco stands in a shining circle of police.
His arms open in welcome.
He promises all dark things
Will be hunted down.

State police yawn in the prisons.
Antonio Machado follows the moon
Down a road of white dust,
To a cave of silent children
Under the Pyrenees.
Wine darkens in stone jars in villages.
Wine sleeps in the mouths of old men, it is a dark red
      color.

Smiles glitter in Madrid.
Eisenhower has touched hands with Franco, embracing
In a glare of photographers.
Clean new bombers from America muffle their engines
And glide down now.
Their wings shine in the searchlights
Of bare fields,
In Spain.

Gregory Corso

1930–2001

When the Beat Generation first announced its presence in the mid-1950s, most commentators viewed the phenomenon as more socio-theatrical than literary: another aspect of the imminently burgeoning 'youthquake' (as evinced by Marlon Brando and James Dean in the movies, by Holden Caulfield in fiction, and even by the emerging Elvis Presley in pop music). Youth, it was perceived, was on the move and in the mood for a new epoch of subversion and delinquency: Beat Generation figures like Jack Kerouac and Neal Cassady were admired for their 'disaffiliated' social postures, and for their willingness to turn aside from postwar rectitudes in search of objectives more exalted and irrational (definitions were never easy to come by in those days, but words like 'exaltation' were habitually close to hand). The Beats' pursuit of the irrational would, it was understood, receive assistance from the already-popular 'drug culture'.

Young Beats like Kerouac and the highly visible Allen Ginsberg nurtured a myth of 'hobo questing', of journeys to whatever lay ahead – journeys both physical and spiritual – and each of these energetic self-promoters was in turn rewarded by the emulative adulation of the young. They also came in for much contempt from the literary establishment, most of whose leaders had taught themselves (in the 1930s) that rebels should have causes. At the same time, though, the literary establishment had to concede that these new writers ought to be explained in literary terms. The recent death of Dylan Thomas, the deepening aridity of the Eliotic New Criticism, the revival of interest in Walt Whitman's yearning for a poetic spaciousness and vigour which would reflect America's own muscular immensity: all this was present – plus a dash of William Blake, a whiff of Eastern philosophy and a general willingness to make mock of their parents' highly prized taboos (against homosexuality and narcotics, in the main, but there were other delinquencies on offer: teen promiscuity, alcohol, 'bad language', and so on). The Whitman connection revitalized old literary quarrels of the past (the Americanist v. European quarrel, in particular), but it also, for Americans, touched on a whole range of social anxieties. The Beats knew how to make such anxieties seem thrilling to the young.

In Britain in the early 1950s, the more intelligent and sophisticated poets were in the process of attempting to live down the Dylan Thomas myth of bohemian excess and to re-establish links with Hardy, rhyme and syntax. They needed to remind themselves that poets did not have to be on drinking terms with God. For some, though, it was just as encouraging to learn – by way of the seductive Beat 'lifestyle' – that the alternative to Dylan Thomas did not need to be, say, Donald Davie. Indeed, by the close of the decade, quite a few of the younger British poets (sensing, no doubt, the imminence of 'poetry-as-performance') were seeking ways of not seeming to resemble Philip Larkin (Larkin could scarcely be thought of as appealing to a 'teenquake'). And by the early 1960s, with 'literate' pop music (i.e., Bob Dylan and the Beatles) well into its stride, there was a strong temptation to seize upon the so-called Beats as representing some new species, almost, of poetic eloquence – and one, moreover, that effected an attractive marriage between Art and Life: loose morals meet loose syntax.

But why were the Beats so called? Nobody seemed quite to

know, and least of all the Beats themselves. On some days, 'Beat' could mean 'beat up', out of it, beyond the pale; on others, it could derive from 'beatific' or 'beatitude'. Sometimes, it referred to drum beats, as in jazz. Sometimes, it just sounded catchy: like 'Lost Generation' in the 1920s. Viewed from across the Atlantic, the Beat movement could easily be taken as a revival of neo-Romantic wartime uplift – with, perhaps, a seasoning of sociology – and seen therefore as a threat. It was all very well for restless young Americans to seek the open road: Britain's highways were in need of recon-struction. And the last thing English poetry needed at this hour was yet another bout of spiritual replanning. 'A neutral tone is nowadays preferred,' wrote Donald Davie. And these shrill, exhorting Beats were anything but neutral. Most of them – and in particular their leader, Allen Ginsberg – had a taste for platform frenzy. Europe had long ago grown tired of slogans. There was a suspicion in some quarters that these hipster Beats were merely tapping into an exhaustion which was not their own.

The Beats, it was pointed out by their opponents, were middle class. Their vagrancies were self-imposed. Both Ginsberg and Fer-linghetti studied literature with Lionel Trilling at Columbia and each of them, over the years, turned out to be a competent businessman: Ferlinghetti with his City Lights publishing house/bookstore, and Ginsberg with his worldwide performance schedules. Neither they nor the Beat novelists Kerouac and Burroughs could truthfully be seen as victims of the social order they so often railed against.

Gregory Corso, in contrast, had the credentials Ginsberg and Co. yearned for. Corso really had been handed the short straw. Born in 1930, of teenage parents who divorced quite early on, Gregorio Nunzio spent much of his childhood in foster homes and institutions. At the age of sixteen, he took to petty crime and was sentenced to three years for robbery. It was during this behind-bars stretch that he discovered drugs. At the same time, though, he discovered poetry. The two interests were interdependent. Most of Corso's verses come across as rather languid and benign, even when they are trying not to be, and he persistently inclines towards the other-worldly.

The poets Corso fastened on to in his cell were, as one might expect, high Romantics like Shelley, Keats and Rimbaud, but he also 'checked out' Homer and the ancients, and throughout his life a taste for debunkery ran parallel to a reverence for High Culture. The poems he himself wrote when in jail knew nothing of the New Criticism or of *Partisan Review*. It was not until 1950, when he first met Allen Ginsberg, that he began to take an interest in current verse – verse which, at this point, was setting itself against the kind of high-toned self-expressiveness that Corso had a taste for. Ginsberg made Corso read Walt Whitman and enrolled him in his troupe of performing poets, a troupe to which Corso contributed much notoriety (Corso was the troupe's clown-figure, always ready to tear off his clothes or chant expletives).

Corso, indeed, turned out to be a showbiz natural: a genuinely offbeat prankster who thrived on direct audience appreciation. His verses, encountered on the page, were no less ramblingly verbose than Allen Ginsberg's, but they had more charm. Hardly ever with Corso do you get the sense of being bludgeoned or 'got at' by a spiritual superior. The drug-haziness does help, of course, but there is also a sense in which Corso was more of an authentic hipster – laid-back, permissive and pacific – than most of his Beat colleagues. Corso's facetiousness can irritate, but it rarely seems faked up. And one feels the same way about his infantile word-games, his taste for wonderful new concepts and commodities like 'Penguin dust', 'Fried shoes', 'Pie glue', etc. Ginsberg called Corso a 'wordslinger', and Corso was content to be so called: he liked to see himself as coming from sound hoodlum stock and whenever possible he played up his New York/Italian origins.

All in all, it could be said, Corso was too deeply attached to histrionic self-presentations of one sort or another for poetry to stand much of a chance. Every so often, though, the footlights darken and Corso shows himself to have possessed a gift which he too rarely used – for direct lyric plaintiveness. In performance, Corso's moments of sorrow or bewilderment would have come across quite feebly, but on the page they carry impact. Without the Beat phenomenon to egg him on, this poet could have been more

than a mere clown: or so one feels by the end of what is surely his
best poem, 'Marriage'. By the time the Beat movement began to
fade from public view, Corso was still in his thirties. He was
irreversibly tagged, though, as a wild man, and he had grown used
to being famous. He was also used to being drugged and drunk.
During his later years, he settled into the role of a historical phenomenon: giving readings, taking on short teaching stints, and so on.
And he was still pulling in some decent crowds throughout the
1990s. By this date, the Beat poets had a niche in the curricula, and
On the Road was heading for the movies. Corso died in January
2001.

Marriage

Should I get married? Should I be good?
Astound the girl next door with my velvet suit and faustus hood?
Don't take her to movies but to cemeteries
tell all about werewolf bathtubs and forked clarinets
then desire her and kiss her and all the preliminaries
and she going just so far and I understanding why
not getting angry saying You must feel! It's beautiful to feel!
Instead take her in my arms lean against an old crooked
    tombstone
and woo her the entire night the constellations in the sky –

When she introduces me to her parents
back straightened, hair finally combed, strangled by a tie,
should I sit knees together on their 3rd degree sofa
and not ask Where's the bathroom?
How else to feel other than I am,
often thinking Flash Gordon soap –
O how terrible it must be for a young man
seated before a family and the family thinking
We never saw him before! He wants our Mary Lou!
After tea and homemade cookies they ask What do you do for a
    living?
Should I tell them? Would they like me then?
Say All right get married, we're losing a daughter
but we're gaining a son –
And should I then ask Where's the bathroom?

O God, and the wedding! All her family and her friends
and only a handful of mine all scroungy and bearded
just wait to get at the drinks and food –
And the priest! he looking at me as if I masturbated
asking me Do you take this woman for your lawful wedded wife?

And I trembling what to say say Pie Glue!
I kiss the bride all those corny men slapping me on the back
She's all yours, boy! Ha-ha-ha!
And in their eyes you could see some obscene honeymoon going
    on –
Then all that absurd rice and clanky cans and shoes
Niagara Falls! Hordes of us! Husbands! Wives! Flowers! Choc-
    olates!
All streaming into cozy hotels
All going to do the same thing tonight
The indifferent clerk he knowing what was going to happen
The lobby zombies they knowing what
The whistling elevator man he knowing
The winking bellboy knowing
Everybody knowing! I'd be almost inclined not to do anything!
Stay up all night! Stare that hotel clerk in the eye!
Screaming: I deny honeymoon! I deny honeymoon!
running rampant into those almost climactic suites
yelling Radio belly! Cat shovel!
O I'd live in Niagara forever! in a dark cave beneath the Falls
I'd sit there the Mad Honeymooner
devising ways to break marriages, a scourge of bigamy
a saint of divorce –

But I should get married I should be good
How nice it'd be to come home to her
and sit by the fireplace and she in the kitchen
aproned young and lovely wanting my baby
and so happy about me she burns the roast beef
and comes crying to me and I get up from my big papa chair
saying Christmas teeth! Radiant brains! Apple deaf!
God what a husband I'd make! Yes, I should get married!
So much to do! like sneaking into Mr Jones' house late at night
and cover his golf clubs with 1920 Norwegian books
Like hanging a picture of Rimbaud on the lawnmower
like pasting Tannu Tuva postage stamps all over the picket fence

like when Mrs Kindhead comes to collect for the Community
    Chest
grab her and tell her There are unfavorable omens in the sky!
And when the mayor comes to get my vote tell him
When are you going to stop people killing whales!
And when the milkman comes leave him a note in the bottle
Penguin dust, bring me penguin dust, I want penguin dust –

Yet if I should get married and it's Connecticut and snow
and she gives birth to a child and I am sleepless, worn,
up for nights, head bowed against a quiet window, the past
    behind me,
finding myself in the most common of situations a trembling man
knowledged with responsibility not twig-smear nor Roman coin
    soup –
O what would that be like!
Surely I'd give it for a nipple a rubber Tacitus
For a rattle a bag of broken Bach records
Tack Della Francesca all over its crib
Sew the Greek alphabet on its bib
And build for its playpen a roofless Parthenon

No, I doubt I'd be that kind of father
not rural not snow no quiet window
but hot smelly tight New York City
seven flights up roaches and rats in the walls
a fat Reichian wife screeching over potatoes Get a job!
And five nose running brats in love with Batman
And the neighbors all toothless and dry haired
like those hag masses of the 18th century
all wanting to come in and watch TV
The landlord wants his rent
Grocery store Blue Cross Gas & Electric Knights of Columbus
Impossible to lie back and dream Telephone snow, ghost
    parking –
No! I should not get married I should never get married!

But – imagine If I were married to a beautiful sophisticated
        woman
tall and pale wearing an elegant black dress and long black gloves
holding a cigarette holder in one hand and a highball in the other
and we lived high up in a penthouse with a huge window
from which we could see all of New York and ever farther on
        clearer days
No, can't imagine myself married to that pleasant prison dream –

O but what about love? I forget love
not that I am incapable of love
it's just that I see love as odd as wearing shoes –
I never wanted to marry a girl who was like my mother
And Ingrid Bergman was always impossible
And there's maybe a girl now but she's already married
And I don't like men and –
but there's got to be somebody!
Because what if I'm 60 years old and not married,
all alone in a furnished room with pee stains on my underwear
and everybody else is married! All the universe married but me!

Ah, yet well I know that were a woman possible as I am possible
then marriage would be possible –
Like SHE in her lonely alien gaud waiting her Egyptian lover
so I wait – bereft of 2,000 years and the bath of life.

Ted Hughes

1930–1998

In some quarters, the name of Ted Hughes cannot be spoken without some accompanying reference to Sylvia Plath, the American poet he married in 1956 and who killed herself in 1963. With Plath's suicide, Hughes's life and, it seemed, his reputation were irreparably altered for the worse. For the remainder of his days – he was thirty-three when Plath died and his own death came in 1998, when he was almost seventy – Hughes was under more or less constant bombardment from feminist and other critics who believed not only that he, by his infidelity, had brought about Plath's death but also that, as her executor, he had manipulated her estate so as to serve his own self-presentation.

For more than thirty years, Hughes withstood such accusations with much dignity. His technique, on the whole, was to stay silent, and at the same time to honour Plath's poetic afterfame by the carefully staged release of her literary remains: edited journals, letters to her mother, unpublished poems, and so on. People grumbled about his gradualist approach, and about his touchiness on the matter of a Plath biography, but, looking back, it seems evident that he managed the whole business fairly well; and this in spite of some quite crazed assaults on his integrity.

Not long before he died, Hughes published *Birthday Letters*, a book of ragged, rather prosy verses which explored his relationship with Plath, and offered new perspectives on her personality. Some critics saw this volume as a kind of whitewash, but most viewed it as a triumph of apologetic candour.

The Hughes persona that emerged from these *Birthday Letters* did not, it must be said, entirely fit with what could be deduced of the poet's personality from works he had already published. The Hughes of *Birthday Letters* is rather meek and put upon by his dynamic, somewhat crazy wife, whereas the Hughes who wrote *Lupercal* and *Crow* was of a violent and eruptive disposition, so it seemed. But speculation of this sort is pretty fruitless and biographers, we must assume, will soon be telling us what really happened. One might spare a thought, though, for a poet whose biography was never quite his own, and never will be.

Ted Hughes was born in 1930 in Yorkshire, where his parents, throughout much of his childhood, ran a small-town newsagent's shop. The setting, though, was semi-rural and Hughes as a child acquired a range of country skills. He attended the local grammar school and went on from there to Pembroke College, Cambridge, where he began publishing his early poems – poems influenced, in their apocalyptic diction, by Hopkins and Dylan Thomas, but with flashes of sharp observation. Some of these poems were brought together in *Hawk in the Rain*, which in 1957 scored a remarkable success, for a first book by an unknown. Here, the feeling seemed to be, was a young poet whose muscular vitality proposed alternatives to the somewhat desiccated commonsense of the emerging Movement poets.

With *Lupercal*, in 1960, Hughes's tense and intimate rapport with the animal kingdom was even more strikingly in evidence. The book was hailed as a significant new work and in the general enthusiasm few critics were ready to take note of the discrepancy between the poet's lively, expert eye for nature's detail and the crudity of most of his ideas. The humans in Ted Hughes's poems tended to be cartoon figures of enfeebled will or misdirected vigour: the pimply clerk, the village boozer, the Mafeking colonel, and so on. The book promoted the brutal, the primitive and the immediate at the expense of the cerebral, the hesitant, the worldly-wise. It was fifteen years since the end of World War Two, and poetry, it seemed, was getting tired of being told that most emotions should be treated with suspicion. Even so, Hughes surely was a little too emphatic in his oppositions. When he spelled them out ('With man it is otherwise'), the effect could be too pushily and simple-mindedly didactic. But when, as in 'Hawk Roosting', Hughes let his animals speak for themselves, or simply *be*, it was entirely clear that he was not in need of any sermonizing rubrics:

> I sit in the top of the wood, my eyes closed.
> Inaction, no falsifying dream
> Between my hooked head and hooked feet:
> Or in sleep rehearse perfect kills and eat.
>
> The convenience of the high trees!
> The air's buoyancy and the sun's ray
> Are of advantage to me;
> And the earth's face upward for my inspection.
>
> My feet are locked upon the rough bark.
> It took the whole of Creation
> To produce my foot, my each feather:
> Now I hold Creation in my foot
>
> Or fly up, and revolve it all slowly –
> I kill where I please because it is all mine.

The absence from Hughes's work of any complex or arresting human personality continued to be notable throughout the ambigu-ously aimed (for adults or for children?) *Earth Owl and Other People* and the somewhat thrown-together package of stories, plays and verse entitled *Wodwo*. In both books, Hughes's gift for piercingly accurate natural description was intermittently in evidence, but so too were his most striking faults: the portentous verbiage, the skimped and shallow dealings with the human world, the relished violence of both word and deed. And these faults were on lavishly egregious display in his next volume, *Crow* (1970) – a book almost laughably blood-soaked and grisly. *Crow* was offered as a sequence but the individual poems did not bear examination: mechanical and formulaic in construction, liturgically repetitive, and altogether without rhythmic subtlety or variation. In the end, the reader simply feels assaulted by a bludgeoning obsessiveness: 'Blood blasts from the crown on his head in a column'; 'Shock-severed eyes watched blood/ Squandering as from a drain-pipe/ Into the blanks between stars'; 'He stands trousered in blood and log-splits/ The lolling body, bifurcates it/ Top to bottom, kicks away the entrails-/ Steps out of the blood-wallow'. One could compile a similar roll-call involving death or disease, or stabbings, smashings, writhings and screamings. *Crow* is full of lists and incantations and seems to mark the beginning of Hughes's later dabblings in black magic, and to prepare the way for his somewhat loopy meditations on the need for us to resurrect 'archaic energies' and to develop a renewed respect for the supernatural, 'its special fears and cruelties'.

In 1970, the year of *Crow*'s publication, Hughes remarried – to Carol Orchard – and made a permanent home in Devon. In 1972 Hughes bought a farm which his new wife's father managed. Hughes's toilings on this farm provide the subject for several sane, direct and detailed poems in *Moortown* (1979), his most impressive book since *Lupercal*. And in 1992, he printed his 'laureate poems' (he'd become Poet Laureate in 1984), and these were generally agreed to be a cut above what is expected from the monarch's wordsmith. Hughes's nostalgia for old tribal instincts together with his own fantasies of kingship came together, seemingly, in his official role. Twelve days before he died, the Queen awarded him the Order of Merit, perhaps the highest, most exclusive honour in her gift. The wild man from the moors had been acknowledged by his sovereign, and it is perhaps a tribute to the forcefulness of Hughes's sense of his high, bardic obligations that this regal recognition seemed entirely fitting. After his death, Hughes's *Birthday Letters* and his *Tales from Ovid* were received with praise and prizes from a grateful nation, and in his fulsome obituaries there was, after all, scant mention of his overshadowing first wife.

Hawk Roosting

I sit in the top of the wood, my eyes closed.
Inaction, no falsifying dream
Between my hooked head and hooked feet:
Or in sleep rehearse perfect kills and eat.

The convenience of the high trees!
The air's buoyancy and the sun's ray
Are of advantage to me;
And the earth's face upward for my inspection.

My feet are locked upon the rough bark.
It took the whole of Creation
To produce my foot, my each feather:
Now I hold Creation in my foot

Or fly up, and revolve it all slowly –
I kill where I please because it is all mine.
There is no sophistry in my body:
My manners are tearing off heads –

The allotment of death.
For the one path of my flight is direct
Through the bones of the living.
No arguments assert my right:

The sun is behind me.
Nothing has changed since I began.
My eye has permitted no change.
I am going to keep things like this.

Pike

Pike, three inches long, perfect
Pike in all parts, green tigering the gold.
Killers from the egg: the malevolent aged grin.
They dance on the surface among the flies.

Or move, stunned by their own grandeur,
Over a bed of emerald, silhouette
Of submarine delicacy and horror,
A hundred feet long in their world.

In ponds, under the heat-struck lily pads –
Gloom of their stillness:
Logged on last year's black leaves, watching upwards.
Or hung in an amber cavern of weeds

The jaws' hooked clamp and fangs
Not to be changed at this date;
A life subdued to its instrument;
The gills kneading quietly, and the pectorals.

Three we kept behind glass,
Jungled in weed: three inches, four,
And four and a half: fed fry to them –
Suddenly there were two. Finally one

With a sag belly and the grin it was born with.
And indeed they spare nobody.
Two, six pounds each, over two feet long,
High and dry and dead in the willow-herb –

One jammed past its gills down the other's gullet:
The outside eye stared: as a vice locks –
The same iron in this eye
Though its film shrank in death.

The pond I fished, fifty yards across,
Whose lilies and muscular tench
Had outlasted every visible stone
Of the monastery that planted them –

Stilled legendary depth:
It was as deep as England. It held
Pike too immense to stir, so immense and old
That past nightfall I dared not cast

But silently cast and fished
With the hair frozen on my head
For what might move, for what eye might move.
The still splashes on the dark pond,

Owls hushing the floating woods
Frail on my ear against the dream
Darkness beneath night's darkness had freed,
That rose slowly towards me, watching.

Sylvia Plath
1932–1963

Sylvia Plath's short life provided the late twentieth century with one of its most compelling literary narratives, dramatizing as it did a body of contentious rivalries: gender rivalries, Anglo-American rivalries, and – subsuming each of these – the rivalry between two gifted poets: Plath and Ted Hughes, her English husband.

When Plath met Hughes at Cambridge in the 1950s, she had already endured a volcanic adolescence, with breakdowns and suicide attempts punctuating her determined, straight-A academic progress from Smith College in Massachusetts to Newnham College, Cambridge. Her father, a German-immigrant entomologist, had died when she was eight and the effect of this loss was momentous. Her mother supervised, with vehemence, her daughter's brilliant academic progress and encouraged her towards some hoped-for literary triumph.

When Sylvia Plath killed herself in 1963, little was known about her life and work. She had published one pseudonymous novel, *The Bell Jar*, and a volume of verse, *The Colossus*, which most reviewers judged to be mannered and derivative – derivative, in part, from her new husband Hughes, who at that time was already being lauded as a talent of some magnitude. Plath had devoted much of her short married life to assisting the growth of Hughes's reputation, but she was fiercely ambitious on her own account and also prone to fits of possessiveness and jealousy, many of which she gave vent to in her *Journals*. For most of her courtship and marriage, Plath was waiting to be hurt – and hurt she was when Hughes took up with another woman. Plath's suicide came only a few months after the couple's separation.

On the Sunday after Sylvia Plath's death, her friend A. Alvarez printed an obituary notice in the *Observer*, together with four poems – poems written during the poem-a-day outburst that preceded Plath's last act. The impact was immediate, and eerie. In one poem, 'Edge', a woman imagines her own suicide: 'The woman is perfected/ Her dead/ Body wears a smile of accomplishment'. In another, 'The Fearful':

> This woman on the telephone
> Says she is a man, not a woman.
>
> The mast increases, eats the worm,
> Stripes for mouth and eyes and nose,
>
> The voice of the woman hollows –
> More and more like a dead one,
>
> Worms in the glottal stops.

Read alongside a terse announcement of Plath's death, at the age of thirty-one, the lines seemed to insist on an inquisitive response: 'How?', 'Why?' and 'Who?' And the inquisition continues to this day, with Hughes as the defendant. As literary executor, Hughes was in charge of his dead wife's posthumous fame – a fame largely based on poems which had been inspired by anger against him – and was widely attacked for his handling of her afterfame.

Throughout all this, Hughes was never in any doubt about Plath's talents. Of these, indeed, there can be little doubt. Even in the elaborate, rhetorical poems of her first book, there were signs of the tormented self-expressiveness that lay ahead. She saw herself as already consigned to the bell jar that she wrote of in her youthful novel of that title. The bell jar links up with all the coffins, the morgues, the beehives, the wombs, the refrigerated babies and so on that swarm throughout her work: it seals her off from a world that she can still just about discern, although distortedly, but it also permits her that suspended, featureless anonymity she seems to crave. How to escape from its imprisonment into the sort of fully expressive self-awareness that poetry demands, how to do this and still function as mother, housewife, villager, and so on? This more and more becomes the basis of Plath's anguished vacillation between a vision of death as something which will efface her silently and benevolently or as a transformation from which she will emerge as a kind of elemental queen, radiant, bountiful, angelic:

> Does not my heat astound you. And my light.
> All by myself I am a huge camellia
> Glowing and coming and going, flush on flush.
>
> I think I am going up,
> I think I may rise –
> The beads of hot metal fly, and I, love, I
>
> Am a pure acetylene
> Virgin
> Attended by roses,
>
> By kisses, by cherubim . . .

One of the most remarkable features of Plath's later work is that she is able to root this conflict, this collision of death-fancies, in the solid details of her daily life, her domestic chores, her bee-keeping and horse-riding; time and again she is plunged into nightmare through what seems a homely trapdoor: as in 'Mary's Song', for instance, where the roasting of the Sunday lamb is made to

scorch across the whole of recent history and be seen finally as a
holocaust.

> The Sunday lamb cracks in its fat.
> The fat
> Sacrifices its opacity . . .
>
> A window, holy gold.
> The fire makes it precious,
> The same fire
>
> Melting the tallow heretics,
> Ousting the Jews.
> Their thick palls float
>
> Over the cicatrix of Poland, burnt-out
> Germany.
> They do not die.
>
> Gray birds obsess my heart,
> Mouth-ash, ash of eye.
> They settle.

This is a difficult transition to make plausible and in other poems
the bid for historical resonance seems forced. But it seems to have
been impossible for Plath simply to stick to what she knew. Towards
the end, she really did see herself as the volunteer arch-victim of
the torments of her century.

When other people appear in Sylvia Plath's poems, they are
usually seen as members of a 'peanut-crunching crowd' who gloat
over the spectacular agonies of the poet, and nearly all the men in
her work appear in black. In one way or another they are in direct
descent from the loved and hated father-figure who dominates all
her writing. Plath spoke once in a broadcast about what she called
her 'Electra complex', and in her poems she often seems to be
doing battle with her father, with his posthumous control over her,

his invitation that she come to him again, in death. In 'Sheep in Fog', Plath finds a metaphor that beautifully reconciles both the threat and the promise of such an invitation:

> My bones hold a stillness, the far
> Fields melt my heart.
>
> They threaten
> To let me through to a heaven
> Starless and fatherless, a dark water.

There is something here, but more nervously and subtly, of what she seems to be saying in her famous cry, 'Daddy, daddy, you bastard, I'm through.' Not only has she had enough of his male power, she has also finally got through to him – via the 'black telephone' that, cut off, becomes a root and then a worm. But as always – and in the end thankfully – no one can get through to her.

Publisher's Note

The Estate of Sylvia Plath refused permission for her poems to appear in this book, in accordance with their standard procedure.

Acknowledgements

The Publishers wish to thank the following copyright holders for permission to quote copyrighted material:

'Dulce et Decorum Est' and 'Futility' from Wilfred Owen, *The Complete Poems and Fragments* (Chatto & Windus), reprinted by permission of Professor Jon Stallworthy.

'Fern Hill' from Dylan Thomas, *Collected Poems* (J M Dent), reprinted by permission of David Higham Associates.

'The Sentry' and 'Dawn on the East Coast' by Alun Lewis, reprinted by permission of Gweno Lewis.

'A Subaltern's Love-song' from John Betjeman, *Collected Poems*, reprinted by permission of John Murray (Publishers) Ltd.

'Adlestrop' from Edward Thomas, *Collected Poems* (Oxford University Press), reprinted by permission of Myfanwy Thomas.

'Pécheresse' and 'The Farmer's Bride' from Charlotte Mew, *Collected Poems and Selected Prose*, reprinted by permission of Carcanet Press Ltd.

'Les Sylphides' and 'Bagpipe Music' from Louis MacNeice, *Collected Poems* (Faber & Faber), reprinted by permission of David Higham Associates.

'Preludes for Memnon, Prelude II' by Conrad Aiken, reprinted by permission of Joseph Killorin.

'Snake' and 'Piano' from *The Complete Poems of D.H. Lawrence*, reprinted by permission of Laurence Pollinger Ltd and the Estate of Frieda Lawrence Ravagli.

'Francesca' and 'Further Instructions' from *Personae* by Ezra Pound, reprinted by permission of Faber & Faber.

'Not Waving but Drowning' and 'Tenuous and Precarious' by Stevie Smith, reprinted by permission of the Estate of James MacGibbon.

'After Apple Picking' and 'Stopping by Woods on a Snowy Evening' from *The Poetry of Robert Frost*, edited by Edward Connery Lathem, the Estate of Robert Frost and Jonathan Cape as publisher, used by permission of the Random House Group Ltd.

'Mr Bleaney' and 'The Whitsun Weddings' from *Collected Poems* by Philip Larkin, reprinted by permission of Faber & Faber.

'The Prisoner' and Syria' from *The Complete Poems of Keith Douglas*, reprinted by permission of Faber & Faber.

'Green, Green is El Aghir' and 'Punishment Enough' by Norman Cameron, reprinted by permission of Jane Aiken Hodge.

'Dirge Without Music' and 'Hearing Your Words, and Not a Word Among Them' by Edna St Vincent Millay, from *Collected Poems* (HarperCollins), copyright 1928, 1931, 1955, 1958 by Edna St Vincent Millay and Norma Millay Ellis. All rights reserved. Reprinted by permission of Elizabeth Barnett, literary executor.

'In Memory of My Cat Domino: 1951–1966' and 'The Middle of a War' by Roy Fuller, reprinted by permission of John Fuller.

'Sea Rose' and 'Evening' from *Collected Poems* by Hilda Doolittle, reprinted by permission of Carcanet Press.

'The Widow's Lament in Springtime' and 'Asphodel, That Greeny Flower' from *Collected Poems* by William Carlos Williams, reprinted by permission of Carcanet Press.

'Old Wife in High Spirits' from *Complete Poems* by Hugh MacDiarmid, reprinted by permission of Carcanet Press.

'Angel' from *Selected Poems 1946–1985* by James Merrill, copyright 1992 by James Merrill, used by permission of Alfred A. Knopf, a division of Random House, Inc.

'Junk Mail' from *Allen Ginsberg: Selected Poems 1947–1995* (Penguin Books), first published in *Ego Confessions* (1974–1977). Copyright © Allen Ginsberg, 1996. Reprinted by permission of Penguin Books.

'Critics and Connoisseurs' and 'The Monkeys' from *The Complete Poems of Marianne Moore*, reprinted by permission of Faber & Faber.

'The Country Clergy' and 'Here' from *Collected Poems* by R.S. Thomas, reprinted by permission of the Orion Publishing Group Ltd.

'Aspects of Robinson' and 'Relating to Robinson' from *Collected Poems* by Weldon Kees, reprinted by permission of Faber & Faber.

'Frau Bauman, Frau Schmidt and Frau Schwartze' and 'Elegy for Jane' from *Collected Poems* by Theodore Roethke, reprinted by permission of Faber & Faber.

'Hawk Roosting' and 'Pike' from *Lupercal* by Ted Hughes, reprinted by permission of Faber & Faber.

'If ' and 'The Long Trail' by Rudyard Kipling, reprinted by permission of A.P. Watt Ltd on behalf of The National Trust for Places of Historical Interest or Natural Beauty.

'Evening Ebb' and 'Gray Weather' from *The Collected Poetry of Robinson Jeffers, 1928–1938*, Volume 2, edited by Tim Hunt, reprinted by permission of Stanford University Press.

'Naming of Parts' by Henry Reed, reprinted by permission of John Tydeman and the Royal Literary Fund. Copyright © Royal Literary Fund.

'The Foreboding' and 'With Her Lips Only' from *Complete Poems* by Robert Graves, reprinted by permission of Carcanet Press.

'Disillusionment of Ten O'Clock' and 'Large Red Man Reading' from *The Collected Poems of Wallace Stevens*, reprinted by permission of Faber & Faber.

'Home After Three Months Away' and 'For the Union Dead' from *Selected Poems* by Robert Lowell, reprinted by permission of Faber & Faber.

'The Woman at the Washington Zoo' and 'The Death of the Ball Turret Gunner', from *The Complete Poems* by Randall Jarrell, reprinted by permission of Faber & Faber.

'He Resigns' from *Collected Poems* and 'Dream Song 29' from *Dreamsongs*, by John Berryman, reprinted by permission of Faber & Faber.

'One Art' and 'Sandpiper' from *The Complete Poems 1927–1979* by Elizabeth Bishop, reprinted by permission of Farrar, Straus and Giroux, LLC.

'my father moved through dooms of love' and 'my sweet old etcetera' from *Complete Poems 1904–1962* by E.E.Cummings, edited by George J. Firmage, reprinted by permission of W.W. Norton & Company. Copyright © the Trustees for the E.E. Cummings Trust and George James Firmage, 1991.

'Missing Dates' and 'Let It Go' from *Complete Poems* by William Empson, edited by John Haffenden, reprinted by permission of Penguin Books.

'Elegy for Margaret' by Stephen Spender, reprinted by permission of Faber & Faber and the Spender Estate.

Picture Credits

Conrad Aiken – Photograph by Eileen Darby © Graphic House, Inc., New York

John Berryman © Rollie McKenna, 1957

John Betjeman © G/M/Camera Press

Elizabeth Bishop © Bettmann/Corbis

Gregory Corso © Francis Miller/TimePix/Rex Features

E.E.Cummings © Marion Morehouse

Hilda Doolittle © Bettmann/Corbis

William Empson © M. Gerson/Camera Press

Robert Frost © Keystone FSP

Allen Ginsberg © Keystone FSP

Robert Graves © H. Grossman/Camera Press

Ted Hughes © Mark Gerson

Randall Jarrell © Rollie McKenna, 1962

Robinson Jeffers © Leigh Wiener

Index of First Lines

Index